# DOCTOR'S AMAZING
# SPEED
# REDUCING DIET

# DOCTOR'S AMAZING SPEED REDUCING DIET

*Rex Adams*

Parker Publishing Company, Inc.

West Nyack, New York

**Library of Congress Cataloging in Publication Data**

Adams, Rex
    Doctor's amazing speed reducing.diet.

    1.  Reducing diets.  2.  Reducing diets--Recipes.
3.  Low-calories diet.  4.  Low-calories diet--
Recipes.  I. Title. II. Title:  Speed reducing
diet.
RM222.2.D72   613.2'5       79-11343
ISBN 0-13-216275-X

*Printed in the United States of America*

# A Word from the Author

Some years ago, a young doctor named Victor Lindlahr was offered a chance to give some diet talks over the radio. What started as a small, local program, attracted such wide attention that, before long, every evening, hundreds of thousands of men and women, of all ages and all walks of life, would set aside a half hour to listen to this man whose advice has helped thousands to healthier, happier living. He spoke in such a simple way that even the most complicated health facts were easy to understand.

For over twenty years, Dr. Lindlahr was heard on his famous radio program, from coast to coast. From the thousands of letters that reached his desk each week, Dr. Lindlahr would select those of widest interest, and in a simple, informal style, answered them for all to hear. He communicated not merely dietetic information, but also hope and courage.

You might say I grew up on Dr. Lindlahr's advice. You see, my mother was one of Dr. Lindlahr's earliest radio fans. And when in 1936, he invited all his listeners to join in a big "Radio Reducing Party," she was an enthusiastic joiner. Many friends and neighbors joined in, too, and the diet was a smashing success. I am too young to remember this, but, as you may well imagine, I have heard a lot about Dr. Lindlahr ever since. The various diet tips my mother passed along to me were always prefaced by, "Dr. Lindlahr said ..."

From time to time, whenever I gained a few pounds, my mother would always prescribe for me what she termed "Dr. Lindlahr's diet"—which would invariably make those excess pounds disappear, almost overnight, like magic! As my interest in health matters grew, I began to question the why and the how of it. A little research at the New York Public Library revealed the missing link, a little-known book by Dr. Lindlahr, explaining his theories, in detail (Eat and Reduce, 1939).

I first became aware of what I call speed reducing foods with reverse calories after reading this book. Of course, Dr. Lindlahr did not call them these things (they are my own expressions). He called them *catabolic foods* (catabolic means "to break down") because they break down fat, or *minus foods* because they have a minus value calorically, they take away rather than add fat, and they do it quickly, he said!

Until I read this book, I was mainly familiar with my mother's home-style variations. But here was the original "radio reducing diet" in detail. In my opinion, as a layman, after much research on popular diets, Dr. Lindlahr's approach is the best yet offered, and just as valid today as when originally written.

In this newly revised version, I have done my best to highlight the most important features of that book and to bring together other related writings by Dr. Lindlahr in books published in the 1940s.

1. In Chapter 1, I summarize these findings and give you a broad overview of things to come, with frequent reference to what Dr. Lindlahr says. This is my own personal interpretation of his writings, my own view or opinion, for what it's worth, and, except as noted, the case histories are my personal experiences, not Lindlahr's.

2. The Lindlahr material is to be found exclusively in Chapters 2 to 8. It is based squarely on what Dr. Lindlahr says in Eat and Reduce, and related books, such as The Natural Way to Health (1939), You Are What You Eat (1940), and The Lindlahr Vitamin Cookbook (1941). It is condensed somewhat, but is mostly verbatim.

Chapter 2 is condensed from Chapters 7 and 8 of Eat and Reduce. Chapter 3 is condensed from Chapters 10 and 11 of the above book.

Chapter 4 is taken from the Appendix of Eat and Reduce, where Dr. Lindlahr lists 100 foods (each marked with an asterisk) that are definitely catabolic—or speed reducing—foods. These foods are recommended by Lindlahr as fat destroying (his words). The facts on these foods, and the menus, were gleaned from his books, You Are What You Eat and The Lindlahr Vitamin Cookbook.

Chapter 5, in the first few pages, summarizes a long chapter (Chapter 9) from Eat and Reduce. After that, I expand on what you can eat, according to Lindlahr. The expanded information on these foods comes from You Are What You Eat and The Lindlahr Vitamin Cookbook.

Chapters 6, 7 and 8 are condensed from Chapters 12, 13 and 14 of Eat and Reduce.

Two additional points: Dr. Lindlahr originally stressed what you can NOT eat in Eat and Reduce. I emphasize what he says you CAN eat. Without distortion, I list every forbidden food. But in every case I place what you CAN eat first. I EXPAND on each permitted food, with background information and recipes from his other books. He has very strong claims on what you CAN eat—and I picked them up in quotes, and placed them up front where you can see them.

The other point is that Dr. Lindlahr had a habit of using distasteful foods in his examples of how fat-destroying foods work. I picked the tasty fat destroying foods he lists, like pineapple, instead of spinach. Where new facts have come to light on the foods he recommends, the book is updated.

In Chapters 10 to 20, you'll find my own personal experiences, including several other speed reducing diets, some with eat-all-you-want features. You'll find further details of my naturally skinny eating method that will permit you to eat anything (absolutely nothing is forbidden) on a daily basis, without gaining weight, for permanent weight loss.

Although I never had the privilege of meeting or consulting with Dr. Lindlahr, it is my sincere hope that this expanded and updated version of his earlier work does it justice—and, as he had long since passed on, no endorsement by him is intended or implied.

**Rex Adams**

# Contents

# DOCTOR'S AMAZING
# SPEED
# REDUCING DIET

# 1

## The Amazing Discovery
## of Reverse Calories:

### A Precis of the Most Important Points
### in the Book, to Be Developed in Detail
### in Later Chapters

In 1936, a medical doctor stunned the world with the incredible discovery of *reverse* calories in certain foods that actually *take* weight from the body. With this new nutritional discovery, he proved for the first time that you can eat many seemingly forbidden foods and lose over a pound a day, safely. And it actually happened for thousands of radio listeners who tested it.

With medically proved safety, men and women shed up to two pounds a day with the amazing discovery of reverse calories in speed reducing foods, foods that permit you to eat fattening foods like bread, potatoes or chocolate cream cake, and never worry about gaining.

We can just imagine their astonishment, as 500,000 radio listeners heard this doctor say: "Is this possible? It is. I am telling you no lies. ... if I want a luscious, appealing (fattening) food with plenty of calories as a main dish, I confuse Devil Fat (with speed reducing foods) in all the other dishes. He is a puzzled foe, Devil Fat, with this system."

The fact is, you can lose up to two pounds a day with speed reducing foods that destroy fat and neutralize the effect of fattening foods. The more you eat, the more you lose. You must eat large amounts of speed reducing foods to lose weight quickly. Speed reducing foods contain what I call reverse calories. These foods have the opposite effect of taking weight from the body. You can well imagine the importance of this discovery. There has never been anything like it—before or since—and the impact of this one great discovery revolutionized the thinking of thousands of scientists all over the world. Reverse calories burn fat.

Yes, the calories in speed reducing foods act like reverse calories. They are so difficult to burn, your body must burn its own fat to digest them. This causes an actual weight loss.

When mixed with regular fattening foods, speed reducing foods make them less fattening, by destroying their fat before it can be stored. They can even neutralize the effect of fattening foods, said this doctor.

Effects are exactly the opposite—in every way—of what you normally expect from food. You don't gain weight from eating them, you lose weight. Speed reducing foods contain reverse calories that are never stored, never turned to fat, for all practical purposes. To burn them, your body needs extra energy from its own fuel reserve, which causes an actual weight loss.

Reverse calories are encased in fibrous armor that makes them so difficult to "get at" that by the time your juices reach this fuel—which is what calories are—your body has already burned so much of its own fuel in the effort that you have lost calories. You lose more than you've eaten. This is the reverse effect of speed reducing foods.

Imagine the startling discovery of reverse calories. The more you eat, the more you lose. It's exactly the opposite of what happens when you eat fattening calories. Eating large amounts of them makes you thin. You can eat them exclusively and lose weight with astounding speed. Or you can mix them with your regular fattening foods to stay slim permanently.

You can eat twice as much as you think. You can dine regally, and even though you eat three pounds of food a day, the weight tumbles off you in record speed. "Many a fat person eats only half of what he really wants to eat," said this doctor. "Too bad! If he only knew, the kind—not the quantity—of the food he eats is what matters."

Just remember: reverse calories burn fat and counter the effects of fattening foods. This doctor called them minus foods—foods that destroy fat faster than anything else, three times faster than starvation. I call them speed reducing foods, with reverse calories (because of this reverse effect). You can lose over a pound a day with speed reducing foods, and then continue eating most of your favorite (fattening) foods, without gaining weight. Spectacular weight-loss is possible, up to two pounds or more a day. They are ordinary foods, all available at your corner grocery or supermarket.

I first became aware of what I call speed reducing foods with reverse calories, after reading a fascinating book on weight-loss by a medical doctor. Of course, he did not call them these things (they are my own expressions). He called them "catabolic foods" because they break down fat, or "minus foods" because they have a minus value, they take away rather than add fat, he said. The doctor's name was Victor Lindlahr.

The first hint that some foods really do take weight from the body was discovered by Dr. Lindlahr in observing his own father's diabetes. Lindlahr's father weighed over 250 pounds. He developed advanced diabetes and was near death when he heard of a famous natural healer, Father Kneipp. (Around the turn of the century.)

He heard wondrous stories of the spectacular cures of this priest who leaned on Nature for his cures. He met patients who were healed of so-called incurable ailments. He consulted the priest, and was given a no-medicine treatment that really worked. His sugar vanished. He lost over 40 pounds. His life had been saved. This was the exciting discovery of speed reducing foods.

Dr. Lindlahr said his father's diet proved excellent for diabetics. Most were overweight—and he could not help noticing the steady and spectacular loss of weight sustained by diabetics who were placed on this diet. Year after year, it reduced patients like magic. It became a routine diet at his Chicago Sanitarium.

Just how fast speed reducing foods worked became clear one day, when a lady arrived at Dr. Lindlahr's office who wanted to lose 30 pounds in 30 days. She was determined to starve it off. She was to be married, and wanted to look extra nice at her wedding. Since she was grossly overweight, Dr. Lindlahr agreed to put her on a fast. Seven days passed, and she lost only four pounds. She was furious. Then Dr.

Lindlahr remembered his father's diet. Of course! This took off pounds more rapidly than a fast. He told her he could definitely reduce her at the pound-a-day rate she wanted.

Starting that night, she went on the Lindlahr diet. She lost 12 pounds the first week, 8 pounds the second, and continued losing. She left for home happy, bestowing a shower of blessings on Dr. Lindlahr. A bit later, she sent a note to report she'd remained on the diet until her wedding day, and had lost a total of 34 pounds.

It seemed impossible that a person eating two-and-a-half to three pounds of food (and more) per day was losing at a rate three times faster than starvation. He had his secretary get out the records. Yes, the rule held. At the very most, patients fasting (starving) on fruit juices lost about three-quarters of a pound a day. But average weight loss on the Lindlahr diet, all cases combined, was over a pound a day.

"Now the study became deeply interesting. Established assumptions in dietetic practice were being given a rude jolt. Fond dietetic beliefs were shattered, and established nutritional principles branded mistakes. I had to look for explanations," said Dr. Lindlahr.

Standard textbooks on food chemistry had to be re-written, said Dr. Lindlahr, for the speed reducing diet destroyed fat, and the how and why was an open sesame to combating overweight.

His search led him through a wilderness of what was not known about food. He had to backtrack to the study of how foods behave when burned in calorimeters. "I had to seek every last morsel of knowledge," he explained. "I had to reclassify foods." Some foods were definitely minus foods and caused an actual weight loss. Effects were exactly the opposite, in every way, of what you normally expect from food. You don't gain from eating them, you lose weight! These foods literally burn fat. Calories in these foods were different in the sense that they are "harder to get at," because speed reducing foods are difficult to burn or digest. They just cannot be made into the same amount of fat as ordinary food. In every case, a speed reducing food requires more calories to burn than it contains. This causes an actual weight loss. This amazing food discovery sends fat rolling out of your body.

"You have to consume large quantities of catabolic (speed reducing) foods in order to lose weight rapidly! ('I can hardly eat all the food given,' said one woman.) Eating large quantities of food to lose weight is something new for the fatty. But it is correct," said Dr. Lindlahr. "See what a good game it is? Understand now why I don't have any worries about fat—why I have fun controlling my weight?"

This is the most incredibly permissive diet, offered by a doctor, you've ever seen. First, to lose weight with maximum speed, you may eat speed reducing foods exclusively—the more you eat, the more you lose—said Dr. Lindlahr. That's no problem, because he lists over 100 fat-destroying, speed reducing foods on the speed reducing diet.

Afterwards, you mix speed reducing foods with your regular fattening foods to stay slim permanently. "When I eat about two-thirds catabolic (speed reducing foods) to one-third anabolic (fattening) foods, my weight stays between 174 and 176 pounds. Just 65 per cent catabolic foods gives me all the leeway I want for eating fattening foods. I can enjoy bread, potatoes, or a piece of chocolate cream cake a la mode if I so desire," said Dr. Lindlahr, who lost thirty pounds with this method. By mixing them with speed reducing foods, said this expert: "Not only have I failed to add calories to my score, I have actually trimmed some off."

Here are some personal experiences that I have heard about, over the years, with amazing speed reducing foods:

Mrs. J.T. weighed 175 pounds, instead of her ideal weight of 125. All other methods had been so slow and discouraging that her will-power snapped. She was convinced if she could only shed those extra pounds quickly, it would give her the confidence she needed to maintain permanent weight loss. With speed reducing foods, she had plenty to eat—felt full all the time—and was able to satisfy her sweet tooth. She could see it happening, as she lost one-and-a-half to two pounds a day. Result: 50 pounds lost in a month.

Mrs. P.N., 64, was so "diet weary" she couldn't face starving and failing again. She'd been on and off diets for years. When she was younger, some worked. But now, no matter how hard she tried, the scales refused to budge. At her age, she felt it was impossible, and had "resigned" herself to being "fat" the rest of her life. After hearing how speed reducing foods explode weight deadlocks—without starvation—she decided on "one last try." To her astonishment, she dropped five pounds overnight, twenty pounds in twelve days. At an age when others are gray and broken, she had a curvaceous new figure—the envy of women half her age.

R.D. said he'd rather starve than eat "diet" foods—and he meant it. He'd been starving on "one glorious meal a day" for a month, lost 15 pounds, and gained half of it back the first time he ate normally. But when he heard that speed reducing foods destroy fat three times faster than starvation—and some were actually "forbidden foods" he thought were fattening—he immediately tried them. Result: 30 pounds gone in two-and-a-half weeks.

You may also eat speed reducing foods during the day, fattening foods at night, or a mixture of them at each meal, or alternate diet and splurging days, whatever seems best to you, said Dr. Lindlahr. This lets you eat many foods you never dreamed possible—things like ice cream, cake, sweet snacks galore, and appetizers for nibblers—and stay reduced. Speed reducing foods destroy fat and counter the effects of fattening foods. You can eat your cake, while slimming down permanently.

How much can you lose? Dr. Lindlahr guaranteed you'll lose over a pound a day, with his method. He said: "Because this diet has almost 90 per cent catabolic (fat destoying) efficiency, the three pounds of food it permits you to eat each day should make moderate overweights lose about a pound of fat per day. Persons considerably overweight," he said, "lose a pound-and-a-half or so daily." I, personally, have lost more. Many have. So can you. In my opinion, you can shed up to two pounds or more a day, every day, day after day with speed reducing foods. Simply mix them with your favorite fattening foods, like French fries, ice cream, cookies, even beer—and you can lose more than you've eaten. I'll show you how in Chapter 10.

Thousands of radio listeners reported spectacular results. By chance Dr. Lindlahr had an opportunity to deliver some diet talks over the radio. Thousands of listeners responded, suggesting that Dr. Lindlahr actually broadcast a complete speed reducing diet, giving the menus day by day. The result was a big radio reducing party. Each day, for a week, hundreds of people who went on the diet phoned, wrote, and even telegraphed their progress. A total of 26,000 participated. When he totalled up the score, average weight loss, all cases combined, was over a pound a day.

This test was positive proof of the speed reducing diet. Many followed the diet a little longer to take off 25, 30, or 40 pounds. In this manner, the speed reducing diet proved itself clinically, blasting the notion that it is not safe to lose over a pound a day, said Dr. Lindlahr.

"Practically the same kind of diet was used successfully to treat certain types of heart trouble, gall bladder crises, and other important ailments," he said. "Imagine it! First and foremost, here is a therapeutic diet which has made sick people well. ... For twenty years patients had lived ... on this diet and *thrived*. Patients had been *cured* of grievous diseases (by these foods).... Secondly, to lose fat efficiently," he said, "you have to eat, not starve yourself as some think."

By popular demand, the speed reducing diet was printed in formal style. The sale was phenomenal. An edition of 200,000 copies was exhausted within a year. In two years, close to a half million copies had been sold.

Medical opinions were revised, and this new system was "approved," said Dr. Lindlahr. While no claim is made that this book reflects recent or majority opinions among doctors, at the time, along with widespread public acceptance of the speed reducing diet, medical doctors began re-examining and re-evaluating long-held beliefs about speed reducing. Finally, in the *Journal of the American Medical Association* (December 10, 1938), a most amazing case was reported in detail. It was a woman weighing nearly 400 pounds who reduced a staggering total of 239 pounds in a matter of months, to 156, on a very similar diet, according to Dr. Lindlahr.

The basic conclusion drawn from the study was: "There is no limit to the extent to which excess weight may be removed" by such foods, as long as essential nutrients are provided. "The medical concept of the dietary treatment of obesity was sharply revised," said Dr. Lindlahr. "Thus a principle went into practice!" This diet was "approved" he said.

Let us look at the reasons behind the speed reducing diet. One reason it works is these reverse calories in speed reducing foods. Your body works harder to digest the calories in speed reducing foods than any other type of food. In this process, excess fat is burned up, too. Adding more speed reducing foods is like adding fuel to a fire. They force the body to burn its own fat.

It is a well-balanced diet that satisfies your body's craving for all the elements it needs, including fats and carbohydrates—but not in excess. It is rich in magic minerals (and all the vitamins that go with them), so you are not compelled to overeat to obtain them.

It satisfies your craving for pleasure at mealtime and between meals, with a rich variety of pleasant tastes. It is rich in natural fiber, which not only aids digestion, but there is startling evidence that bulk foods actually prevent many calories from being absorbed (this means that you may actually eat more and still lose, if you can manage it, because bulk foods are also very filling). In addition to relieving constipation, speed reducing foods actually force fat out of your body, and this has been scientifically proven.

It is a catabolic eating system that causes more fuel to be burned than is taken in. In other words, it causes your metabolism—the rate (BMR) at which food is burned—to run at a higher speed, so to speak. Catabolism is the breaking down of body fat for energy. During this diet, your catabolic combustion is high. This is a proven biochemical fact.

Speed reducing foods have slow absorbing sugar. Dr. Lindlahr found that some people gain weight more easily than others because of the *type* of sugars and starches they ate. The sugar content of speed reducing foods, he found, has a much lower absorption rate than other types of sugar, and will not put on weight so easily. Nature's saccharin!

Speed reducing foods destroy hard-to-melt fat. That "spare tire" will melt away on the speed reducing diet. Fat stored in the lower abdomen and the midriff is difficult to break up. But speed reducing foods stir up and stimulate the catabolic processes, and this so heightens the destruction of fat that even the tougher kinds are blown up, said Dr. Lindlahr. The thyroid and other glands are stimulated to greater activity, he said. Hundreds and hundreds of radio listeners who followed the speed reducing diet reported that the spare tire, the extra chins, had obligingly disappeared.

Speed reducing foods prevent water weight gain. Most fatties are waterlogged, said Dr. Lindlahr. Jowls that wibble and wobble, hips that billow and surge, abdomens that undulate soon become firm on the speed reducing diet—watch and see—he claimed. To a great extent, waterlogging made these portions of the anatomy flabby and floppy. The speed reducing diet changes them to solid, natural flesh, not by dehydration, but by making the tissue water balance normal.

You shed pounds without exhausting exercise. "To take weight down via exercise is to choose the hard way," said Dr. Lindlahr. "It is the most difficult and unsatisfactory method of getting rid of a pound of fat. A 200-pound man, for example, would have to play handball furiously for almost six hours really to burn up a pound of fat. Though he might sweat two pounds of perspiration ... this is not losing fat ... Drinking water puts it back ... I'll take the food way to slimness ... it's easy to dissolve that extra fat with foods."

Speed reducing foods do not dehydrate. Here is a little-known fact. Adding fat to the diet prevents water storage. Some very dangerous reducing diets have been formulated because of this fact, said Dr. Lindlahr. Dehydration causes a miserable string of symptoms ranging from headaches to exhaustion. The speed reducing diet does not dehydrate. It causes the greedy, exaggerated water metabolism of overweight to calm down. Water balance is corrected, he said.

Acidosis is prevented. The speed reducing diet is carefully calculated to provide such an excess of alkaline or base ash that it will neutralize roughly two pounds of tissue breakdown a day—a guarantee that you cannot suffer from acidemia on the diet, said Dr. Lindlahr. And each one of these foods (except the proteins) is literally a mine of minerals and vitamins. The speed reducing diet is good for you, fat or no fat, he emphasized. It lets you "starve" the fat off your body, while eating like a king.

Best of all, it's easy to follow. In most cases, it's no-cook cooking all the way—no muss, no fuss, no bother. You get daily menus for 7 days, and substitution lists (in case you don't like some food mentioned). There are over 100 speed reducing foods. This makes it possible for you to eat out and take the menu in stride. You never have to eat the same food twice. The variety and endless combinations make it a pleasant, easy diet to follow.

Lastly, and most fascinating of all, only speed reducing foods release *glucagon*, the reducing hormone. The speed reducing diet accomplished this 20 years before glucagon was discovered. Glucagon causes fat to be released. It is produced by the pancreas. Dr. Lindlahr noted that overweights have an unusual tendency to store fat: "I consider fat men and women as specially gifted people.... They are able to transform food into fat (which is stored energy) at a much more efficient rate than the thin or normal individual." Now it may be stated that this is due to a lack of glucagon.

In 1960, it was proven that the alpha-2 cells of the pancreas can be forced to produce glucagon, which causes fat to be released. This hormone is a fat mobilizing substance (FMS) that forces the release of fat from fat tissues, say medical doctors. This fat-dissolving hormone mobilizes inner fat stores—sets them rolling out of your cells—and actually enables you to consume your own fat.

The speed reducing diet stimulates the alpha-2 cells of the pancreas to release glucagon—whereas the only other way to do this is by strenuous exercise. It does this through certain foods like beef. In scientific tests, for example, in healthy adults who ate two ounces of lean beef, blood glucagon levels rose gradually, nearly doubled within ninety minutes, and stayed high for at least four hours. You can concentrate on speed reducing foods exclusively, to keep your glucagon level high all the time—even while you sleep—to accelerate your weight loss.

Everything is done for you, on the speed reducing diet. No matter how you look at it, with this system, output exceeds input, resulting in the negative nitrogen balance (NNB) necessary for quick weight loss, without draining energy from vital organs. It works in all cases, cannot fail, said Dr. Lindlahr, and even if this specific menu plan does not suit you, future chapters will show you how to adjust this diet to your specific needs.

Dr. Lindlahr, a trained nutritionist, spent 20 years perfecting the speed reducing diet. It requires a trained nutritionist, plus years of careful study and consideration, to formulate a healthfully balanced reducing diet—providing for almost 40 different elements you need for health.

These include food minerals, various vitamins, essential amino acids, water balance, bulk, and the acid-alkaline ash qualities. Certain minerals and vitamins must definitely be provided to carry on rapid fat destruction without harm, said Dr. Lindlahr. Careful protein balance must be maintained to prevent destruction of tissues other than fat. It has all been done for you on the speed reducing diet.

This is *not* the water diet. Here's the inside story of the original speed reducing diet, 30 years before the so-called "water diet." Dr. Lindlahr called it the 7-day reducing diet, using minus foods (with what I call reverse calories). And speed reducing is my term for this rapid reducing system.

By contrast, this is a diet of good, solid foods. Why starve, when you can satisfy your craving for pleasure at mealtime and between meals with a rich variety of pleasant tastes ... with flavorful roast meats, tempting egg dishes, cheese souffle, custards, sherbets, sweet snacks, hors d'oeuvres, cocktails, appetizers, even caviar!

Dr. Lindlahr's diet was encouraging to the extent that many forbidden foods could be eaten—after the initial loss of 10, 20, or 30 pounds. An eating method, a way of life, was evolved that would permit anyone to partake of his or her favorite fattening foods (and let's face it, the fattening ones are often the most delicious), on a daily basis, without gaining, losing a few pounds if necessary, and maintaining permanent weight loss.

I call this the naturally-skinny eating secret. To do this, all you have to realize is that certain foods burn fat—and they do it faster and more effectively than starvation. You can easily prove this to yourself by going on a fast (fruit juices permitted), and then the speed reducing diet, and comparing results. You may lose four pounds a week on the fast. But you'll lose up to two pounds a *day* on the speed reducing diet.

Here's a very simple way of remembering it. Ice cream and potatoes may have the exact same number of calories, but they are not the same *kind* of calories, said Dr. Lindlahr. A potato calorie is much harder to digest—hence more reducing, because more energy is needed to assimilate it.

This makes it possible for you to eat anything you want, in moderation, and still reduce and stay reduced. Many doctors recommend this as an alternative to starvation diets, or skimpy ones, that are hard to follow. And there are certain eat-all-you-want foods. Once you understand the basic principles more clearly, you can tailor the system to fit your own needs. Speed reducing foods during the day, fattening foods in the evening, or a mixture of them at each meal, or alternate diet and splurging days, whatever seems best for you.

Why speed reducing? Because it's satisfying and encouraging to see your weight drop rapidly each day. That is the essential fact in this revolutionary speed reducing diet. You lose pounds and inches fast, fast, fast. The reason it will—it must—work for you, no matter how many times you have failed up till now, is simple: you see immediate results.

Immediate results make reducing a joy. You're slim before you have time to grow diet weary. Before you know it, ugly, unwanted bulges disappear overnight. That's why speed reducing has succeeded in thousands of seemingly hopeless cases. With speed reducing foods, you can lose five to six pounds immediately, and then shed weight at the rate of one-and-half to two pounds or more daily.

It gives you something to look forward to each day. For example, on conventional diets, it takes so long, the foods are so bland, and there's nothing to look forward to at mealtime for such a long time, you are soon easily discouraged. But on the speed reducing diet, you eat to satisfy your taste as well as your hunger. You dine regally, and even though you eat three pounds of food a day—the weight tumbles off you in record speed.

You don't miss anything. You never really abandon the foods you enjoy. There are special treats. And you won't mind it because you don't have to wait long. You see results immediately, not in weeks or months. That's the crucial fact that will make it work for you.

You can see it happening. You'll be delighted and impressed by the speed of the decided drop in your weight when you step on the scale each morning—yes, each morning— it can change that fast. Every single day you'll be sure you're reducing, starting the very first day, in most cases. You can see it happening as you drop up to six pounds immediately, and then shed weight at the rate of one-and-a-half to two pounds or more daily.

You stay slim permanently. On conventional diets, what happens when you reach your ideal weight? All too often, you fall back on old eating patterns, and gain it all back. But with this method, you'll never have to worry about regaining lost weight. You never really abandon the foods you enjoy. If you gain a few pounds, it's a simple matter to shed them quickly—often in as little as one day—with amazing speed reducing foods. You can use this secret successfully the rest of your life.

Starting today, you can lose pounds and inches quickly, and have a slimmer, more attractive figure in a hurry—and stay slim forever. Specifically, you'll lose the bulges you want to be pleased with your image in the mirror, and the fit of your clothes. You'll look and feel like a new person, almost overnight. Men and women have shed up to two pounds or more a day, as much as twenty pounds in a week, with speed reducing foods. And when you reach your ideal weight, you can stay slim permanently, without starvation.

But here's a word of advice. Frankly, if you believe yourself to be overweight, the first step in any sensible diet is discuss it with a qualified doctor. Let him check you out, and fill you in on certain facts about yourself that neither you, nor I, nor any stranger is qualified to tell you. Since I am neither a physician, consultant, or medical practitioner, I can only report what others have done. By discussing your diet with your doctor, you can tailor it to meet your needs in perfect safety. Self-treatment is not recommended without a doctor's permission.

Here are the most powerful fat-dissolving foods known to science. In the following chapters, Dr. Lindlahr's original speed reducing diet that shocked the world is given in full detail. Many fat-blasting, fat-demolishing foods are given. Here are foods that melt away pounds for you simply by eating them, with no exercise, pills or torture therapies of any kind. The more you eat of them, the more you lose. It's as simple as that. They will enable you to stop dieting and start living by eating a wide variety of delicious foods you never thought possible. They are the crucial difference between months of painful starvation diets with little weight loss—and dramatic weight loss eating satisfying gourmet meals.

# 2

## The Diet Discovery
## That Shocked the World!

Victor H. Lindlahr grew up observing his father's pioneering work in the science of nutrition. In the early 1880's when men ate heartily, at 5'7", Lindlahr's father weighed over 250 pounds. He developed diabetes of the serious type. His condition grew worse. Advised, finally, to settle his affairs, Henry Lindlahr disposed of his business, and sought a cure. Various treatments and "cures" at different spas proved unavailing. He made his peace with God and prepared to die. Then he heard about a famous natural healer—Father Kneipp.

He heard wondrous stories of the spectacular cures of this priest who leaned on Nature for his methods. He met patients who were healed of so-called incurable ailments. Faither Kneipp gave him a no-medicine treatment that really worked. Springtime greeted a new Henry Lindlahr. His sugar was gone. He had lost over forty pounds. His life had been saved.

But something else had happened to Henry Lindlahr. The miracle of diet absorbed him, body and soul. He mourned that *his* overweight father might yet have been alive had he been told how to eat. He had lost a sister who was obese, and died before she reached 30. He had seen loved friends die, and from what little he knew, he suspected that some of them might have been saved if they had been told how to eat. In short, he became a full-fledged diet enthusiast. He wanted to help other people. He made up his mind to study medicine, becoming a medical doctor in 1904.

Lindlahr's father left no page unturned in the lore of foods and diet. He pored over the writings of Hippocrates, who had used the livers of birds and animals to cure night blindness and certain inflammatory diseases of the eyes. He marvelled over the discoveries of Lind of Great Britain, who had advised Captain Cook to carry sauerkraut and lemons on his ships to cure the sailors of scurvy. He heard how rice hulls cured beriberi. He studied diet, diet, diet.

As a result, when Lindlahr's father became a doctor, he knew much about diet—far more than any other doctor of his time. Within a few months he was very busy, helping patients with knowledge many of his medical colleagues did not possess. In 1905 he started the Lindlahr Sanitarium. There he used his diet ideas and knowledge with such skill that his reputation quickly grew.

His son, Victor Lindlahr, grew up in this little world that revolved around nutrition, foods, and the treatment of disease by diet, surrounded by patients who were gravely—sometimes terminally—ill. Watching his father's work inspired him, and as a young man he enrolled in the Chicago College of Osteopathy, and was graduated and licensed as an osteopathic physician and surgeon, in 1918. He continued his studies at the Jenner Medical College, and was graduated as a doctor of medicine in 1924. When he succeeded his father, the Sanitarium had been established for 19 years.

Those who came to the Lindlahr Sanitarium were chiefly cases that could be helped by diet. A good many of them were diabetics. Victor Lindlahr had four years of practice among this group before the advent of insulin. It was marvelous training, as a prelude to understanding the dietetic problems of reducing.

The Lindlahr diet, like any good diet for diabetes, was composed mainly of low starch and low sugar vegetables and fruits. The L.C. diet, they called it (low carbohydrate). Dr. Lindlahr observed, as anyone who sees many diabetic cases will note, that most diabetics are overweight. And he could not help noticing the steady and spectacular loss of weight sustained by diabetics who were placed on the L.C. diet. Year after year, this diet reduced patients like magic!

Occasionally, Dr. Lindlahr—like his father—prescribed a fast. The harsher name for this is starvation (only fruit juice allowed, one quart daily). In the few types of sickness where this drastic treatment was indicated, it really worked marvelously well. Patients lost excess weight, along with their ailments.

All of this is important to remember, for time finally brought this startling fact to light: *A person on an L.C. diet lost weight more quickly than one who was fasting*. Not until some time later did the significance of that simple rule dawn on him, Dr. Lindlahr recalled ...

## 30 POUNDS IN 30 DAYS!

A portly lady from Philadelphia arrived at Dr. Lindlahr's office. She said she wanted to lose 30 pounds in 30 days. She was determined to starve to lose weight. She was to be married in a little over a month, and wanted to look extra nice at her wedding. Since she weighed 240 pounds, Dr. Lindlahr saw no harm in the idea. So she began a carefully supervised fast. Seven days passed with the result that she lost only four pounds. She was furious! Dr. Lindlahr told her to be patient, and retreated, a bit uncomfortable. He did some thinking.

Then a great light dawned on him! The L.C. diet! Of course! The L.C. diet took off pounds more rapidly than a fast. Actually there is a similarity between the problems of sugar chemistry in diabetes and fat chemistry in obesity. So he stopped back to see the lady from Philadelphia. He told her he would put her on a diet which, he was sure, would definitely reduce her at the pound-a-day rate she wanted. That week, she lost at the rate of nearly two pounds a day!

Beginning that night, the lady from Philadelphia went on the L.C. diet (speed reducing foods). She lost twelve pounds the first week, eight pounds the second, and a little over six the third. She left for Philadelphia happy, bestowing a shower of blessings on Dr. Lindlahr. A bit later, she sent a note to report that she had remained on the diet until her wedding day—and had lost thirty-four pounds!

## THE IMPOSSIBLE HAD HAPPENED!

After the lady from Philadelphia left, Dr. Lindlahr was stunned. *It seemed impossible* that a person eating two-and-a-half to three pounds of food (and more) per day on the Lindlahr diet lost more weight, and lost it more consistently, than the person who was starved—the person on a fast.

He had his secretary cull out, from treatment records of the past twelve months, the histories of patients who had been on a fast (they numbered 152) and on the L.C. diet (206). *Yes, the rule held!*

This fact stuck out like the Empire State Building: *the L.C. diet was more reducing than a fast!* It became apparent that the greater the accumulation of body fat, the greater the weight loss!

A fasting patient (on fruit juices) lost about ¾ of a pound a day (2500 calories). The average weight loss on the Lindlahr speed reducing diet, *all cases combined*, was over a pound a day! Heavyweights lost about a pound-and-a-half or so daily!

## EXISTING BELIEFS SHATTERED!

"Now the study became deeply interesting," said Dr. Lindlahr. "Established assumptions in dietetic practice were being given a rude jolt. Fond dietetic beliefs were shattered, and established nutritional principles branded mistakes. I had to look for explanations.

"The trail led through a wilderness of what we didn't know about food metabolism. I had to back-track to the study of how foods behave when burned in calorimeters. I had to seek every last morsel of knowledge about the behavior of nitrogen and the mineral elements in foods during metabolism.

"The complex problems of what is called the respiratory quotient in food chemistry gave a light. The intricate workings of the water metabolism of the body gave more clues. Strangely enough, the best clue came from following the steps by which a cow makes cream out of grass.

"I had to reclassify foods. Standard textbooks still applied the term carbohydrates (starch) to lettuce, mushrooms, and half a hundred other foods which have more water content than milk, and very little starch and sugar."

Established works on food chemistry had to be rewritten, for the speed reducing diet destroyed fat, and the how and why was an open sesame to combatting overweight. Here's why the speed reducing diet works!

## WHY SOME FOODS BURN FAT!

It costs body heat and energy to digest food. When you eat a piece of food, your teeth must grind it. Esophageal muscles carry the chewed morsels to your stomach, where they are rocked to and fro for a few hours, while little glands provide ferments which partly digest them.

Later, 33 feet of intestines will mold and enfold what was once a piece of food, and a few other digestive juices will change the material into more simple chemical forms.

Finally, tiny suction pumps will carry some of the digested food to lymph glands in your body for further use. Blood cells will patiently load a microscopic bit into their hollows, and carry it to hungry cells throughout the body.

The liver, the spleen and the pancreas will play a part in this process. The heart will beat harder for it. Even the lungs will take in more air because you have eaten a bit of food. All told, you use a considerable amount of body heat and energy (calories) in this complicated process of chewing and digesting food, and assimilating its ultimate fractions for body use.

There is no way to calculate, in exact calorie value, the amount of heat and energy a given person will use in metabolizing a piece of food. The calorie cost will vary with the individual, for we all behave just a little bit differently.

We do know, however, that it does not require nearly as much body energy to digest some foods as the foods themselves provide. We make an energy (calorie) profit out of the transaction.

To illustrate: A four-ounce piece of cake may supply about 300 calories. If we assume, for the sake of simplicity, that the average person uses about 25 calories of body energy preparing this cake for body use, he will make a net profit of 275 calories. If these are used up in exercise, work, sleep or play, good enough. If not, they may be stored as an ounce of fat.

Now let us consider the metabolic fate of four ounces of a speed reducing food—pineapple! All those processes involved in the digestion of a piece of cake must also take place to digest a slice of pineapple. The same whirling and twirling of the digestive system, the same physical and chemical commotion—there is not much difference. *But it costs the body much more heat and energy to digest a slice of pineapple* than a piece of cake!

*Pineapple is much harder to digest,* owing to its relatively high mineral value and roughage content. (There is practically no metabolic cost in digesting the sugar and flour in a piece of cake—remember that.)

Four ounces of pineapple will yield 76 calories of energy value. However, if it takes 100 calories of energy to digest the pineapple, we find that the pineapple eater would lose heat and energy, in the transaction, to the extent of 24 calories! Where are these extra calories of energy to come from? The body cannot find them in the pineapple, so they must come eventually from stored fat in the body.

That is why eating pineapple alone would cause an actual weight (calorie) loss to the body. There are many foods of the same nature. Obviously, they come in very handy for reducing diets.

## "CATABOLIC FOODS" ARE BORN!

After he arrived at this fundamental fact in the metabolic behavior of certain foods, a convenient term to designate them as a class was needed. Dr. Lindlahr used the expression, "catabolic foods."

Body metabolism is composed of two separate divisions of activity: one is the breaking down of tissues, called catabolism; the other is the building up of tissues, called anabolism. In youth the body grows and develops; anabolism is then greater than catabolism.

When foods create a deficit in the body fat, they may properly be called catabolic foods because the process of losing weight is a catabolic process. Adding fat to the body is an anabolic process and foods which will perform this function may be called the anabolic foods.

After growth has been completed, anabolism and catabolism remain equal; the body tissues retain a status quo as far as growth is concerned. In the later years of life, the catabolic processes increase, the tissues shrink, and the weight grows less.

Generally speaking, the person who puts on extra fat is receiving too generous treatment from the anabolic processes. If anabolism could be tamed down some and remain equal to catabolism, body weight would stay at a normal level.

When Dr. Lindlahr found that some foods were definitely catabolic—or speed reducing—he realized they were excellent weapons to regulate metabolism.

## SOME FOODS REALLY TAKE WEIGHT FROM THE BODY!

"At first glance, it might seem strange that some foods really take weight from the body, but when the facts are appreciated, it is understandable, for some foods have a very specific purpose in nutrition. They supply rare but vitally needed minerals ... or extraordinary quantities of some particular vitamin," said Dr. Lindlahr. *Nature put these things in food long before multi-vitamin and mineral tablets were invented, and foods still contain many undiscovered nutrients we need!*

For example, an apricot gives us relatively tremendous quantities of vitamin A, iron, and other minerals, considering its high water content and minute percentage of solids.

Nature is apparently willing that the body be forced to expend extra energy and work to dig out these precious properties. Hence a catabolic (speed reducing) food, while costing us a little fat and extra body energy, really gives a valuable return in the form of minerals and vitamins. Nature makes us work for the good things in food.

You may say: "Can't the same thing be accomplished by taking vitamin pills?" *The answer is "No!"* Vitamin pills are an instant form of nutrition that require no effort to absorb or digest. The same is true of minerals and other food supplements. Taking them will do no harm—and really may be of decided benefit—on *any* diet. *But it is the nutrients in foods, in their natural form (unprocessed) that cause the catabolic effect.*

Study and consideration of the catabolic foods showed them to consist, chiefly, of those with a very high water content (pineapples and watermelon, for example, are well over 90 per cent water). The seventy-five really excellent catabolic foods are in the class called protective foods—those exceedingly rich in mineral and vitamin values, "healthful" foods.

Here was a stroke of luck. Imagine it: the very foods that contribute valuable vitamins and food minerals to the body turned out to be reducing foods.

A person twenty pounds overweight has 70,000 calories of stored fat. He could live for 35 days without any food—just water—and still do moderate work. Hence, it would seem decidedly beneficial for such a person to starve and use some of his burdening fat. But even a grossly overweight person must eat because food provides other necessary factors to life—many not even mentioned yet! We must eat, even when reducing!

## CATABOLIC FOODS ARE HEALING!

Additional inquiry into the catabolic foods showed not just mineral and vitamin values. Many of them were foods that provide an alkaline ash, very useful in offsetting the acid residue of fat destruction in the body. Furthermore, some of the catabolic foods were very rich in the food factors that have a favorable influence on the internal secretory glands—such as the pancreas, which as was discovered years later, produces *glucagon,* the fat-dissolving hormone, only in the presence of catabolic foods!

The catabolic foods, as might be expected, were all very low in calorie value. When Dr. Lindlahr figured up the daily calorie value of the speed reducing diet, the three pounds of food totalled only 600 calories on the average, *but since many of them are sweet and have practically no caloric value, 600 reverse calories seem like 6,000 fattening ones*!

Here was another revolutionary turn. Many a dietician vowed then that it was impossible to support life in an adult with only 600 calories per day. Dr. Lindlahr knew that it *was* possible. For twenty years patients had lived for weeks and months on this speed reducing diet, and *thrived*. Patients had been cured of grievous disease by the speed reducing diet, notwithstanding its low calorie content.

"Just take a general view of the connotations of this discovery. First and foremost, here is a therapeutic diet which has made sick people well. Secondly, to lose fat efficiently on this diet, you have to eat, not starve yourself as some think. Furthermore, you have to consume large quantities of food to lose weight rapidly. Eating large quantities of food to lose weight is something new for the fatty. But it is correct," said Dr. Lindlahr!

## *REVERSE* CALORIES IN SPEED REDUCING FOODS!

If the word catabolic is unwieldy or strange to you, call the catabolic foods *speed reducing foods*, if you please. That is what they are. These foods actually have a "*minus*" value calorically, said Dr. Lindlahr. Instead of adding, they take away fat. These calories act like *reverse* calories in every way: *eating large amounts of them makes you thin!*

"Every time I eat a minus food I am just that much ahead of Devil Fat for the day," said Dr. Lindlahr. "Not only have I failed to add calories to my score, but I have actually trimmed some off." *In addition, speed reducing foods counter the effect of fattening foods!* "If I want a luscious, appealing food with plenty of calories as a main dish," he continued, "I confound Devil Fat by compensating for my choice, somewhat, with minus foods in all the other menu roles. He is a puzzled foe, Devil Fat, with this system."

"See what a good game it is?" said Dr. Lindlahr. "Understand now why I don't have any worries about fat—why I have fun controlling my weight?"

# 3

## The Speed Reducing Diet
## Makes Its Debut!

One summer—quite unexpectedly—Dr. Lindlahr had the opportunity to deliver some diet talks over the radio. Thousands of listeners responded with such enthusiasm that the program was extended, by public demand. People were fascinated! Questions on reducing were the most popular part of the show. For six years, Dr. Lindlahr sent out hundreds of copies of his reducing diet, explaining speed reducing to interested listeners. People reported spectacular results with this diet!

In this manner, the 10-day speed reducing diet—as it was then known—proved itself clinically, blasting the notion that it is not safe to lose more than 2-3 pounds a month, demolishing the argument that losing over a pound a day must be deadly and dangerous.

Then something happened. A group of radio listeners suggested that Dr. Lindlahr actually broadcast a complete speed reducing diet, giving the menus day by day in detail. "I jumped at the idea," says Dr. Lindlahr. "If a considerable number of the audience would go on the diet, follow it faithfully, and then report, we would really accumulate irrefutable evidence and the not-to-be-denied attention value of the spectacular."

So, Dr. Lindlahr announced that he would give a test reducing diet, if a thousand listeners would promise to follow it. And he promised that if the test were satisfactory, if the listeners liked it, if it actually helped procrastinating, weak-willed overweights to undertake a "mass" reducing effort—he would follow the test with a reducing party for all of the audience who wished to speed reduce.

A few weeks later, they began the test diet. About 1100 people volunteered. Before long, Dr. Lindlahr received 438 reports. Within a month, 936 had reported—the average weight loss had been a pound a day for ten days.

### Reported Results (10 Days):

* "Thanks to you for the reducing diet. It has worked wonders with me. I lost eight pounds in ten days. I didn't lose anything until three days after I started, and then lost an average of a pound or more a day. I had plenty to eat and did not feel hungry at all during the ten days." —H.E.G., Hempstead, L.I.

* "Am I happy that I went on that ten-day diet! I lost 12 lbs. Never really felt hungry all during the diet . . ."—M.L.C., Bronx, N.Y.

* "I think I owe it to you to make a report on my success with the diet. I lost nine pounds. Did not suffer any ill effects like headaches or lack of food. Am feeling fine and never felt better in my life. It was a grand diet and crowned with success."—H.L.M., Croton-on-Hudson, N.Y.

* "I weighed two hundred pounds when I started on your diet and lost sixteen pounds. I can't tell you how good I feel. Before I had lots of aches and pains and now they are all gone. I wish every stout person would follow your diet and get the good results I did."—C.G., Ridgewood, N.J.

* "I lost two pounds the first day and a pound every day since. I have been the same weight for five years and did not believe that any impression could be made on my fat, but the diet worked like magic. I suffered no headaches." — M.K., Woodside, N.Y.

* "I started the diet by weighing 207 pounds and finished at 195½. I am very happy to say that I never felt better in my life, and will continue with your three-day alternate diet." —H.G., New York, N.Y.

* "I lost thirteen pounds and am still on the diet. I did not cheat even once. I am feeling so much better and my eyes have improved a lot." —M.C., Audubon, N.J.

* "I remained on the diet for one week and lost ten pounds, and stopped. I felt fine all throughout the period of the diet . . ." —M.C., New York, N.Y.

* "I lost sixteen pounds. I want to lose seven more. My husband was so pleased that he gave me a pair of scales to watch my weight. I felt fine all throughout the diet, and even worked harder than usual, as our house was being painted. I feel so much better since I lost that excess weight." —G.J.P., Nutley, N.J.

This test was positive proof of the speed reducing diet! Dr. Lindlahr now shortened the diet to seven days, in preparation for the first big radio reducing party. In April 1936, the party began and 26,000 listeners participated!

## REPORTED RESULTS (7 DAYS)!

On April 27, 1936, Dr. Lindlahr broadcasted the 7-day speed reducing diet on the radio. Each day, for a week, he gave the daily menus and encouraged listeners to try it. Hundreds of people who went on the diet phoned, wrote, and even telegraphed their progress. Let us now look at some of these letters, to give you who are hesitating, with fears of what might happen if you were to follow the speed reducing diet, an actual view of what really happens.

### Fifth Day of the Diet (May 1):

* "I am on your list of reducers. I weighed 192 on Monday (such a surprise when I got on the scales). I weighed 190 on

Tuesday, and boy, was I feeling good! I house-cleaned for
four hours, then went to the movies.... I've pulled my
girdle about three inches ... Puffiness out of my ankles and
shin bones ... rediscovering the buoyancy of health, head
clear as a crystal. I vowed I was going to get my girlish
figure back, and I'll show some certain snooty young ladies
that they don't know it all...." —Mrs. R.H.G.,
Hoesburg, Pa.

*"Well, I, for one, feel it's a real duty to tell you the results of
the present reducing diet. Am I losing? Well, I certainly
am. I'm one of the great army of fat night nurses ... I have
to have a bite with the family and eat at home, too.... I
am perfectly satisfied with the reducing meals.... No
need to tell you I'm feeling 100% fit. I can hardly eat all the
food given in a meal and the feeling of satiety stays with
me ...."—from a night nurse in Brooklyn.

## Sixth Day of the Diet (May 2):

*"I wish to report a loss of four pounds on the fourth day. Isn't
that grand? I'm the lady who inquired how I could go on the
diet when ... I couldn't chew because of lack of teeth. A
friend suggested that I grind the vegetables. That's just what
I'm doing, and here I am, losing at the rate of a pound a day.
I'm going to take off thirty pounds before I get through."—
a lady in New York City.

*"On April 27, I weighed 231 pounds. Waistline 40 inches,
calf 18, thigh 27, hip 45, height six feet one, age 43. On
May 2, I weighed 224 pounds, waist 38½, calf 17, thigh
25, hips 44. I lost exactly eight pounds. I possess a heavy,
bony structure, and I want to add ... that your diet is
unquestionably the best organized, most scientific of any I
have seen." —from a man in New York City.

*"Lost six and one-half pounds from Monday until Friday. ...
As I wrote you previously, I have diabetes. During the five
days, my blood sugar dropped from 220 to 137½. I was so
surprised that I asked my doctor if that were possible. He
said of course it was, and that I was doing fine."—a lady in
Philadelphia.

## The Following Monday:

*"I am 50 years old, five feet two, and weighed 259. Began
the diet April 27, without much hope, as I had been told

that it was impossible for me to reduce. Tuesday morning, I hadn't lost an ounce.... Wednesday, I almost popped off the scales from surprise, because I had registered a three-pound loss. I couldn't believe it. Happy? No words to describe it! By Thursday, I had lost 5 pounds.... By Saturday I had lost nine pounds. I told my butcher; he wouldn't believe me. And now, Monday morning, after a net loss of 12½ pounds, I feel splendid and have a big day's work mapped out." —from Philadelphia.

There you are! That's the inside story of the beginning days of the diet. The final survey of that week's adventures showed that the speed reducing diet, when used in thousands of cases, worked—really worked—with the accuracy of an oiled Swiss clock. Average loss was 8 pounds in seven days, *all cases combined!* Following the "big" party, the 7-day speed reducing diet was printed in formal style. The sale was phenomenal. An edition of 200,000 copies was exhausted within a year. Additional printings were made. By the Fall of 1938, close to a half million copies had been sold.

## MEDICAL OPINIONS REVISED, NEW SYSTEM "APPROVED"!

Along with widespread public acceptance of the speed reducing diet, medical doctors began re-examining and re-evaluating long-held beliefs about speed reducing. Finally, in the *Journal of the American Medical Association* (December 10, 1938), a most amazing case was reported in detail. It was the history of a woman who had reduced from 395 to 156 pounds in twenty months, with a very similar diet. The basic conclusion drawn from the study was: "There is no limit to the extent to which excess weight may be removed" by such foods, as long as essential nutrients are provided. "The medical concept of the dietary treatment of obesity was sharply revised," said Dr. Lindlahr. "Thus a principle went into practice!" This diet was "approved" he said!

## MORE AMAZING DISCOVERIES!

The aftermath of Dr. Lindlahr's speed reducing diet brought thousands upon thousands of letters. Here was experience more valuable than gold—better, even, than a searching laboratory experiment. More amazing discoveries came to light. Here are some of them.

## SPEED REDUCING FOODS HAVE SLOW ABSORBING SUGAR!

Dr. Lindlahr found that some people gain weight more rapidly than others because of the *type* of fatty foods or sugars and starches they ate. The sugar content of speed reducing foods, he found, has a much *lower absorption rate* than cane sugar or other types, and will not put on weight so easily.

## SPEED REDUCING FOODS DESTROY HARD-TO-MELT FAT!

On ordinary diets, or where exercise is depended upon, very often a fat person will lose fat mainly in the skin and neck, becomes drawn and haggard looking, but still exhibits the fat paunch, the "spare tire." Fat stored in the lower abdomen and the midriff is difficult to break up. But speed reducing foods stir up and stimulate the catabolic processes, and this so heightens the destruction of fat that even the tougher kinds are blown up, says Dr. Lindlahr. The thyroid and other glands are stimulated to greater activity. At any rate, hundreds and hundreds of radio listeners who followed the speed reducing diet, and began eating more and more speed reducing foods, reported that the spare tire, the extra chins, had obligingly disappeared. Amazingly, Dr. Lindlahr found that those in their 70's and older, reduced the easiest of all!

## MANY AILMENTS RELIEVED!

By far the greatest gains in health, well being, and general fitness were made by overweights who were beyond the age of 50. Those beyond 50 are likely to have rheumatism, high blood pressure, gall bladder trouble, and the degenerative diseases. The connection between overweight and degenerative diseases is so close that reducing becomes an essential part of the alleviation of these ailments, says Dr. Lindlahr. Not suprisingly, a vast number of reducers reported that high blood pressure went down from ten to fifty points ... blood sugar diminished 10, 20, 50, or even 100 per cent. Dr. Lindlahr wrote to several hundred of his regular radio listeners who had kept their weight loss, to ask them why. What was the impelling reason? A great majority reported that they held their weight down because they felt better.

## MENOPAUSAL SYMPTOMS RELIEVED!

Those who felt best after weight loss were women in change of life—and they lost weight more easily, too! Twenty-five women in the New York, New Jersey, and Philadelphia areas who were more than 35 pounds overweight and definitely in the change of life reduced an average of 9¾ pounds on the 7-day speed reducing diet, according to their letters.

## HOW TO STAY SLIM PERMANENTLY!

Many speed reducers began to crave speed reducing foods. Many followed this diet a little longer to take off 25, 30, or 40 pounds! Some used an alternate system of dieting one day and "letting go" the next day. Many preferred to eat a reducing breakfast, a reducing lunch, and relax their dietary vigilance at dinner. However they achieved it was the right way for them, Dr. Lindlahr declared. A number reported that they prevented fat accumulation by eating a "lot of speed reducing foods" or by replacing fat-adding foods with fat-demolishing foods, and this may have increased their metabolism.

It must obviously be possible for most overweight people to keep from gaining weight by the simple expedient of adding more speed reducing foods to their diet, Dr. Lindlahr declared. For example, if you should eat some food which gives you 150 net (or unburned) calories of excess fat, you can offset that gain by eating goodly portions of speed reducing foods, he pointed out.

# 4

## 100 Speed Reducing Foods
## with Reverse Calories!

Speed reducing foods contain what I call *reverse calories!* These foods have the opposite effect of *taking weight from the body!* The calories in speed reducing foods are different from ordinary calories, in one respect. They are encased in what you might call a deflector shield, a non-caloric fibrous mass that makes them much harder to get at or burn up!

**This fibrous armor makes them so difficult to "get at" that by the time your juices reach this fuel—which is what calories are—your body has already burned so much of its own fuel in the effort that you have *lost calories!* You lose more than you've eaten!**

This causes an actual weight loss! When mixed with regular fattening foods, speed reducing foods make them *less fattening*, by destroying their fat before it can be stored! They can even *neutralize the effect of fattening foods!* In effect, speed reducing foods contain reverse calories that are never stored, never turned to fat, for all practical purposes. Effects are exactly the opposite—in every way—of what you normally expect from food. You don't gain weight from eating them, you *lose weight*. Large amounts of speed reducing foods *make you thin!*

## 100 SPEED REDUCING FOODS!

Dr. Lindlahr listed over 100 fat-destroying, speed reducing foods—foods that actually take weight from the body. In this list of speed reducing foods, most meats are omitted, because they are not catabolic. In burning them, the body is left with excess calories. But lean meats *are* speed reducing. Excess meat calories are *excreted rather than stored*. They help the body burn its own fat by not contributing calories to any significant degree. Lean meat is essential on the speed reducing diet. You need some every day. In addition to all its other body building functions, lean meat stimulates the production of glucagon, the fat dissolving hormone that forces the release of fat from inner fat stores so that it can be burned. However, this can only happen in the presence of speed reducing foods with reverse calories. It's like pressing a gas pedal—fuel (fat) is released for burning. Speed reducing foods make sure that *more is burned* than normally happens! Eating speed reducing foods with reverse calories is like adding fuel to a fire. Here are the 100 fat-destroying foods Dr. Lindlahr discovered:

*Fruits*

apples
apricots
blackberries
blueberries
cantaloupe
cherries (fresh or canned)
crabapples
cranberries
currants (fresh)
Damson plum

fruit salad (fresh or canned)
grapefruit
grapes (Concord)
honeydew
huckleberries
kumquats
lemons (ice, juice)
limes (fresh)
loganberries
mangoes

muskmelons
nectarines
oranges (Florida, ice or juice)
papaya (fresh)
peaches (fresh, canned)
pears (Bartlett, fresh or canned)

pineapple (fresh)
pomegranates
prunes (fresh, canned)
quince
raspberries (fresh, red)
strawberries (fresh)
tangerines
watermelon

*Vegetables*
artichokes
asparagus
green beans
  (canned)
string beans
beets (raw,
  canned)
beet greens
  (cooked)
broccoli
  (cooked)
Brussels
  sprouts
  (canned)
cabbage (raw)
Chinese
  cabbage
  (raw,
  cooked)
caper
carrots (raw,
  cooked,
  tops, and
  peas,
  cooked)
cauliflower
  (raw,
  cooked)
celeriac
  (cooked)
celery (raw,
  cooked)
chervil
  (leaves)
chicory
  (leaves,
  green)

chives (fresh)
corn (sweet,
  canned, on
  cob,
  succotash,
  canned)
cucumbers
  (cooked)
Dandelion
  greens
dill pickles
  (with
  onions)
eggplant
endive
garlic
greens, beet
kale (cooked)
kohlrabi
  (cooked)
leeks (cooked)
lettuce (raw,
  cooked)
macédoine
mushrooms
  (raw,
  cooked)
mustard
  greens
okra (cooked,
  canned)
onions (fresh,
  boiled)
parsley leaves
parsnips (raw,
  boiled)
peas (raw,

canned,
  cooked,
  with
  carrots)
peppers,
  green,
  sweet, red
  (fresh)
pickles, dill,
  sweet, sour
pumpkin
radishes
red cabbage
rhubarb (raw)
rutabagas
sauerkraut
salsify
  (cooked)
scallions
sorrel
spinach
  (fresh,
  cooked)
squash
  (canned,
  summer,
  cooked)
tomato (fresh,
  canned)
turnips (raw,
  cooked)
vegetable
  salad
watercress

*Fish*
bass, sea

buffalo
clams
  (cooked)
cod steaks
crabs
flounder
frogs legs
lobster
  (cooked)
mussels
oysters (raw,
  cocktail,
  half shell)
shrimps (raw,
  boiled,
  canned)
terrapin


*Drinks*
(unsweetened)

juices
  apple
  apricot
  cherry
  grapefruit
  grape
  lemonade
  (dash
    sugar)
  orange
  papaya
  pineapple
  tomato
milk*

*Whole milk, acidophilus milk, buttermilk and skim milk are not catabolic, strictly speaking, but they provide such excellent food values, and are so useful in any reducing diet, that Dr. Lindlahr recommends them as speed reducing foods—especially skim milk, which has all the food value of whole milk, without the fat or cream.

On the following pages, you'll find recipes—recommended by Dr. Lindlahr—that contain a high percentage of speed reducing foods. The recipes may be used in any combination, for lunch, supper, or between meal snacks, on a speed reducing diet of your own creation (more details on the *original* speed reducing diet, with exact menus, are given later on in this book). Dr. Lindlahr used butter and various salad dressings in his recipes. I suggest the following: use diet margarine, diet salad dressings, omit salt or use it sparingly, and limit yourself to one slice of bread per meal (or 2 slices of high fiber bread which has half the calories).

## Apples

Raw, scraped apples are of particular benefit to adults suffering various intestinal disturbances, such as diarrhea and certain forms of colitis. The active principle is pectin. Raw, scraped apples can be used therapeutically alone without any other food. They are a good source of Vitamin B-1, excellent for increasing hemoglobin in the blood (good for anemia). They are alkaline, but may cause allergic reaction. If allergic, of course, avoid them. Apples are suitable for eating as fresh fruit and should be used as table fruit, or diced or sliced for salads and fruit cups. Store in cool, dry place.

## Apricots

Apricots are rich in Vitamin A, which makes them a good food to help ward off colds and other such infections. They are also rich in B vitamins. Apricots are alkaline. Fresh or canned, they have medium calorie content, but are definitely catabolic, when fresh or canned (but not dried). They are available fresh (short season, June to August). Select ripe, plump fruit, bright orange-yellow in color. Store at room temperature until ripe before chilling. Apricots are best eaten fresh—uncooked. Serve as breakfast fruit, table fruit, simple dessert or as part of fruit cup.

## Artichokes

Their high catabolic nature makes artichokes good for reducers—and they are low in calories, too, when no butter or rich sauce is served with them. Artichokes are high in roughage, and should not be used on a soft diet, unless puréed. They generally do not cause allergic reactions. Use with heavy meats or starches.

*Quick-Cooked Artichokes*

6 small or medium-sized
    artichokes
4 tablespoons diet margarine

Wash thoroughly; remove any discolored outer leaves. Cut off sharp tips of leaves and stem about ½ inch below base of leaves. Drop artichokes into 2 inches of boiling water. As soon as water boils again, cover utensil tightly; cook about 20 to 30 minutes, just until artichokes are tender (when outer leaf can easily be pulled from stem). Time of cooking depends upon size and freshness of artichokes. Serve whole with melted margarine. Eat only white flesh part of leaves and heart.

## Asparagus

Apart from excellent vitamin values in B-1, C and G, asparagus contains a food factor called asparagin, which gently stimulates kidney function. In addition, high water content makes asparagus of particular value in cases of kidney disease, as it helps normalize water balance of body. High mineral content of asparagus is helpful to sufferers from nutritional anemia. It is best to buy green, unblanched stalks. Calorie content is very low. Asparagus is a good reducing dish if not served with butter or rich sauce. Serve as main vegetable dish at dinner. Hot asparagus on toast, garnished with pimiento strips, makes an excellent luncheon dish. Cold asparagus may be used for salads.

*Quick-Cooked Asparagus*

30 stalks asparagus salt         3 tablespoons melted diet
                                           margarine

Wash stalks thoroughly under running water. Remove all of stem end which is hard and woody. Tie stalks in bunch with white cotton string; place stem-end down in bottom of double boiler containing 2 inches boiling water. Cover with upper part of double boiler (inverted), and cook 12 to 20 minutes, until tender. Add salt just before removing from heat. Drain asparagus, remove string, and dress with melted margarine.

*Asparagus Loaf*

| | |
|---|---|
| 2 cups cooked or canned asparagus | ½ cup soft bread crumbs |
| 2 eggs | 1 tablespoon minced onion |
| ½ cup asparagus pot liquor | ½ teaspoon salt (optional) |
| ½ cup milk (skim) | ⅛ teaspoon paprika |
| 1 tablespoon melted diet margarine | 3 teaspoons minced parsley |

Quick-cook asparagus according to basic recipe, or open canned asparagus and drain, reserving pot liquor. Cut asparagus into 1-inch pieces. Combine eggs, pot liquor, milk and melted margarine; beat well. Add bread crumbs, onion, seasoning, parsley and asparagus, and turn into buttered casserole or loaf pan. Bake in moderate oven (375° F.) about 25 to 30 minutes, just until center is firm and top is delicately browned. Garnish with pimiento strips.

## Bass—See Fish

## Beans (Green String Beans)

Green string (snap) beans are a good source of all the vitamins; yellow wax beans contain smaller amounts—both are highly catabolic (fat breaking). Many persons feel that string beans are difficult to digest. The answer is usually that beans are improperly prepared with lots of grease or meat. Quick-cooked beans rarely cause distress, except in persons allergic to them.

*Quick-Cooked String Beans*

| | |
|---|---|
| 2 pounds green or yellow (wax string beans) | salt (optional) |
| | 2 tablespoons diet margarine |
| 2 teaspoons grated onion | 2 tablespoons minced parsley |

Wash thoroughly; break or cut off ends of beans. Shred by cutting each bean into fine strips or slivers (slice lengthwise or sidewise diagonally). Drop slivers into 1 inch of boiling water. When water again reaches full boil, cover utensil and cook beans until just tender. Add onion (or chives) during last 5 minutes of cooking. Cook 15-20 minutes. Add salt just before removing from heat (never during cooking). Serve in individual dishes with pot liquor and margarine, and garnish with minced parsley.

*String Beans and Corn*—Quick-cook 1 pound shredded green or yellow string beans as directed in basic recipe. Separately, quick-cook 1½ cups fresh-cut corn in 1 inch boiling water about 6 minutes. Combine vegetables with pot liquors, add 2 tablespoons diet margarine and 2 teaspoons of salt (optional). Serve in individual dishes. If canned or leftover cooked corn (cut from cob) is used, add to beans 5 minutes before they have finished cooking.

*String Beans and Chard Stalks*—Combine 1½ pounds shredded green or yellow string beans and 2½ cups diced chard stalks (from 3 pounds chard). Quick-cook as directed in basic recipe. If canned string beans are used, add to saucepan after chard stalks have cooked 10 minutes. This dish is a good way to serve chard to those who may not like it plain. (Chard is a good diet food.)

## Beets

Beets contain an easily available sugar which is readily burned as fuel, not stored as fat. They are, therefore, good as a quick source of energy. High water content makes beets an excellent food for balancing concentrated (high starch or protein) foods. They are an excellent source of Vitamin B-1, thus helpful in keeping the nerves healthy. They are also an excellent source of Vitamin A and B-2. They are alkaline. Use in soft diets only when puréed, as fairly high in roughage. Beets are low in calories, excellent for reducers (occasionally cause allergic reactions). It's best to quick-cook beets (see below). Serve them to balance a dinner protein dish. They should not accompany another sweet vegetable, like carrots, or be eaten with a sweet dessert, or the meal as a whole will be too sweet. Leftover beets, chilled and pickled, are appetizing in salads. Beet greens should not be thrown away if young and crisp, as they are even higher in vitamins (especially A) than the root, and very rich in the blood building minerals, iron and manganese. Serve them cooked with beets, with mixed greens, or alone.

### Quick-Cooked Beets

| | |
|---|---|
| 18 small beets | 2 tablespoons lemon juice (or |
| 2 tablespoons diet margarine | 6 orange segments, diced) |
| 1 teaspoon salt (optional) | |

Remove leaves and stems. Scrub beets. Scrape or pare thin skin from beets; dice, slice, or cut into quarters. Drop prepared beets into boiling water to cover. When water has again reached full boil, cover utensil and cook 20 to 25 minutes, just until beets are tender. Add margarine and salt to taste, and fruit or fruit juice just before serving. Serve in individual dishes with pot liquor.

*Young Fresh Beets*—Rub thoroughly washed beets across fine shredder or grater, and place slivers in saucepan with only enough water to prevent burning. Cover and cook over low heat about 8 to 10 minutes, stirring occasionally. Season with salt and a few drops of lemon juice. Serve dotted with butter in individual dishes.

*Beets Piquant*

| | |
|---|---|
| 8 medium-sized cooked (or 1 No. 2 can) beets | ½ teaspoon salt |
| | ⅛ teaspoon pepper |
| 1 cup beet liquor | 1 teaspoon sugar |
| ¼ cup lemon juice | 1 tablespoon minced onion |

Prepare, cook and drain beets (reserving liquid) as directed in basic recipe. Add beet liquor to remaining ingredients and stir until sugar dissolves. Pour over beets. Reheat to serve hot, or chill thoroughly to serve as cold pickled beets.

*Quick-Cooked Beet Greens*

| | |
|---|---|
| 1½ pounds beet greens | 2 tablespoons diet margarine |
| 1 teaspoon salt (optional) | 6 lemon wedges (1 lemon) |

Remove any coarse, wilted or discolored leaves and stems. Wash well in several waters to remove all traces of sand. Place greens in utensil containing ½ inch boiling water. Cover pan when water has again begun to boil and cook about 7 minutes—just until tender. Season with salt just before removing from heat. Drain, chop and add margarine. Serve with lemon.

## Blackberries

Blackberries and blackberry juice are highly catabolic, low in calories, and excellent for reducing. Canned berries (Standard pack) are medium in calorie content, but still catabolic; reducers should choose water-packed fruit or wash and drain Standard-pack variety. This fruit seldom causes allergic reactions. It is a good source of Vitamin A and B-1. Blackberries are alkaline. They should not be eaten on soft diets unless puréed (force through fine sieve), because they are high in roughage.

Blackberries contain a chemical which relieves dysentery (diarrhea) and digestive complaints arising from eating spoiled food. During the Civil War, a truce was once declared so that men suffering from intestinal complaints could forage openly for blackberries. Avoid bruised berries or stained containers. Blackberries are best eaten as fresh fruit, or mixed in fruit cups, or in cereals.

## Blueberries (Huckleberries)

Blueberries contain a substance called "neomyrtillin," used in treating diabetes. Neomyrtillin does help reduce excess sugar in the blood in a manner similar to that of insulin. They are a good source of Vitamins B-1 and C, rich in manganese, and alkaline. Exclude them from soft diets, as they are fairly high in roughage. Use blackberry juice, instead. Medium in calorie content, they are still highly catabolic and good for reducers.

Their calories are derived chiefly from a natural sugar which is readily transformed into energy, capable of burning up fat. The whole fruit is preferable to juice for reducers. Choose water-packed fruit in the canned type, or drain and wash berries from Standard-pack cans. Blueberries seldom cause allergic reactions. They are best eaten as a fresh fruit or mixed in fruit cups, or in cereals.

## Broccoli

Because of extremely high Vitamin C content, broccoli is an excellent food for those suffering with arthritis or rheumatism. It is particularly good for persons who tend to bleed readily from the surface capillaries (tiny blood vessels close to the skin surface). It is also a good food to build up the blood. It is alkaline and generally does not cause allergic reactions; in fact, it is used in elimination diets for allergic patients. Tends to produce flatulence when overcooked; hence, quick-cooking is best.

Low in calorie content—and highly catabolic—broccoli is especially good for reducers, and for all others to balance a heavy or concentrated meal. Tender stalks of broccoli may be used raw as an appetizer, and tender leaves may be added to soup stock or cooked in mixed greens.

*Quick-Cooked Broccoli*

3 pounds broccoli                    2 tablespoons diet margarine
   (approximate)
1 teaspoon salt

Discard only the largest and heaviest leaves, and any woody part of stems if present. Separate flowers into suitable portions for serving. Wash well. Tie sections into bunch with white cotton string. Place stems downward in utensil containing 3 inches of boiling water. When water has again reached a full boil, cover utensil and cook 15 to 30 minutes, depending on tenderness of stems. Salt just before removing from heat. Remove from water, remove string and serve with margarine and pot liquor.

## Brussels Sprouts

Brussels sprouts are an outstanding source of Vitamin C; thus a good food for those suffering from blood pressure disorders, pyorrhea or bleeding gums. It is also excellent for arthritics (the pot liquor is especially beneficial). Do not use on soft diets, since Brussels sprouts are high in roughage and difficult to purée. Highly catabolic and very low in calories, they are an excellent dish for reducers. Many persons who suffer digestive distress after eating Brussels sprouts may be sensitive merely to improperly cooked sprouts. Overcooking generates sulphur compounds and often makes sprouts difficult to digest. Finely shredded raw sprouts, or quick-cooked ones, rarely cause distress, except in those actually allergic to this vegetable.

*Quick-Cooked Brussels Sprouts*

1 quart Brussels sprouts          ½ teaspoon pepper
1 teaspoon minced onion           2 tablespoons minced parsley
1 teaspoon salt                   2 tablespoons diet margarine

Remove any wilted leaves and stems; cut into quarters and wash well. Soaking is unnecessary and destroys vitamins. Remove hard stem. Drop quartered sprouts and onion into enough boiling water to cover. Do not cover utensil. Cook 8 to 10 minutes, just until tender. Add salt, pepper and parsley just before removing from heat. Never salt during cooking. Dress with margarine; serve with pot liquor in individual dishes.

*Brussels Sprouts and Celery*—Quick-cook 1½ cups diced celery as directed on page 62. After it has boiled about 5 minutes, add 1 pint quartered Brussels sprouts and 1 teaspoon minced onion with just enough boiling water to cover. Continue cooking as in basic recipe for Brussels sprouts. Season, add margarine and minced parsley, and serve in individual dishes with pot liquor.

## Cabbage

Cabbage contains the anti-ulcer vitamin U, plus chlorine and sulphur which help cleanse the mucous membranes of the stomach. This, say medical authorities, is only possible if eaten raw or its fresh juice drunk. The value of raw cabbage juice as a cure for ulcers is now recognized by many doctors, since it was first announced by Dr. Garnett Cheney of the Department of Medicine, Stanford University Medical School, around 1950. Raw, shredded cabbage (green, red, Chinese) is one of the cheapest and best sources of Vitamin C. One generous six-ounce serving of coleslaw will fulfill the day's Vitamin C requirement.

It is highly catabolic, low in calories, and good for reducers. Properly quick-cooked cabbage and *finely* shredded raw cabbage have been shown in clinical experiments to be well tolerated by persons who previously had suffered digestive distress upon eating cabbage. Never overcook. Serve as raw salad to introduce any meal, or use in combination with other vegetables to make a large luncheon salad.

### Quick-Cooked Cabbage

| | |
|---|---|
| 1 large head cabbage | 2 tablespoons diet margarine |
| ¼ teaspoon salt | ½ cup rich milk (optional) |
| ¼ teaspoon pepper | |

Remove any damaged leaves. Quarter, slice or shred (depending upon use) and wash under running water. Place in boiling water to cover and cook uncovered just until tender, 7 to 12 minutes, depending upon size of pieces. Quartered sections require longest cooking time. Add salt and pepper just before removing from heat. Drain, reserving pot liquor for future use. Add margarine, and milk if desired.

*Cantaloupe—See Melons*

*Carrots*

Carrots cooked or raw, and especially the pot liquor (when cooked) have brought miraculous results in restoring sight to near-blind glaucoma victims. They are higher in vitamin value when eaten raw in salads or as an appetizer. They are highly catabolic, low in calories, and recommended for reducers. Their high water content makes them ideal for serving at a meal with concentrated foods. One of the best "combiners" among vegetables, their flavor blends well with almost any green vegetable. *Carrot tops* are too often thrown away by housewives. They are a fine source of vitamins and minerals, and should always be saved for use in cooked mixed greens, soups (especially spring consommé and cream of spinach soups) or stews. Use tender leaves and stems. Flavor is characteristically strong and somewhat bitter; hence, combination dishes are recommended.

### Quick-Cooked Carrots

| | |
|---|---|
| 2 pounds (about 12 medium-sized) carrots | ½ teaspoon salt<br>2 tablespoons diet margarine |

Small-sized carrots can be served whole and need not be scraped; larger, more mature ones can be skinned after cooking. Carrots to be sliced or diced should be scraped before cooking. Slice or quarter lengthwise. Drop into 1 inch boiling water. When water has again reached full boil, cover utensil; cook about 15 to 25 minutes, just until tender, depending upon size and maturity of carrots. Add salt and margarine just before removing from heat. Serve with pot liquor in individual dishes.

*Parsley Carrots*—Quick-cook carrots as directed in basic recipe. When tender, drain, reserving pot liquor for future use. Add diet margarine to drained carrots in pan. Gently turn carrots in melted butter until well coated. Sprinkle with 4 tablespoons minced parsley.

*Carrots and Onions*—Shred very fine 10 medium-sized carrots and mince 2 medium-sized onion. Place in pan with 1 cup boiling water, cover tightly and quick-cook about 8 to 10 minutes, just until tender. Add ½ teaspoon salt, 2 tablespoons diet margarine, 2 tablespoons minced parsley and 1 cup rich milk just long enough before serving to heat milk. Serve in individual dishes with pot liquor.

*Carrots and Peas*—Dice 6 medium-sized carrots. Combine with 1½ cups shelled peas and quick-cook, according to directions in basic recipe, about 15 minutes. Sprinkle with 2 tablespoons minced parsley, season, dress with diet margarine and serve in individual dishes with pot liquor.

### Carrot Ring

| | |
|---|---|
| 3 cups diced carrots | ⅛ teaspoon pepper |
| 2 tablespoons diet margarine | 2 tablespoons minced parsley |
| ¼ teaspoon salt | |

Quick-cook carrots as directed in basic recipe. Drain, reserving pot liquor for future use, and mash. Stir in remaining ingredients. Place in buttered ring mold (using diet margarine) and reheat in moderate oven (375° F.) about 10 minutes. Unmold and serve garnished with parsley.

## Casaba—See Melons

## Cauliflower

Cauliflower is an excellent source of Vitamin C, and is good for high blood pressure, pyorrhea or bleeding gums. It is also rich in Vitamin B-1, B-2, calcium and sulphur, which make it cleansing and soothing to the nerves. High water content makes it excellent for balancing concentrated (high starch or protein) foods at a meal. It is alkaline, not recommended for soft diets unless strained, as it is high in roughage.

It is highly catabolic, low in calories, and good for reducers. Like other members of the cabbage family, it may cause allergic reactions. However, the digestive distress some people suffer is often due to improper cooking. Correctly cooked, it rarely disturbs those not allergic to it. Make Vitamin C pot liquor by dropping outside leaves into boiling water and boiling for 2 minutes.

### Quick-Cooked Cauliflower

| | |
|---|---|
| 2-pound head of cauliflower | 1 tablespoon diet margarine |
| 1 teaspoon salt | 2 tablespoons minced parsley |

Remove leaves, stalks, stem and any discoloration on flowerets. Save leaves for making soups or pot liquors, and stems for eating raw. Break head into flowerets and wash well under running water; do not soak. Drop flowerets into 2 inches of boiling water, and cook uncovered 15 to 20 minutes. Salt just before removing from heat. Serve in individual dishes with pot liquor to which has been added diet margarine and parsley.

## Celery

Celery was brewed by ancient Oriental peoples as a medicinal herb for stomach upsets. Green celery is 100 times richer in Vitamin A than white or blanched celery. It is highly catabolic, low in calories, and good for reducing. Its high water content makes it good for balancing concentrated foods at a meal. It adds to the alkaline reserves of the body. It is fairly high in roughage; not recommended for soft diets.

### Quick-Cooked Celery

| | |
|---|---|
| 3 cups diced celery | 1 tablespoon diet margarine |
| 1 teaspoon salt | 2 tablespoons minced parsley |

Scrub celery and remove any damaged stalks or leaves. Trim root. Quarter bunch and, holding quarters together, cut through all four sections at once to dice. Place diced celery in cold water to cover and move pieces about to remove any remaining sand. Drain. Drop diced celery into ½ inch boiling water. When water has again reached full boil, cover pan and cook 10 to 12 minutes, just until celery is tender. Salt before removing from heat. Serve in individual dishes with pot liquor to which has been added margarine and minced parsley.

## Cherries

Cherries have brought amazing pain relief in arthritic and rheumatic ailments, especially gout. They are a good source of Vitamins A and B-1, and are among the foods highest in iron, copper and manganese (important for building up blood and good for anemia). They are alkaline, recommended for soft diets, as they are low in roughage. They seldom cause allergic reactions.

Cherries are medium in calorie content, but very catabolic and good for reducing. Canned water-packed cherries may be used on reducing diets to better advantage than fresh or Standard-pack canned cherries (the latter, however, may be washed off and used by reducers). Use sweet cherries for eating as fresh fruit, and sour ones for cooking. The sweeter varieties are the larger, heart-shaped fruit. Some smaller types, deep red to almost black, are also sweet. Sour ones are usually smaller. Choose ripe, well-colored, plump, firm cherries. Avoid bruised ones or stained containers.

## Chicory

Chicory is good for warding off colds and other respiratory infections, and to maintain normal eyesight. Its high Vitamin C makes it of some value to sufferers from blood pressure disorders, pyorrhea or bleeding gums.

Chicory is highly catabolic, low in calories, excellent for reducers. Its high water content makes it suitable for balancing concentrated (heavy starch or protein) foods at a meal. It generally does not cause allergic reactions. Chicory is best eaten raw as salad or salad ingredient. It may be cooked and mixed with other greens such as spinach. To cook, cover leaves with boiling water in covered utensil. Cooking time will depend upon texture of leaves. Drain, chop, season and mix with spinach or any milder green, if too strong. It is often cut fine and cooked in soups or stews.

## Clams—See Shellfish

## Cod—See Fish

## Corn

Yellow corn is an excellent source of Vitamin A, which makes it good food to help ward off colds and other respiratory infections, and to maintain normal eyesight. It is an acid-ash food, and should be avoided by those suffering with hyperacidity, or those on a special alkaline diet. It is not recommended for soft diets unless puréed, as it is high in roughage.

Corn itself is not especially high in calorie content, as is usually supposed, and not very much of it is digested—but it is highly catabolic (fat breaking). Actually, the butter used with corn is what makes it taboo for reducers, who could eat corn safely with a bare minimum of butter (or diet margarine).

*Quick-Cooked Corn*

6-12 ears corn

In large kettle, boil enough water to cover ears of corn. Remove husks and silk or ears, trimming ends if necessary. Drop corn into boiling water and cover when water starts boiling again. Cook 5-10 minutes, until milk in kernels is set; overcooking will make corn tough. Serve ears piping hot, to be buttered and seasoned individually at table.

*Scalloped Corn and Tomatoes*—Combine 2 cups canned (whole kernel style) or fresh-cut cooked corn, 1 cup canned or fresh tomatoes and ½ cup grated sharp cheese in a greased casserole dish. Bake in medium oven (375° F.) about 10 minutes, until cheese is melted. For additional flavor, add 3 tablespoons minced and sautéed onion before baking.

## Crabs—See Shellfish

## Cranberries

Cranberries contain a substance which stimulates the flow of gastric juice, aiding digestion. They are particularly helpful in digesting heavy meat! They are highly catabolic, low in calories, a good source of B-1 and C. They are one of the few fruits with an acid effect on the body, and should be avoided by those suffering with hypersensitivity, or those on a special alkaline diet. Choose dark red rather than lighter colored berries. Ripe fruit is firm and well-colored; avoid soft, bruised, over-ripe berries. Cooked cranberries make delightful cranberry ice, sherbets or gelatin salads.

## Cucumbers

Cucumbers contain an enzyme called erepsin, which aids digestion of proteins. Cucumber purée or juice is sometimes advised for digestive difficulties. Should be used raw or broiled (after parboiling) with all heavy protein foods to aid in digesting them. Their actual protein-digesting value is comparable to that of papaya. They are an excellent source of Vitamin B-1, very useful as a balancer of concentrated (heavy starch or protein) foods at a meal. They are alkaline, highly catabolic, low in calories, ideal for reducers. Cucumbers may cause allergic reactions (some people are sensitive to raw but not cooked cucumbers). It may be possible to avoid sensitivity by not soaking them in salt water. They are best eaten raw, as salad ingredient, or cut into strips for appetizer. Very young ones need not be pared. If skin is old and tough, pare, as it may cause digestive distress for anyone with a delicate stomach (however, the peeling is not poisonous). If slightly wilted, crisp in ice water 10 to 15 minutes. Do not oversoak or use salt water. If desired cooked, pare and boil like summer squash. Season with salt, pepper, butter. Sprinkle with grated cheese for extra flavor.

## Currants

Black currants are an outstanding source of Vitamin C; red currants are a good source of B-1 and C. Although currants are sometimes eaten as fresh fruit, they are most commonly used in jams, jellies, pies or tarts. Most dried currants are eaten like raisins. They are rich in iron, copper and manganese, which makes them a good food for building up the blood. They are alkaline (especially dried currants). Fresh currants and currant juice have low calorie content—and are highly catabolic. However, since they are eaten by the handful, it is wiser to stick to fresh currant juice, if you are reducing, and avoid jam, jelly and dried currants, which lose their catabolic effect.

## Damson Plum

Plums are valued chiefly for their delicious flavor and refreshing qualities—a pleasant variation in fruit desserts and fruit cups. All fresh plums are a good source of Vitamin B-1 and G (B-2). High water content and low calorie value make plums a good food for reducers. They are highly catabolic. They should not be eaten to excess because—although alkaline—they contain substances which increase the acidity of the urine. They are not permissible for those suffering hyperacidity or those on a special alkaline diet. They are high in pectin—which helps detoxify the digestive tract. Reducers should choose waterpacked fruit or rinse off syrup from Standard pack ones. Plums seldom cause allergic reactions. Damson plums are comparatively small, purple in color. Choose firm, ripe plums of good color. Larger ones are preferable. Fully ripe plums are suitable for immediate table use. Chill before serving, or use in salads and fruit cups.

## Dandelion Greens

This vegetable is a kidney stimulant. A tea derived from dandelion greens is used as an old-time remedy for kidney disease and dropsy. It was also prescribed in ancient times to help treat stones. Today we know that dandelion greens are an outstanding source of Vitamin A, the factor known to help ward off and dissolve stones and gravel—also good for the complexion, especially when eaten with other mixed greens. They are alkaline, and may be used on soft diets as they are low in roughage. Low in calories and highly catabolic, they may be used liberally by those on a reducing diet. They usually do not cause allergic reactions. Choose young, green, unwilted leaves. Clip from plant before blossom appears (older ones have bitter taste), and use at once. They are best eaten raw, chopped and mixed with milder-flavored greens as a salad ingredient. Serve with favorite diet dressing. To cook, place dandelion greens in ½ inch boiling water and cook 7 minutes, stirring occasionally. Combine for best flavor, with cooked spinach, lettuce or other mild greens. Chop, season and dress with diet margarine and lemon juice.

## Chives and Garlic

Chives stimulate the flow of saliva and gastric juice. They are an outstanding source of Vitamin C, A, B-1 and B-2. Garlic contains a bactericide called crotonaldehyde, and is a good germ-killer. It is particularly excellent for disease of the nose and respiratory tract. It is often recommended for patients with high blood pressure. Garlic is also a digestive stimulant and antiseptic, a good source of Vitamin C. Both garlic and chives are alkaline, high in roughage—but since they are used solely as flavoring agents in tiny amounts, this factor is unimportant. They contain practically no calories, but may cause allergic reactions, due to sulphur content.

In chives, the fine grass-like shoots should be unwilted and unspotted (no yellowed or dried-out tips). Use only for seasoning. A few minced shoots are sufficient for any purpose. In garlic, choose firm, mature bulbs with dry, brittle skins. Avoid those with cracked skins or double-growth splits. Use chives as you would onion for seasoning green salads, cottage cheese, soups, stews, meat, egg and vegetable dishes—but use sparingly. Garlic, too, is used solely as a flavoring agent (except for medicinal purposes). Rub cut end of clove over roasts, steaks, poultry, etc., or over salad bowl or utensil in which food is to be cooked. Use whole clove for flavoring in basting liquids of meats.

## Eggplant

Eggplant is an outstanding source of Vitamin B-2, hence good for nervous conditions like sore tongue, shingles, etc. This vitamin is not found in great abundance in any other vegetable except turnip greens. Eggplant is highly catabolic, low in calories, and excellent for reducers. The reputation eggplant has for being difficult to digest is the result of improper cooking. Old-fashioned cooks always fried or sautéed eggplant, thus making it a greasy dish. It is much better nutritionally to add needed flavor with tomatoes, onion, mushrooms, etc., as in Eggplant Creole.

### Eggplant Creole

| | |
|---|---|
| 1 medium-sized eggplant | 1½ cups fresh or canned |
| ½ pound (2 cups) mushrooms | tomatoes |
| 4 tablespoons diet margarine | ½ teaspoon salt |
| 1 medium-sized onion, | ½ teaspoon sugar |
| minced | ⅛ teaspoon pepper |
| 1 green pepper, chopped | |

Pare eggplant and chop or dice into small pieces. Wash and slice mushrooms. Melt margarine in large skillet, add onions, peppers and mushrooms, and sauté until onions are yellow, about 3 minutes. Add eggplant and tomatoes, cover and simmer about 20 to 25 minutes, just until eggplant is tender. Add seasoning and serve.

## Fish

   Fish are flesh (protein) food consisting of two broad groups: those with scales (fish), and those without (shellfish). There are more than 140 edible fish available in the United States, although the average person is familiar with perhaps only ten varieties. The leading types common to most markets may be classified as lean or fat fish.

| Lean Fish | | Fat Fish | |
|-----------|----------|-----------|----------|
| black fish | king fish | bonito | salmon |
| bluefish | perch | butterfish | sardines |
| cod | pickerel | herring | shad |
| flounder | smelt | swordfish | tuna |
| haddock | trout | mackerel | whitefish |
| halibut | weakfish | pompano | |

   Lean fish, of course, are helpful in any reducing diet. But of all fish and seafood products, only the following may be classified as speed reducing foods (with reverse calories):

| | |
|---|---|
| bass, sea | frogs legs |
| buffalo | lobster (cooked) |
| clams (cooked) | mussels |
| cod steaks | oysters (raw, |
| crabs | cocktail, half shell) |
| flounder | shrimps (raw, boiled, canned) |

   Lean fish have about 2 per cent fat; all others have 5 per cent or more. Very fat fish, such as salmon, butterfish, etc., contain as much as 15 to 20 per cent fat. All fish have a high mineral content and are apt to be richer in certain of the vitamins than meats. Fish oils and livers (cod liver, halibut, tuna or salmon oil) are exceptional sources of vitamins A and D. Fish—especially salt-water fish—is our most important source of iodine, needed for proper functioning of glands. Everyone should eat fish at least once a week. Freshness is all important. Fish never has a strong (or tainted) odor, if fresh. Fish spoils quickly, but can be kept for a short time if packed in ice (cleaned, salted, and wrapped securely).
   Fish is cooked just until it flakes (separates easily). Generally speaking, fat fish should be broiled or baked; lean fish, poached or broiled. Fillets are small strips of boned and skinned fish. Brush lean fish with butter or oil before cooking. The simplest ways to cook fish

are usually the best. Use almost any fillet (halibut, haddock, cod, perch, fluke, etc.) for baking or broiling; use large fish (bluefish, bonito, etc.) for stuffing. Use leftover or canned fish for flaked fish salad, casserole dishes, etc.

Fish lends itself well to garnishing with catabolic (speed reducing) foods like parsley and lemon. Where possible, incorporate garnish in dish (sprinkle minced parsley on top of fish, rather than serve sprigs as decoration), so that it is more likely to be eaten. Always serve fish on a hot platter, as it cools rapidly.

## Broiled Fish

| | |
|---|---|
| 1 3-to-4-pound fish (or 6 small fish) | 1 teaspoon paprika |
| | ¼ cup melted diet margarine |
| 1 teaspoon salt | Lemon Butter (see below) |

Have dealer split and clean whole fish. Wash thoroughly and blot with paper towel or cloth. Be sure fish is dry before cooking. Mix salt and paprika with melted margarine, and brush over fish. Place fish, skin-side down, on well-greased broiler pan (or rack, if fish is fatty). Broil 2 inches from moderate heat about 10 to 15 minutes, until fish is brown and flakes when tried with a fork. Small fish or thick fillets may be turned to brown both sides. Serve on hot platter with Lemon Butter.

## Lemon Butter

| | |
|---|---|
| 4 tablespoons diet margarine | 1 tablespoon minced parsley |
| 1 tablespoon lemon juice | dash of paprika |

Place margarine in small skillet and stir constantly over low heat just until it melts. Remove from heat and stir in remaining ingredients. Serve at once.

## Fillets Baked in Milk

| | |
|---|---|
| 2 pounds fish fillets | 3 tablespoons diet margarine |
| 1 cup milk (or sour cream) | 2 tablespoons minced parsley |
| 1 teaspoon salt | (or chives) |
| ⅛ teaspoon pepper | |

Wash fillets, cut into pieces for serving and arrange in greased baking dish. Pour over just enough milk or sour cream to cover. Sprinkle with salt and pepper and dot with butter. Bake in moderate oven (375° F.) about 15 minutes, or until fish flakes when tested with fork. Serve garnished with minced parsley or chives.

*Baked Fish*

| | |
|---|---|
| 1 3-to-4-pound fish | ¼ cup melted diet margarine |
| 1 teaspoon salt | 6 lemon quarters |
| 1 teaspoon paprika | watercress |
| 1 teaspoon onion juice | Parsley Butter |

Have fish split and cleaned at dealer's. Wash thoroughly. Place in greased shallow baking pan. Mix salt, paprika and onion juice with margarine, and brush over fish. Bake, skin-side down, in a moderately hot oven (424° F.) 30 to 40 minutes, until fish is well browned and flakes from bone when tried with a fork. Garnish with quartered lemon and watercress, and serve with Parsley Butter.

*Parsley Butter*

Follow basic recipe for Lemon Butter, but increase parsley to 3 tablespoons and omit lemon juice or decrease to ½ teaspoon.

*Baked Fish Suggestion*

If you have a plank or oven-proof platter, arrange fish in center of plank and bake as directed. After fish has baked 25 minutes, surround with 12 halves buttered (use diet margarine), quick-cooked carrots, 12 buttered mushroom caps, 6 halves of fresh tomatoes and 3 cups mashed potatoes (for border). Continue baking about 5 to 10 minutes longer.

## Flounder—See Fish

## Garlic—See Chives

## Grapefruit

Many physicians advocate the grapefruit treatment for influenza, colds and fevers; no solid food whatsoever, plenty of water and 5 to 15 grapefruits a day. This is probably effective due to its high alkalizing effect and excellent Vitamin C values. High blood pressure caused by acidemia may often be relieved with grapefruit. Grapefruits have low calorie content, are highly catabolic, and good for reducers. Reducers will do well to eat the whole fruit, rather than drink the juice, and to purchase water-packed grapefruit in canned variety or wash-off Standard-pack type. The juice is very low in roughage and may be used on soft diets. Grapefruit seldom causes allergic reactions. They are best eaten fresh, in halves, with or without sugar, or in segments or slices for salads, fruit cups, desserts, etc.

### Honeydew—See Melons

### Kale

Kale is one of the most outstanding sources of Vitamin A; in fact, it is superior in all vitamins except D. Kale should be eaten often when in season, as one serving will supply more than the daily Vitamin A requirement, and go far toward satisfying all the other vitamin needs. Kale is rich in minerals as well. It is low in calorie content and alkaline in reaction. Onion cooked with kale adds a pleasant flavor for those who may not like kale alone. Use it either plain and quick-cooked, or mixed with other vegetables.

#### Quick-Cooked Kale

| | |
|---|---|
| 2 pounds kale | ¼ teaspoon pepper |
| salt | 2 tablespoons diet margarine |

Remove root ends, coarse stems and any wilted or discolored leaves. Wash thoroughly in several waters. If leaves are large, cut into smaller pieces. Drop leaves into enough boiling water to cover and cook covered about 15 to 20 minutes, just until tender. Drain, reserving pot liquor, and chop. Add seasonings and margarine to a little of the pot liquor (save most of it for other uses). Pour over chopped kale.

### Kohlrabi

Kohlrabi is unusually high in Vitamin C. Nutritionally, it is best eaten raw, cut into strips. It is highly catabolic and excellent for reducers. Use as main dinner vegetable to offset concentrated foods at a meal. Serve along with yellow or white vegetable for color contrast.

*Quick-Cooked Kohlrabi*

1½ pounds kohlrabi (about 12         1 tablespoon diet margarine
  medium-sized kohlrabies)          3 tablespoons evaporated or
1 teaspoon salt                          rich milk (optional)

Remove root ends, stems and leaves of kohlrabi, reserving tender stems and leaves for future use. Wash, pare and dice or slice thin. Drop into enough boiling water to cover, and cook uncovered about 20 to 30 minutes, just until tender. Drain and place in individual dishes. To a little of the pot liquor (save most of it for other uses), add seasoning, margarine and, if desired, evaporated or rich milk.

## Leeks

The germicidal quality of the whole onion family (garlic, scallions, etc.) is shared by leeks. They have good protective vitamin values, too. They are highly catabolic, low in calories, and of great value to reducers. Excellent in soups.

*Quick-Cooked Leeks*

12 leeks                              3 tablespoons evaporated or
½ teaspoon salt                          rich milk (optional)
1 teaspoon diet margarine

Remove green tops from leeks to within 2 inches of white stalks (save tops for use in soups, stews and gravies). Remove root end and thin, paper-like covering of stalks and any wilted or discolored portions. Wash thoroughly. Cut into 1-inch slices. Drop sliced leeks into enough boiling water to cover vegetable, and cook uncovered about 10 to 15 minutes. Salt just before removing from heat. Drain, reserving liquid, and place leek slices in individual dishes. To part of pot liquor (save most of it for other uses), add margarine, and milk if desired. Pour over leeks and serve.

## Lemon

Lemons were the first-known, as well as the most effective, remedy for Vitamin C deficiency (scurvy). A few drops of lemon juice in a glass of water can be used as an aid to digestion upon arising or after meals. Lemon juice is alkaline, and this plus high Vitamin C content are beneficial to arthritic and rheumatic sufferers. Lemons are rich in potassium, B-1 and B-2. The juice has no roughage, and can be used on soft diets. Lemons rarely cause allergic reactions. Use lemon juice often to fortify other foods (fish, salads, melons, fruit cups, meats, drinks). Both the lemon and its juice are highly catabolic and excellent for reducers. Heavy lemons are more likely to be juicy with a minimum of seeds. They should be deep greenish-yellow, and not dried-out or leathery looking, firm but not hard. Keep in refrigerator (hydrator if possible). Lemons and limes have the same characteristics and uses.

### Lettuce

Ancient physicians used lettuce both as a sedative and as bulk food for constipation. Its sedative qualities derive from a milky juice extracted from the plant. Green lettuce is superior to white iceberg lettuce in vitamins. All lettuce is rich in potassium and in elements of value to anemic patients. It is alkaline, high in roughage, but the chief component of the roughage is hemicellulose, which can be used on soft diets. It is very low in calories, good for reducers, highly catabolic, but may cause allergic reactions. Serve head lettuce as salad (sliced or shredded). Use leaves in sandwiches, or as salad base. Lettuce is best eaten raw. To cook it as a green vegetable: wash, quarter or separate leaves, place in 1 inch boiling water, cover, and cook only 1 to 2 minutes—just long enough to wilt leaves. Season and serve with pot liquor sauce.

### Lime—See Lemon

### Lobster—See Shellfish

### Melons (Muskmelons or Cantaloupes, Including Honeydews and Casabas)

As early as the first century, most melons were believed to have kidney-stimulating qualities. Very high water content makes them useful for persons suffering from dehydration. They are an excellent source of Vitamin C—⅖ as rich as orange juice—and can well be used as a substitute for citrus fruits during seasons when muskmelons are cheap and oranges expensive. They are a good source of Vitamins A and B-1. Melons are highly alkalinizing. They are not permissible on soft diets as they are fairly high in roughage. But they are very low in calories, highly catabolic, and excellent for reducers. Some people are allergic to melons, although some distress is due to overeating or improper meal balance rather than to sensitivity.

True muskmelons (the word cantaloupe is mistakenly, though commonly, applied to these gourds) should have coarse and prominent netting on the outer surface. Ripe melons, the best kind, will have a depressed and calloused scar at the stem end, and—whether gray or yellow—will be lighter than unripe fruit. Judge ripeness by smell. Fully ripe muskmelons have a sweet fragrance.

Casaba melons have a golden color with either smooth or deeply ridged rinds. Appearance of stem-end scar is not important, as casabas are usually picked before maturity and ripened on the vine. They do not have the distinguishing aroma of muskmelons. They should be heavy.

Honeydews are usually ripened off the vine. They should be yellowish-cream in color, with smooth skins only slightly nettled, rinds somewhat less firm than those of cantaloupes. They have a sweet aroma.

All melons should be free from moist spots (especially near stem end), soft depressions, and mold—which may have penetrated rind. Allow ½ ordinary muskmelons per serving. Store all ripe melons in refrigerator. If not fully ripe, melons should be kept at about 70° F. until ripe. All melons should be served in their natural form as fresh fruit. Serve casabas and honeydews with a slice or a wedge of lemon or lime. The meat of all melons may be scooped into balls or small pieces and combined with other fruits in fruit cups or salads; or melons can be filled with fruit mixtures or ice cream.

## Mixed Greens

Many greens usually served raw (dandelion, escarole, lettuce, etc.) are excellent when mixed with others in a cooked mixed greens dish. Because of the bland flavor or some greens (lettuce, spinach, chard, kale, kohlrabi and broccoli) and strong flavors of others (chicory, endive, escarole, turnip tops, beet greens, carrot greens, dandelion greens and mustard greens), a combination of greens is often desirable. However, usually only two greens are combined—never more than three—as individual allergies must be guarded against.

From a nutritional point of view, greens are a superior dish. They supply Vitamins A and C, and the minerals iron and copper. They are highly catabolic, low in calories, and excellent for reducers. Many vegetable tops normally thrown away as just so much waste may go into a mixed greens dish. Since tops are often even better protective foods than roots, a mixed dish is practical. Serve at dinner to balance concentrated foods.

### Quick-Cooked Greens

| | |
|---|---|
| 3 pounds greens | 2 tablespoons diet margarine |
| 1 teaspoon salt | 1 teaspoon onion juice |

Prepare desired greens as directed under individual listing of vegetables, and wash thoroughly in several waters, removing any wilted or damaged leaves. Boil just enough water to cover greens in saucepan, then add selected greens and cook as follows: escarole, chicory, endive, kale, kohlrabi and carrot tops about 15 to 20 minutes; beet greens, spinach, chard and dandelion greens about 7 to 10 minutes; lettuce about 5 minutes. It should take no longer than about 20 minutes for the coarsest leaves to become tender. Drain, reserving pot liquor for future use. Chop together and place in individual dishes with seasoned pot liquor to which margarine and onion juice have also been added.

## Mushrooms

Mushrooms are highly catabolic, and low in calories (in fact, there are almost no calories in cooked mushrooms, excluding butter or cream sauce). Hence, they are excellent for reducers. Their high water content makes them good to balance concentrated foods. This factor, plus the easy digestibility of mushrooms, makes them ideal for convalescents. Mushrooms are used most frequently to give additional flavor to meat, vegetable or soup combinations, or to serve with steak, but are delicious as a separate vegetable, and may be eaten by the can. Fortification of mushrooms with foods rich in Vitamin A (peppers, pimiento, etc.) rounds out the protective value of this vegetable.

*Broiled Mushrooms*

| | |
|---|---|
| 1 pound mushrooms | salt and pepper to taste |
| 3 tablespoons diet margarine, melted | |

Cut off woody ends of stems if present. Wash thoroughly under running water, using a soft brush to remove dirt from top and bottom of rounded tops if necessary. Move back and forth in cold water several times. Drain and dry. Remove stems, reserving for other dishes. Dip caps in melted margarine, and place round-side up on broiling pan. Broil for 2 minutes. Turn, drop small piece of melted margarine into hollows, and season; broil about 7 or 8 minutes longer, just until tender.

## Muskmelons—See Melons

## Okra

Okra is important chiefly for its vegetable mucin content. This substance is of therapeutic value in cases of digestive disturbances, like stomach ulcers, because it is soothing and helps to neutralize hydrochloric acid. Okra is highly catabolic, low in calories, and excellent for reducers. Because of its bland flavor, okra is generally eaten in combination dishes, such as Okra Creole, other mixtures of tomatoes, corn, green peppers and onions, or in soups (particularly chicken-rice). Its nutritive value—as well as taste appeal—are enhanced by such methods of cooking.

*Okra Creole*

| | |
|---|---|
| ½ pound okra (or 2 cups canned okra) | 1 cup cut or canned whole kernel corn |
| 1 cup green lima beans | ½ teaspoon salt |
| 6 large tomatoes (or 2 cups canned tomatoes) | ¼ teaspoon pepper |
| | 2 tablespoons diet margarine |

Cut okra into ¼-inch slices and shell beans. Place in saucepan with just enough boiling water to cover. Cook in tightly covered pan 20 minutes. Add tomatoes and corn and simmer just until all fresh vegetables are tender or canned vegetables are thoroughly heated, about 10 minutes longer. If all vegetables used are canned, combine vegetables and simmer about 15 minutes. Add seasoning and margarine and serve.

## Onions

Mild onions and scallions are used primarily as additions (raw or cooked) to other vegetables, soups, salads, stews, meat dishes, etc., but both stronger flavored onions and scallions may be served plain boiled or creamed. All onions contain protective vitamin values as well as a special chemical called allyl aldehyde which makes onions a natural bactericide. Quick-cooked onion soup is valuable therapeutically for both these reasons. Sulphur compounds in onions are not well tolerated by some people. It is best for such individuals to eat mature onions cooked or young onions (or scallions) raw. Onions, fresh or boiled, are highly catabolic and excellent for reducers. Onions intended for flavoring agents in soups, vegetable combination dishes, etc., should be sautéed in a slight amount of butter or diet margarine for two or three minutes before adding to dish. This makes onions tender without long cooking.

### Boiled Onions

| | |
|---|---|
| 1½ pounds white onions | Vegetable Pot Liquor |
| salt and pepper | Cream Sauce |
| 2 tablespoons diet margarine | 3 tablespoons minced parsley |

Wash and peel onions. Cook uncovered in plenty of water 20 to 30 minutes, until tender. Drain, reserve pot liquor, season and dress with margarine. Serve with pot liquor and minced parsley in individual dishes. Or prepare Pot Liquor Cream Sauce, combine sauce and onions, and garnish with minced parsley.

## Oranges

Oranges are an outstanding source of Vitamin C, particularly since they are almost always eaten raw, or in fruit cups and salads. Oranges help relieve fevers. They are a good source of B-1 and B-2. Orange juice appears to improve retention of calcium in the body. They are highly alkalinizing. The juice has no roughage and can be used on soft diets. Oranges are highly catabolic, low in calories. The fruit is better than the juice on reducing diets. The peel may cause allergic reactions. Distress from the juice itself may be avoided by diluting with water. Buy thin-skinned Valencia type (either Florida or California) for juice; these have few seeds, but are hard to separate into segments. Buy thicker-skinned, seedless Navel oranges for slicing and segmenting. Store in cool, unheated pantry where temperature ranges 40 to 60° F.

## Oysters—See Shellfish

## Parsnips

In ancient records, it is hard to distinguish between carrots and parsnips. Pliny advised parsnips for anemia and certain eye disorders; he might have meant what we know today to be carrots, as carrots do contain the Vitamin A helpful for these two ailments, while parsnips do not. The chief value of parsnips today is to balance concentrated heavy starch or protein foods at a meal. They are very high in water content, also an excellent source of B-1 if eaten raw, a good source of C and B-2, rich in potassium. They are alkaline, highly catabolic, low in calories, and good for reducers, who can eat them alone or add them to potatoes to lower the calorie count of the latter. They are not recommended for soft diets unless puréed, as they are fairly high in roughage. They generally do not cause allergic reactions in normal individuals.

### Quick-Cooked Parsnips

| | |
|---|---|
| 6 medium-sized parsnips | 2 tablespoons melted diet |
| 1 teaspoon salt | margarine |
| | 2 tablespoons minced parsley |

Wash well. If old, pare very thin. If young, scraping is unnecessary as thin skin may be easily removed by peeling under cold water after boiling. Cut in halves, or pare and dice or cut into strips. Cook uncovered, in boiling water to cover, about 30 to 50 minutes, until tender. Salt before removing from heat. Drain, reserving pot liquor; remove woody core. Peel, if this has not previously been done. Serve with melted butter and minced parsley.

*Parsnips and Potatoes*—Dice 3 medium-sized parsnips and 3 medium-sized potatoes. Quick-cook together as directed in basic recipe. Drain, and mash or rice. Season with 1 teaspoon salt and dash of pepper. Add ½ cup heated milk, 1 tablespoon diet margarine and beat.

### Parsnips Loaf

| | |
|---|---|
| 4 cups cooked mashed parsnips | ½ cup parsnip pot liquor |
| 2 tablespoons diet margarine | 3 tablespoons minced parsley |
| 1 teaspoon salt | ½ cup buttered bread crumbs |
| ¼ teaspoon pepper | 2 tablespoons finely minced |
| 2 eggs | green pepper (or pimiento) |

Quick-cook parsnips as directed in basic recipe and drain, reserving pot liquor. Scrape skins and mash parsnips with butter and seasonings. Combine pot liquor and eggs and beat well, then add to mashed parsnips with minced parsley. Stir until thoroughly mixed. Place in buttered casserole or loaf pan and top with buttered crumbs. Bake in hot oven (400° F.) about 20 to 25 minutes, until center is firm and top is delicately browned. Unmold on hot platter and garnish with finely minced green peppers or pimiento.

## Peaches

The peach is one of the fruits and vegetables most capable of increasing the hemoglobin content of the blood. Yellow peaches are an excellent source of Vitamin A, which helps ward off colds. Peaches are alkaline. Fresh ones should be peeled, and all should be puréed (pressed through a coarse sieve) for soft diets, because they are fairly high in roughage. Fresh peaches have a low calorie content—are highly catabolic—and recommended for reducers. Canned and dried peaches are not as desirable. Reducers should choose water-packed canned peaches or rinse the syrup off Standard-pack fruit. Peaches seldom cause allergic reactions. Serve whole, unpeeled, in fruit bowl at table; or peel, remove pit and slice to serve with cereals, or in fruit cups or salads.

## Pears

Pears are known to be helpful in stimulating peristalsis—and are therefore an aid to constipation. They are very alkalinizing. Fresh pears are low in calories, highly catabolic, and recommended for reducers. Canned and dried pears are not as desirable. Reducers should choose water-packed canned pears or rinse the syrup off Standard-pack fruit. Pears seldom cause allergic reaction. Unlike other fruits, the finest-quality pears are picked when still slightly green and allowed to ripen in a cool, dry place. If allowed to ripen on the tree, they will be coarse-grained and gritty. Pears are best eaten as a fresh fruit dessert. They may be used as a salad ingredient, and can be pared, diced and added to fresh fruit cups. They may also be stewed or baked.

## Peas

Peas are among the most popular of all vegetables. They are comparatively high in vegetable protein, medium in calorie content (not low, like leafy, watery greens, tomatoes, etc.), but highly catabolic. Reducers should choose very young peas—the younger they are, the lower their calorie content, the more catabolic. Peas should be used with less concentrated vegetables in a meal. They may be served occasionally as a meat substitute. They lend themselves admirably to combining with other vegetables, meats, etc.

### Quick-Cooked Green Peas

3 pounds (3 cups shelled)
   peas
2 tablespoons diet margarine
½ teaspoon salt

¼ teaspoon pepper
4 tablespoons rich milk
   (optional)

Shell peas. Discard all but a few pods. Place in 1 inch boiling water; let water return to full boil and cover; cook 10 to 15 minutes, just until tender. Add margarine, salt and pepper and, if desired, rich milk to pot liquor; bring to boil and serve pot liquor with peas in individual dishes.

*Peas and Lettuce*—Reduce peas in basic recipe to 2 cups shelled peas. Melt margarine in heavy utensil. Add 1 tablespoon water, 1 medium-sized minced onion, 1 tablespoon minced parsley and ¼ teaspoon nutmeg, and cook over low heat 2 minutes. Add peas and ½ cup boiling water and cook covered about 8 to 12 minutes, until peas are almost tender. Add 8 shredded lettuce leaves and cook about 5 minutes longer, until peas are tender. Add seasoning and margarine to taste.

*Peas and Onions*—Follow directions in basic recipe for quick-cooked peas. Add 1 minced onion with the peas at start of cooking. Increase amount of rich milk to ½ cup. Serve in individual dishes with pot liquor.

## Peppers (Green and Red, Sweet and Hot)

Peppers have the highest Vitamin C content of all foods. The Vitamin C in peppers helps protect against hardening of the arteries. They also are a rich source of Vitamin A. Peppers are best eaten raw (minced and added to salads, sauces, other vegetables, dressings, etc.).

Plain cooked peppers are not particularly palatable. They are best when stuffed whole, or minced and used as an ingredient of loaves, stews and vegetable combination dishes. They are highly catabolic, low in calories, and excellent for reducers—and good to balance starchy or concentrated foods.

*Stuffed Green Peppers*

| | |
|---|---|
| 6 green peppers | 1½ cups Boiled Rice |
| 4 tablespoons diet margarine | 3 tablespoons minced parsley |
| 1 cup (¼ pound) chopped mushrooms | 1 teaspoon salt |
| | ¼ teaspoon pepper |
| ¼ cup minced onion | ¼ cup buttered bread crumbs |
| ¼ cup diced celery | (use diet margarine) |

Remove stem end of each pepper by slicing crosswise, or cut peppers (if large) lengthwise. Remove seeds and white fibrous portions. Melt margarine in large skillet. Add mushrooms, onion and celery, and sauté over medium heat about 3 minutes, stirring occasionally to prevent burning. Stir in rice, parsley and seasoning, and mix well. (If desired, add a bit of ketchup or tomato soup to moisten stuffing.) Stuff peppers, cover with buttered bread crumbs and place in buttered baking dish. Bake uncovered in hot oven (400° F.) about 25 minutes.

*Additional Stuffings*—Other suggested stuffings for green peppers are cooked rice, tomatoes and mushrooms; cooked or canned corn and tomatoes; okra, rice and tomatoes, peas and mushrooms.

## Pineapple

The juice of fresh pineapple has been used for centuries as an anthelmintic. The active principle is an enzyme called bromelin. Bromelin also serves to digest proteins, in the same way as does pepsin, a substance normally secreted in the human stomach. Pineapple is good in helping to digest meat and egg dishes. It is one of the fruits and vegetables most capable of increasing the hemoglobin content of the blood, excellent for anemia. Pineapple is alkaline. The juice, either fresh or canned, is preferable to the whole fruit for those on soft diets. All forms have low calorie content, but the whole fruit is preferable to the juice for reducers, who should choose water-packed fruit or rinse off syrup of fruit packed in light syrup. Pineapple seldom causes allergic reactions. Pineapple is best eaten as a fresh fruit dessert, or cut into cubes for adding to fruit cups. Canned pineapple should be served plain as a simple dessert, or dressed with cheese as a salad, or in vegetable, chicken or fruit salads. Canned slices or wedges may also be broiled to serve with meats.

## Prunes

Prunes have been known for centuries to have a mildly stimulating effect on the intestines. Hence, they are a good remedy for constipation. They are also good for increasing the hemoglobin content of the blood (good for anemia). They should not be eaten to excess because, although alkaline, prunes contain substances which increase the acidity of the urine. The whole fruit is fairly high in roughage. Reducers should use the canned variety only, and rinse off the syrup. They are catabolic and seldom cause allergic reactions.

## Pumpkin

Pumpkins were used by American Indians to treat stones and gravel. Since they are an excellent source of Vitamin A, they are a good food to help prevent the formation of stones. The seeds are also an excellent worm remedy. High water content makes pumpkins excellent for balancing concentrated (heavy starch or protein) foods at a meal. Pumpkins are alkaline. They are not recommended for soft diets, unless puréed, as they are fairly high in roughage. But they are very low in calories—highly catabolic—and excellent for reducing. Pumpkins generally do not cause allergic reactions.

Since pumpkin is not popular with most people as a vegetable, its chief purpose seems to be to serve as pie filling. The recipe given for boiled pumpkin may be used as a basis for such a filling.

### Baked Pumpkin

To bake, break into pieces for serving; remove seeds and stringy portions. Place in greased casserole dish, dot with diet margarine and season. Cover dish and bake in moderate oven (375° F.) until flesh is tender (40 to 50 minutes). Do not pare, but serve in rind. May be baked whole like Hubbard Squash.

*Quick-cooked (Boiled) Pumpkin*

3 pounds pumpkin        salt and pepper
  (approximate)
3 tablespoons diet margarine

Cut or break pumpkin into small pieces. Remove seeds and stringy portions and pare. Cover with boiling water. Cook covered about 20 to 30 minutes, until tender. Drain. Mash or put through ricer. Season with salt and pepper, and dot with margarine. If mashed pumpkin is to be used for pumpkin pie, do not add seasoning or margarine.

## Radishes

Black radishes were known in olden times to have specific therapeutic value in treating gallstones. The juice of one radish was pounded out, mixed with white wine or grape juice and drunk once a day. Radishes are a good source of Vitamin B and C. The tops are eight times higher in Vitamin C than the roots, and contain appreciable quantities of Vitamin A. Radishes are alkaline. They are not recommended for soft diets, as they are fairly high in roughage. They are very low in calories—highly catabolic—and excellent for reducing. Many persons find radishes difficult to digest because they tend to produce flatulence. Although they do contain sulphur, they can usually be tolerated if eaten in a salad served *first* —before the rest of a meal—and are minced, grated fine, or sliced very thin. They rarely produce allergic reactions. Radishes are best eaten raw, minced in salads. The same is true of radish greens. Both roots and greens are very low in calories, highly catabolic, excellent for reducers.

*Creamed Radishes*

3 cups red radishes (about 3     1 cup radish pot liquor and
  bunches)                 milk
2 tablespoons diet margarine   salt and pepper to taste
2 tablespoons flour          3 tablespoons minced parsley

Wash radishes and slice (not too thin). Reserve greens. Place sliced radishes in saucepan, add boiling water to cover and let come to a boil again. Reduce heat, cover pan and cook about 5 minutes, just until radishes are tender. Drain, reserving pot liquor (there should be about ½ cup of liquid). Melt margarine in large skillet, reduce heat and add flour, stirring constantly until well blended. Add reserved pot liquor and milk (to make 1 cup of liquid) gradually, stirring constantly until mixture boils and thickens. Add seasoning and radishes, and cook just until radishes are reheated, about 2 minutes. Serve garnished with minced parsley.

## Raspberries

Valued chiefly for their high water content, which makes them excellent for balancing concentrated (heavy starch or protein) foods at a meal. Raspberries are alkaline. They are not recommended for soft diets, as they are fairly high in roughage, but they can be puréed. They are low in calories—highly catabolic—and good for reducing. Reducers should use the whole fruit, and choose waterpacked fruit or rinse off syrup of Standard-pack cans. Raspberries seldom cause allergic reactions. They are best eaten as fresh fruit, or with milk as a breakfast fruit or simple dessert, or combined with other fruits in salads or fruit cups.

## Salad

Raw vegetable salads serve the serious purpose of introducing some of the richest vitamin foods into the diet in a delicious way. On the speed reducing diet, you should eat some fresh raw foods every day. A salad should be served first, as an appetizing introduction to the meal—or as a snack you may enjoy any time, in any quantity. Simple salads are often the most flavorful. A few ingredients may be quickly prepared, easily crisped and chilled. If allergic to certain leafy vegetables, simply omit them.

Green leafy salad ingredients are prepared by shredding, cutting into thin strips. Tender, crisp vegetables like green cabbage leaves, escarole or chicory, green lettuce, watercress, are suitable salad greens. Serve them singly or combined—with your favorite diet dressing. Sharp-flavored and less tender greens, such as beet greens, dandelion greens, spinach, etc., are best when used as cooked greens, since they may cause digestive upsets if eaten raw.

Mixed salads consist of leafy green vegetables as a base, covered with any or all of the following garden vegetables (diced, sliced or minced): carrots, celery, cucumbers, red and green peppers, radishes, scallions, tomatoes—all high catabolic, fat breaking, speed reducing foods.

*Raw* cauliflower, turnips, beets, etc., are sometimes used in raw vegetable salads, but many people are unable to digest them, due to their high cellulose content. It is best to quick-cook and chill the following vegetables before using them as salad ingredients: asparagus, beets, cauliflower. Cooked vegetable salads are very filling, and should not be served with heavy meats. Use them as main luncheon or supper dishes. Such cooked vegetable salad ingredients include string beans, carrots and peas.

Certain vegetables themselves may be used as salad dressing. These include chives, onions, parsley, pimientos, and scallions. Fresh herbs such as tarragon, sorrel, dill, chervil, etc., may also be used for this purpose. They, too, are highly catabolic.

With these basic principles in mind, you can prepare dozens of delicious and delightful vegetable salads to suit your taste, purse, and convenience.

*Combination Salad*

1 cucumber, diced
6 scallions (or 1 small onion), minced
6 radishes, thinly sliced (optional)
2 tablespoons minced parsley
2 medium-sized tomatoes coarsely chopped
2 cups shredded or chopped green lettuce (or cabbage)
¼ cup French dressing or diet dressing

Combine thoroughly chilled ingredients with dressing, and toss together lightly until evenly coated.

*Asparagus Salad*

18 cooked (or 1 can) asparagus tips
6 to 12 lettuce leaves
2 pimientos, cut into strips
¼ cup French dressing or diet dressing

Marinate asparagus, arrange on shredded salad greens and garnish with pimiento strips.

*Carrot-Raisin Salad*

1½ cups shredded carrots
½ cup seedless (or seeded) raisins
4 tablespoons lemon juice
6 to 12 lettuce leaves (or 1½ cups shredded cabbage)
¼ cup Mayonnaise (or diet Mayonnaise)

Shred carrots. Soak raisins in lemon juice. Combine ingredients, mix with dressing, and serve in lettuce cups or on shredded cabbage. (Or simply shred carrots, soak raisins in water a while to make them juicy, mix with carrots and Mayonnaise and serve.)

*Coleslaw (Cabbage)*

3 cups finely shredded          ¾ cup dressing
   cabbage
1 tablespoon minced onion

Select young, tender, green head. Remove wilted or coarse leaves. Cut in wedges and slice (or shred) very fine with slaw center or sharp knife. Wash thoroughly by shaking shredded cabbage in pan of cold water (ice water preferred). Drain until almost dry and place in refrigerator to chill and crisp. Cooked salad dressing, sour cream dressing, French dressing, Mayonnaise or diet Mayonnaise may be used. Any dressing will be refreshed by addition of 1 tablespoon lemon juice just before serving. Combine cabbage, onion and dressing, and garnish with pimiento or green pepper strips, if desired.

*Apple Coleslaw*—Reduce shredded cabbage of basic recipe to 2 cups. Shred or chop fine 2 medium-sized apples, and drop into dressing as prepared. Mince 2 pimientos. Combine and serve.

*Cucumber Coleslaw*—Reduce shredded cabbage of basic recipe to 2 cups. Chop coarsely 1 medium-sized cucumber and proceed as in basic recipe.

*Parsley Coleslaw*—Add ¼ cup minced parsley to basic recipe. Parsley adds a large amount of Vitamin A to Coleslaw.

*Green Pepper Coleslaw*—Mince 1 green pepper and add to ingredients in basic recipe. Green pepper makes Coleslaw exceptionally high in Vitamins A and C.

*Pimiento Coleslaw*—Mince 3 canned pimientos and add to ingredients in basic recipe. Pimientos add considerable amounts of Vitamins A and C to coleslaw.

*Pineapple Coleslaw*—Reduce shredded cabbage of basic recipe to 2 cups. Omit onion. Add 1 cup drained, crushed pineapple. Combine all ingredients with ¾ cup cooked fruit juice dressing.

*Sliced Cucumber Salad*

2 medium-sized cucumbers, sliced thin

6 to 12 lettuce leaves (or 1½ cups shredded cabbage)

2 tablespoons minced parsley, chives, or watercress

¼ cup French dressing (or diet dressing)

Slice cucumbers on salad greens. Garnish with minced parsley, chives or watercress. Serve dressing separately. If Mayonnaise is used, thin with lemon juice.

*Mixed Greens Salad*

2 cups shredded or chopped lettuce (escarole, chicory or cabbage)

1 bunch watercress, shredded

½ cup minced parsley

½ cup chopped celery

1 green pepper, minced

2 tomatoes, cut in eighths

¼ cup French dressing (or diet French dressing)

Combine thoroughly chilled ingredients with dressing and toss together lightly until evenly coated.

*Tomato Salad*

4 medium-sized tomatoes

6 to 12 lettuce leaves (or 1½ cups shredded cabbage)

2 tablespoons minced parsley

¼ cup French dressing (or diet French dressing) or Mayonnaise (or diet Mayonnaise)

Slice or cut peeled or unpeeled tomatoes into eighths. Serve on salad greens. Sprinkle with minced parsley. Serve dressing separately.

*Vegetable Gelatin Salad (basic recipe)*

1 envelope (1 tablespoon) granulated gelatin

½ cup cold water

1 cup boiling water

⅓ cup sugar (or less)

¼ teaspoon salt

¼ cup lemon juice (or cider vinegar)

¼ cup chopped or shredded carrots

1 cup chopped celery

2 tablespoons chopped green pepper

2 tablespoons chopped pimiento

Soften gelatin in cold water and dissolve in boiling water. Add sugar; stir until dissolved. Stir in lemon juice and place in refrigerator to chill. (Up to this point, this recipe is the foundation for all jellied vegetable or fruit salads. Any desired vegetables may be used, not merely the ones suggested in this list of ingredients.)

When mixture begins to set, add vegetables. Turn into 1-quart mold or individual molds and chill until set. Turn out on bed of lettuce, watercress or any other salad green; serve with Mayonnaise.

### Cantaloupe Salad

1½ cups cantaloupe balls
1 cup sliced fresh strawberries
1 cup diced pineapple

¼ cup cooked fruit juice dressing
salad greens

Prepare thoroughly chilled fruit. Combine with dressing and serve on salad greens. Garnish with watercress, if desired.

### Grapefruit Salad

2 grapefruits (or 1 can grapefruit wedges)
6 to 12 lettuce leaves (or 1½ cups shredded cabbage)

2 pimientos, cut into strips
¼ cup French dressing (or diet French dressing)

Prepare grapefruit and segment sections. Arrange grapefruit on greens and garnish with pimiento. Serve dressing separately.

### Pear (Peach or Pineapple) Salad

6 fresh or canned pears (peaches or pineapple slices)
2 medium-sized apples
2 tablespoons lemon juice
¼ cup seedless raisins

¼ cup Mayonnaise (or diet Mayonnaise)
6 to 12 lettuce leaves (or 1½ cups shredded cabbage)

Dice pears and apples. Add lemon juice. Chill. Soak raisins in just enough water to cover and place in refrigerator about 30 minutes to plump. Combine fruit with dressing and serve on salad greens. Pears also combine well with citrus fruits, grapes or cooked cranberries.

### Waldorf Salad

3 medium-sized apples, diced
2 tablespoons lemon juice
1½ cups diced celery
¼ cup nut meats (optional)

¾ cup cooked salad or fruit or fruit juice dressing or Mayonnaise (or diet Mayonnaise)
shredded salad greens

Use firm "eating" apples. If skins are red and free from blemishes, they need not be pared. Sprinkle apples with lemon juice and combine with celery, nuts and dressing. Toss lightly and serve on shredded salad greens.

*Fruit Gelatin Salad*

1 tablespoon (1 envelope) granulated gelatin
½ cup cold water
1 cup boiling water (or fruit juice drained from fruit)
¼ cup sugar
¼ teaspoon salt

¼ cup lemon juice
1½ cups diced fresh or canned fruit (except fresh pineapple)
salad greens
¼ cup Mayonnaise (or diet Mayonnaise)

Soften gelatin in cold water and dissolve in boiling water or fruit juice. Add sugar and salt; stir until dissolved. Cool. Stir in lemon juice and place in refrigerator to chill. When mixture begins to set, add fruit (if canned, drained of juice). Any of the following fruits may be used, alone or in combination: cherries, oranges, grapes, canned (not fresh) pineapple, apples. Turn into mold or individual molds and chill until set. Turn out on bed of lettuce, watercress or any suitable salad green. Serve dressing separately.

*Shrimp Salad*

2 cups cooked or canned shrimp
½ cup finely chopped celery
¼ cup minced pimiento
1 small onion, minced or grated
½ cup diced cucumber

¼ cup minced green pepper
3 tablespoons lemon juice
2 tablespoons minced parsley
salt and pepper to taste
½ pimiento, cut into strips

Drain fish, reserving liquor, and separate into flakes with a fork. Combine with celery, minced pimientos, onion, cucumber and green pepper. Use fork to toss together lightly. Add lemon juice, parsley and seasoning to 4 tablespoons reserved fish liquor and mix thoroughly. Combine with fish and vegetables and chill at least 30 minutes before serving. Place on large platter, garnish with pimiento strips and surround with salad greens, tomato slices, etc.

## Shellfish

Shellfish fall into two groups: mollusks and crustaceans. Mollusks are of soft structure, and include clams, oysters and scallops. As long as they are absolutely fresh and correctly prepared, the latter are easily digested. Like vegetables, they are low in calorie content and fairly high in water content, which makes them excellent foods for balancing an otherwise heavy meal. Their character in these respects is very unusual for protein food, and should be taken advantage of by reducers and persons with digestive difficulties. Those allergic to these foods, of course, should avoid them. Use them just as you would any fish, as a main dish for dinner or supper. The usual method of preparing oysters or scallops is to dip them in flour or crumbs and fry. Such a cooking procedure adds indigestible material, which explains many cases of digestive distress attributed to shellfish themselves.

Like other shellfish, the crustacean group, which include shrimp, crabs and lobster are very easy to digest, if fresh and cooked properly. They are good for reducers and those needing concentrated foods (in contrast to fatty meats, fowl, cheese, etc., which may produce digestive distress). Of all shellfish, the following are definitely catabolic (fat destroying) with reverse calories: *clam, crab, lobster, oyster, shrimp*.

### Steamed Clams

| | |
|---|---|
| 4 quarts unshelled clams | ¾ cup melted diet margarine |
| 1 cup boiling water | 2 tablespoons lemon juice |

Be certain clams are absolutely fresh and alive when purchased. If they are alive, shells will be tightly closed. If shells happen to be open, they should snap closed when touched. If they do not close, clams are no longer alive and should not be purchased.

Wash and scrub clams well. Put into a large kettle with water, cover kettle and steam just until shells open, about 10 to 15 minutes. Do not overcook, as long cooking will make clams tough. Serve with individual dishes of diet margarine seasoned with lemon juice or celery salt. Strain clam broth remaining in kettle, season with celery salt and minced parsley, and serve hot with clams, or chill and use cold as clam juice cocktail. Mixing equal parts of clam juice and tomato juice provides good variation.

*Baked Oysters*

| | |
|---|---|
| 36 oysters in shells | 1 small onion, finely minced |
| 1 small green pepper, finely minced | 2 tablespoons lemon juice |
| | 3 tablespoons diet margarine |

Be certain oysters are absolutely fresh when purchased. If bought in shells, they should be alive, which is indicated by tightly closed shells. If shells happen to be open, they should snap closed when touched. If they do not snap, oysters are no longer alive and should not be purchased. Have dealer open oysters and give you half the shells. Arrange oysters on half-shells in baking pan. Sprinkle tops with green pepper, onion and lemon juice, and dot with diet margarine. Bake in hot oven (450° F.) about 10 minutes, or just until oysters puff up.

*Broiled Scallops*

| | |
|---|---|
| 1 quart small scallops | 1½ cups fine, dry bread or cracker crumbs |
| 1 egg, slightly beaten | 1 lemon, sliced |
| 2 tablespoons water | 2 tablespoons minced parsley |
| 1 teaspoon salt | |
| ¼ teaspoon pepper | |

Be certain scallops are absolutely fresh when purchased. Wash scallops, drain and dry. Dip in slightly beaten egg diluted with water, and roll in seasoned crumbs. Place scallops on buttered broiler pan, or on buttered heat-proof platter (using diet margarine), dot with margarine and broil 3 inches from moderate heat about 15 minutes, turning once during cooking. Serve with sliced lemon and garnish with minced parsley.

*Boiled Shrimps*

| | |
|---|---|
| 1½ pounds fresh shrimps (2¾ cups boiled) | 1 quart water |
| 2 teaspoons salt | 2 slices lemon |

Be certain shrimps are absolutely fresh (or properly refrigerated during shipping) when purchased. Drop shrimps into boiling salted water. Add lemon slices to water. Boil 10 to 15 minutes, just until shrimps turn pink. Drain to serve hot, or let cool in cooking water to use cold. Remove shells and black intestinal vein running along back. Serve hot with tartar sauce. To use cold, chill in fish stock, drain and clean before serving in salad.

*Shrimp Creole*

½ medium-sized onion,          ⅛ teaspoon pepper
   chopped                    ¼ teaspoon thyme
1 green pepper, chopped        1 small bay leaf
2 tablespoons diet margarine   2 tablespoons chopped
2 tablespoons flour               pimiento
2 cups (1 can) condensed       2 cups cooked or canned
   mushroom soup                shrimps
½ teaspoon salt                3 tablespoons minced parsley

Sauté onion and green peppers in margarine 3 minutes, stirring occasionally. Stir in flour until smooth and well blended, then add soup gradually and cook until thick, stirring constantly. Add seasonings and shrimps and cook about 5 minutes, just until shrimps are heated. Remove bay leaf. Serve on toast made of high fiber bread (has half the calories of regular bread, but may not be tolerated if you are on a soft diet) or boiled rice, and garnish with minced parsley.

*Boiled Hard-Shelled Crabs*

12 live hard-shelled crabs          salt (to measure)
boiling water

Be certain crabs are still alive when purchased, as indicated by movement of claws and feelers. Wash crabs under running water until free from sand. Fill large kettle ¾ full of boiling water. Add 2 tablespoons salt for each quart water. Handle live crabs with tongs, or hold firmly just behind claws, and plunge head first into water. Cover and boil rapidly about 20 to 25 minutes. Remove from kettle and plunge into cold water after cooking to cool before removing meat. Break off claws and apron, or tail. Open and fold back shells at tail end, and remove spongy substance (gills, stomach and intestine) between two halves of body and between sides of top shell and body. Remove meat, flake and pick over carefully to remove bits of cartilage. Crack claws with nut cracker or hammer and remove meat. Serve hot in shell with melted butter, or use meat cold for salad.

*Deviled Crabs*

| | |
|---|---|
| 1 pound (2 cups) cooked or canned crabmeat | ½ teaspoon paprika |
| | 1 cup milk |
| 6 crab shells | 2 tablespoons chopped parsley |
| 4 tablespoons butter | 1 tablespoon lemon juice |
| 2 tablespoons flour | 1 cup bread crumbs |
| ½ teaspoon salt | 2 tablespoons melted diet |
| ½ teaspoon dry mustard | margarine |

Pick over crabmeat to remove cartilage, and flake. In a large saucepan, melt margarine, stir in flour, salt, mustard and paprika. When well blended, add milk slowly, stirring constantly over low heat until mixture thickens and boils. Stir in parsley, lemon juice and crabmeat. Fill crab shells or place in greased 1½ quart baking dish. Top with bread crumbs and melted margarine. Bake in a moderate oven (375° F.) about 10 minutes.

*Broiled Live Lobster*

| | |
|---|---|
| 6 small or 3 large lobsters | salt and pepper |
| melted diet margarine | |

Be certain lobster is alive when purchased, as indicated by movement of claws and feelers. Make sure the wooden plugs remain in claws. Place live lobster on its back on a board, and hold body between claws and tail. Then with large sharp knife, split from head to tip of tail. Remove sac near head, and intestinal vein. Crack large claws with hammer. Put lobster on greased broiler, brush meat with melted margarine, and sprinkle with salt and pepper. Broil shell side down 2 inches from heat about 5 minutes, until lobster turns pink. Serve with melted margarine.

## Shrimp—See Shellfish

## Spinach

Spinach was used centuries ago, by Arabian physicians, for kidney disorders. The Vitamin A in spinach is known to help prevent formation of kidney stones and gravel. Its Vitamin C helps keep small blood vessels supple, and thus indirectly protects against hardening of the arteries. Spinach contains relatively large amounts of oxalic acid; however, tests reveal that ordinary quantities of spinach eaten (up to 100 grams a day) are not harmful. There is some evidence that oxalic acid forms compounds with calcium to make that mineral unavailable to the body; hence, it is probably wise to include many calcium-rich foods (milk and cheese) in the diet when eating foods known to contain oxalic acid. Oxalic acid, however, is essential to the body in the coagulation of the blood.

Spinach is highly catabolic (fat destroying), low in calories. Its lack of popularity usually results from poor cooking; it should never be overcooked. Always serve spinach with a more concentrated vegetable, as it does not have much "staying" quality. Spinach combined with eggs naturally is high in protein, and should be served as a main luncheon or supper dish.

### Quick-Cooked Spinach

2 pounds spinach
1 tablespoon diet margarine

salt to taste
bits of garlic or garlic powder
(optional)

Wash spinach thoroughly under running water. Cut off roots and coarse stems, and remove any discolored or wilted leaves. Shake spinach leaves in large pan of cold water. Lift leaves to another can of cold water, and continue this procedure, changing water each time, until spinach is free of sand. When leaves are clean, no sand will appear in bottom of pan. Usually 4 rinse waters will suffice. Place spinach in ½ inch boiling water and cook covered about 7 minutes, stirring occasionally. Chop, add diet margarine and season. Add 1 tablespoon lemon juice for further flavor, if desired.

## Strawberries

Early Romans used strawberries to prevent and cure scurvy. They are an outstanding source of Vitamin C. They are also a good blood builder. Strawberries are alkaline. They are not recommended for soft diets unless puréed, as they are fairly high in roughage. They are low in calories—highly catabolic—good for reducing if not sugared. Reducers should choose water-packed fruit or rinse off syrup of Standard-pack cans. Strawberries may produce allergic reactions, however these may be avoided if partially cooked (place in pan with a little honey and remove just before boiling point is reached, chill and serve as usual). Strawberries are best eaten as a fresh fruit or dessert, in salads, fruit cups, and other mixtures.

## Squash

Squash is an excellent food for reducers. It is highly catabolic and low in calories. High water content makes it excellent for maintaining normal water balance and avoiding dehydration. It is also good to balance concentrated (heavy starch or protein) foods. It is alkaline, very easy to digest, but occasionally causes allergic reactions. It should not be used on soft diets unless pared (seeds must be removed) and then mashed and puréed, as it is fairly high in roughage. Summer squash is best when well-fortified with other vegetables.

### Baked Hubbard Squash

3 pounds Hubbard squash      salt and pepper
2 tablespoons diet margarine

Wash squash and break into pieces for serving, removing seeds and stringy portion. Arrange in greased baking dish, dot with diet margarine, season and cover. Bake in moderate oven (375° F.) about 40 to 50 minutes.

### Baked Acorn Squash

Scrub 6 small acorn squash. Leave whole for better flavor and texture. Place in baking dish and add water to depth of ½ inch. Bake in hot oven (400° F.) about 30 minutes, until skin is soft when touched. Serve like baked potatoes—to be dressed at table with seasonings.

### Boiled Summer Squash

3 pounds squash      salt and pepper
2 tablespoons diet margarine

Wash squash. Do not pare or remove seeds. Slice thin and drop into ½ inch boiling water. Cook covered about 8 to 10 minutes, just until tender. Mash if desired. Add seasoning and diet margarine, and serve with pot liquor in individual dishes.

### Creole Squash

2 tablespoons diet margarine      6 tomatoes, peeled and sliced
1 onion, minced                  (or two cups canned
1 green pepper, minced          tomatoes)
salt and pepper                 1 yellow or zucchini squash
                                 (approximately 2 cups
                                 sliced)

Melt margarine in large skillet. Add onion and pepper, and sauté about 3 minutes, just until onion is yellow. Add tomatoes. While tomatoes are heating, slice or dice squash without peeling. When tomatoes come to a boil, add squash, cover, and simmer about 8 minutes, just until squash is tender. Season and serve in individual dishes.

*Baked Zucchini*—Cut 6 zucchinis in halves lengthwise. Place in greased baking dish. Bake in moderately hot oven (400° F.) 15 to 25 minutes, until tender. Season and butter (with diet margarine).

## Tangerines

Tangerines have a higher Vitamin C content than certain vegetables that must be cooked (which destroys Vitamin C). Therefore, tangerines are a good food for those suffering with blood pressure disorders, pyorrhea or bleeding gums. They are recommended as an alternative to oranges for relieving fevers. They are an excellent between-meal snack. Tangerines are alkaline, low in calories—highly catabolic—good for reducers, who should eat the whole fruit. Tangerines are best eaten fresh, in salads, fruit cups, desserts.

### Tangerine Fruit Cup

A mixture of fresh fruits, or canned fruits combined with fresh fruits, in whatever proportion desired. A few suggested combinations are: tangerines (or oranges), red grapes and pineapple; tangerines (or oranges), grapefruit, banana and green minted cherries (not for reducing); tangerines (or oranges), apples, bananas and cherries (red, black or green).

## Tomatoes

Tomatoes are highly catabolic (fat destroying), low in calories, and excellent for reducers. They should be used, either raw or cooked, to offset heavy, concentrated foods. They are alkaline, and easily digested (unless allergy is present). Tomatoes are well-liked by nearly everyone, and can be combined tastily with numerous other vegetables. They are best nutritionally when eaten raw, but still valuable when quick-cooked.

*Stewed Tomatoes*

| | |
|---|---|
| 8 large tomatoes (or 3 cups canned tomatoes) | salt and pepper |
| 1 small onion, minced | 3 tablespoons diet margarine |

Peel and quarter tomatoes; place in saucepan with minced onion. Cover and cook 10 minutes over medium heat. Add remaining ingredients; stir until margarine is melted. If desired, serve with whole wheat toast, cut into cubes, and a sprinkling of sharp cheese. Tomatoes may be combined and cooked with any or all of the following vegetables: diced celery; whole-kernel canned, fresh or quick-frozen corn, minced green peppers, minced onions or summer squash.

*Tomato-Egg a la Mode*

Prepare stewed tomatoes as in basic recipe, reducing tomatoes to 4 (or 1½ cups canned tomatoes). Then prepare a flour-water paste by gradually adding 3 tablespoons water to 1 tablespoon flour, stirring until smooth and well blended. Stir into stewed tomatoes and cook 2 minutes, pour over slices of toast and top each slice with a poached egg.

*Baked Tomatoes*

| | |
|---|---|
| 6 tomatoes | 3 tablespoons diet margarine |
| salt and pepper | 2 tablespoons, minced parsley |
| ¼ cup finely minced onion | |

Cut tomatoes into halves and place in shallow baking pan. Season, sprinkle with minced onion (or onion juice), and dot with butter. Bake in hot oven (450° F.) about 15 to 20 minutes, just until tender but still firm. Sprinkle with minced parsley. If desired, omit onion and sprinkle each tomato with 1 teaspoon grated cheese after 10 minutes' baking.

*Broiled Tomatoes*

| | |
|---|---|
| 6 tomatoes | ¼ cup grated sharp cheese |
| salt and pepper | 3 tablespoons minced parsley |
| 2 tablespoons onion juice | |

Peel and cut tomatoes into ¼-inch slices. Place in greased broiler pan. Season and sprinkle with onion juice and sharp grated cheese. Broil 3 inches from medium heat, about 3 minutes. Sprinkle with parsley.

## Turnips

Turnips are highly catabolic and excellent for reducers (both roots and greens). Because of sharp, somewhat bitter flavor, they should be combined with mild greens, like spinach, in mixed greens. The roots are an excellent source of Vitamin C, but the long cooking time needed to make them palatable causes this vitamin to be dissolved into cooking water. Its pot liquor is thus very valuable. The greens are even higher in vitamin and mineral content than the roots, and very inexpensive, too.

### Quick-Cooked Turnips

2 pounds white or yellow           salt and pepper
   turnips (approximate)           3 tablespoons diet margarine

Scrub thoroughly; pare, slice or dice. Place in boiling water to cover; cook uncovered about 20 to 30 minutes (until soft) if young—about 50 minutes or longer if old. Drain, rice or mash and season with salt, pepper and margarine.

*Turnips with Green Peppers*—Cook as directed in basic recipe, drain and mash with 4 tablespoons minced green pepper which has been sautéed in 2 tablespoons diet margarine over low heat for 5 minutes.

*Turnips with Peas*—Dice 1 pound turnips and cook as directed in basic recipe. Quick-cook 1 cup shelled green peas separately, then drain (reserving liquid). To ½ cup milk, add cooking water drained from peas and turnips to make 1½ cups liquid. Use to make pot liquor sauce. Reheat and add 2 tablespoons minced parsley before serving.

## Watercress

Watercress is high in Vitamin C, and was once an outstanding scurvy remedy. It is often used as a garnish, like parsley. Nutritionally, it is one of the most valuable foods, and should always be eaten. It stimulates the digestive tract, is one of the richest sources of vitamins and minerals, good for blood building. Watercress is alkaline. It is not recommended for soft diets unless chopped very fine, as it is high in roughage. Watercress is very low in calories—highly catabolic—good for reducers. Generally, it does not cause allergic reactions. It is almost always used raw either in mixed salads or as an appetizer or garnish with meats, fish, soups, etc. Suggested salad: chopped onions, chopped dandelion greens, quartered tomatoes and cut watercress. It may also be minced and mixed with diet margarine, cottage cheese, and diet mayonnaise as a sandwich filling. In France, watercress soup is popular.

## Watermelon

Watermelon has been used for centuries as a mild stimulant to kidney action. A decoction of watermelon seeds is also used as a simple folk remedy by sufferers from high blood pressure. Watermelon seeds contain a substance called cucurbocitrin, of value in dilating the very small blood vessels—the capillaries—thus reducing pressure in the large blood vessels and sometimes improving kidney function. Watermelons are alkaline. They are not recommended for soft diets as they are fairly high in roughage and difficult to purée. They are very low in calories—highly catabolic—excellent for reducers. They may cause allergic reactions, or "repeating" if overeaten. Watermelon is best eaten fresh, in slices, or add watermelon balls or diced pieces to fruit salads and cups. Lemon or lime juice may be added for extra flavor, and these may be garnished with mint sprigs.

# 5

## Your Secret Friends
## Help You Lose Weight Quickly!

You know now that the secret of reducing is to eat the right kinds of foods. As Dr. Lindlahr said: "Proper reducing is not a question of starvation—of cutting your meals in half." Best of all, you know that foods are not your enemies. You need not be afraid to eat now. As Dr. Lindlahr stated many times: *You have to eat large amounts of speed reducing foods to lose weight rapidly!*

Speed reducing foods are your friends—always your friends, the best friends you have. "I don't suppose there is any food which does not contribute something of value to man's diet. But foods have virtues and faults. Foods, like people, are individualistic. Some foods fit us;

some foods fit the other fellow. So we must choose our friends wisely,'' said Dr. Lindlahr.

Catabolic—or speed reducing—foods are overwhelmingly our best friends. Cultivate their companionship. You are going to be fashioned by the food you eat. Take salads, as an example. ''Here is Nature's gracious gift to the overweight, the best and most pleasant foods with which to fight fat. This type of food is thinning, and the best fat-blasting food on the list,'' said Dr. Lindlahr. Tasty, too. And this question of flavor is important, because we are entitled to enjoy every bit of food we eat.

## YOU HAVE FRIENDS
## YOU NEVER KNEW EXISTED!

But there are other foods—not necessarily catabolic—that are our friends, as well. They are helpful on any speed reducing diet. Take soups, for example. Many are tasty and non-fattening, too. They are a decided help. All you have to do is steer away from thick, rich or creamy soups, and you're in good shape, in that department.

Then we have muscle meats, tender and flavorful, and broiled meats which are fine if lean, including chopped steak. We can enjoy gravy, made from seasoned juices and water (fat-free gravy is fine). Then there are broiled chicken, stewed chicken and fish. Fish is an excellent speed reducing food, just loaded with food minerals, and you may eat it frequently, baked or broiled (see pages 68-70). Lobsters, oysters, shrimp and clams are—as a matter of fact—speed reducing foods with reverse calories. In addition, they are rich in iodine, which spurs along metabolism. They are best used as dinner appetizers or salads. We can have lobster salad, made with chili sauce dressing! Oysters are delightful baked with a little dab of chopped greens, a brisk brush of garlic and a few buttered cracker crumbs. Or we can have shrimp for salads and cocktails.

Glandular meats (kidney, liver, tripe, sweetbreads, tongue) are man's finest sources of Class A protein. (Other sources are certain fish, eggs, milk, and soy beans.) These are the chief meats which possess real vitamin and mineral value. The curative power of calf liver is well known. Eat them frequently. Broil them. Enjoy a tasty, non-fattening, lip-smacking good Sunday breakfast of broiled lamb kidney with eggs.

Eggs, perhaps the most dependable source of protein, are among our trusted allies. Probably the most nearly perfect food nutritionally, they outrank milk (which is excellent, too). There are scores of tempting egg dishes: boiled eggs (to any degree we desire), baked eggs, eggs scrambled slowly and lightly in a pan dabbed with just enough butter. Eggs are our friends. We can also stave off Devil Fat with a plain omelette. Chipped beef may be served with eggs in place of bacon or ham.

The dairy products include an assortment of food friends that rate aces high. Here are man's most dependable sources of food calcium. Dairy foods should comprise a sizeable portion of man's meals. Two of our best choices in dairyland are skim milk and buttermilk. Light cream or whole milk are fine for coffee and cereal. Butter is permitted on your maintenance diet. In moderate amounts it is one of the best foods. Cheese is a far better protein than muscle meat. It is worth more, in essential amino acid value, than any steak, chop or roast you ever ate. To collect such extra food dividends, we can have a cheese souffle, or a bowl of pot cheese, frequently, for lunch or dinner.

Vegetables, together with fruits, are, all told, our richest source of vitamins and minerals. Not the least amazing feature of vegetables is their variety and abundance. The biological function of vegetables is to supply us with vital vitamins and minerals. All recommended vegetables—without exception—are low in calories, and can be prepared in such delicious fashions.

Fruits are probably the masterpieces among protective foods, put by Nature into such attractive packages that we are tempted to eat them raw, which is best. Have them for breakfast (and a dandy one, at that). They provide an escape for the fatty who is not satisfied by a snack and a cup of coffee for that meal. Fruits can also solve the dessert problem. Most people with any sort of appetite want a sweet at the end of a meal. A fruit cup is comforting, satiating, yet not calorically dangerous. The handsome varieties we can eat, we should enjoy chilled, stewed, fresh, or in fruit cups of endless combinations. Prunes, pineapples and apples help "cut" rich meats and may be served with them. Rhubarb and stewed fruits of various kinds as side dishes lend variety, too. Nibblers are offered an escape by fruits. An apple or orange can always be eaten, between meals, or when time hangs heavy on our hands. In fact, fruits can be served instead of vegetable dishes. Fruits help solve the problem of hors d'oeuvres and meal beginnings, too. Melon or fruit juice cocktail makes a perfectly delicious appetizer.

## EATING OUT IS NO PROBLEM!

Not on the speed reducing diet! Of course, you have to cut your starches and carbohydrates to lose weight speedily—you can't gorge yourself on crackers, breads, cakes, fancy ice creams, candy, tidbits, alcoholic beverages and hors d'oeuvres. But afterwards, you can reasonably indulge in some of these things.

Take bread, for example. Let us have no misunderstanding. Bread is a very good food. Since bread is good to the taste, we naturally want some. You can have a slice at each meal, no harm done—*two slices*, if you are using high fiber bread, which has half the calories! And cake! After all, a person has to have a piece of cake once in a while. You can have pound cake, raisin cake, angel food cake, sponge cake, if you must. Don't overdo it.

"If you are at a soda fountain to tickle your taste buds a bit, order some plain ice cream. It is toothsome, and a dandy food, as foods go, despite its calories," said Dr. Lindlahr. Fruit ice cream is even better, since the little wedges of fruit displace the full amount of ice cream you'd normally get. At the soda fountain, you can order plain ice cream, phosphates, plain sodas (strawberry, for example) or some drink such as Coca-Cola. You can also order lemonade, orange juice, milk, tomato juice—which are actually speed reducing—whereas Coke is not catabolic, just reasonably low in calories (about sixty per glass). The best in tidbits is popcorn; most of it is indigestible (less caloric value, too)—only the butter makes it fattening, but you can use diet margarine, which has half the calories, or just cooking oil, if you make it yourself. Either way, it makes a delicious TV snack! (Unbuttered popcorn is just 65 calories a cup!) In hors d'oeuvres, smoked haddock is acceptable. Caviar is not so bad as you might think. And hard candy is acceptable, too!

When dining out, on your maintenance diet, bear these things in mind—and stick closely to the above foods, if you feel you must indulge. Avoid rich, thick, creamy soups, salty ones, or those filled with noodles. Have them served clear, if you can. Avoid crackers if you can't stop at one or two. Breads are fattening, no question of that. In the breads avoid corn bread, rolls (even paper thin ones), and biscuits. Strangely enough, whole wheat and rye breads are usually higher in calories per slice than white varieties—except gluten bread, which has only ⅔ the caloric value of the others, and high fiber bread, which has ½. Avoid heavy buttering. Avoid cakes with icing, layer cakes and certain others, like walnut cake, which are extremely high in calories that are not catabolic, since they require almost no energy to digest. This is especially true of soda fountain seducers, like malted milk, chocolate syrup, ice cream mixed with flavors like strawberry, or nuts (which are very fattening). Cocktail crackers, potato chips, pretzels, peanuts, cocktail frankfurters, including those wrapped in bacon, olives, smoked fish, creamed cheese, soft candies, are all, unfortunately, to be avoided. They are all too easy to digest, hence fattening, even in small quantities (and who can stop at one). Think, rather, of all the things you can eat—the list of speed reducing foods, which is infinitely greater!

## THESE FOODS ARE FRIENDS!

Many of the following foods are not catabolic—but they are your friends—and you can eat them on a speed reducing diet of your own! Together with the 100 fat destroying foods just listed in Chapter 3, they present a formidable and impressive army of foods you *can* eat, while losing weight in record speed!

### Desserts

Lunches, dinners and suppers need some form of dessert—a "sweet" to complete the meal and give a feeling of satisfaction. Of all desserts, the best from the nutritive standpoint are simple fruit dishes, such as those suggested, or various fresh fruits arranged attractively as a centerpiece, from which everyone can help him or herself. These are recommended for the entire family, because they are low in calories.

The heavier the meal, the lighter the dessert should be. Fruit is your best choice. Others are included. Be sure that all fruits are chilled before being peeled, segmented, taken from the can, etc. Crushed or finely chopped mint, contrasting fruit juices, particularly lemon juice, or nut meats and raisins may be added to most fruit cups for extra flavor. Do not sweeten fruit unless necessary.

#### Citrus Cup

1½ cups diced, seeded orange (or tangerine) segments

1½ cups diced, seeded fresh (or canned) grapefruit segments

Combine chilled fruit; serve in individual dessert dishes, with diced, unpeeled red apple or a few mint leaves to give color, if desired.

*Grapefruit-Strawberry Cup*

3 small grapefruits (or 1 No. 2 can unsweetened grapefruit segments)

1½ cups fresh sliced strawberries
2 tablespoons sugar (optional)

Cut grapefruits in halves. Carefully remove membrane, seeds and grapefruit sections, reserving shells to use as cups. Combine grapefruit sections and berries, and refill grapefruit shells with mixture. Sprinkle fruit with sugar just before serving, unless fruit is naturally sweet enough. If canned grapefruit is used, serve in individual dessert dishes. In winter, cranberry sauce may replace strawberries; in that case, omit sugar.

## Frozen and Gelatin Desserts

Simple fruit ice and gelatin desserts—light ices, such as orange, lemon and pineapple—are high in Vitamin C and water content, low in protein, carbohydrates and fats. Thus they are ideal desserts for heavy or concentrated meals, and are especially valuable to reducers at all times, since they are low in calorie content. Use ices often in summer, as they are cooling foods—not only because of their appetizing, refreshing qualities, but because they contain few heat-producing calories. Ice creams and mousses should be used with caution on a reducing diet.

*Orange Ice*

2 cups boiling water
2 cups sugar
1 orange rind, grated

⅓ cup lemon juice
2 cups orange juice

Combine water and sugar and stir constantly until sugar is dissolved. Boil 5 minutes without stirring. Cool, then add fruit juices and orange rind. Strain, pour in freezing trays of automatic refrigerator and freeze until firm, stirring occasionally. *Lemon Ice*—Omit orange rind and juice and increase lemon juice ¾ cup. For a more definite lemon flavor, add 1 tablespoon grated lemon rind.

## Custards

Simple custards make excellent desserts for practically everyone, especially convalescents or other people on a light diet. Consisting chiefly of eggs and milk, they supply important Class A protein, high in quality but not very great in quantity. They are excellent sources of all the vitamins except Vitamin C, and they are particularly rich in minerals like iron and copper, needed for blood building. Custards are an excellent way of getting milk into the diet. Use them as dessert for lunch or supper, after almost any meal, except one with other egg or milk dishes in it. The soft custard combined or served with crushed or sliced fruit is especially good, from the nutritional standpoint. While some sort of fruit should be eaten in almost all luncheon and dinner menus, custards are ideal desserts for those meals already containing fruit—fruit salad or fruit canapés, for example. Do not overdo it, if reducing.

### Baked Custard

| | |
|---|---|
| 3 eggs | 3 cups milk |
| 3 tablespoons sugar | 1 teaspoon vanilla extract |
| ¼ teaspoon salt | ⅛ teaspoon nutmeg |

Beat eggs enough to mix the yolks and whites thoroughly, and add remaining ingredients, beating until sugar is dissolved. Strain into individual custard cups and set in pan of hot water. If custard is to be removed from cup when served, butter cup before filling with custard. Bake in a moderate oven (375° F.) about 25 to 30 minutes, just until custard is firm in the center. Test by inserting silver knife blade; if knife comes out clean, custard is done. Do not overcook, causing custard to separate and ruining its delicate texture. Set cups in cold water immediately to prevent custard from continuing to cook from heat retained in cups. Chill and serve.

### Soft (or Stirred) Custard

| | |
|---|---|
| 2 cups scalded milk | ¼ teaspoon salt |
| 2 eggs or 4 egg yolks, slightly beaten | ½ teaspoon vanilla extract (or sherry to taste) |
| 4 tablespoons sugar | |

Scald milk in top part of double boiler. In a mixing bowl, beat eggs or egg yolks with sugar and salt until well mixed. Pour scalded milk gradually into egg mixture, stirring constantly until thoroughly mixed. Return to double boiler and stir constantly over hot water until mixture stops foaming and begins to coat silver spoon, about 2 minutes. Dip silver spoon into custard and take it out. If custard forms a straight line across spoon, mixture should be removed from hot water immediately. If the line is wavy, custard is not quite done. Be very careful not to overcook.

When custard is finished (in about 3 to 5 minutes), remove from heat and set pan in cold water immediately. This will prevent overcooking or curdling, as custard continues cooking after it is removed from heat unelss the pan containing it is cooled at once. Strain, add flavoring, and chill. Serve as simple dessert or as sauce over fruit or simple cake. For a slightly thicker custard and deeper yellow color, use 3 eggs or 6 egg yolks. For a fuller-bodied custard sauce, use 3 egg yolks.

*Fruit Custard*—Prepare custard according to directions in basic recipe. Place about 3 tablespoons diced or crushed fresh or canned fruit in each of 6 parfait glasses, cover with custard and chill. Serve garnished with diced fruit. This fruit adds Vitamin C to the custard.

## Sweet Beverages

Orange, lemon, lime, grapefruit, pineapple, and tomato juice are highly catabolic, fat breaking, speed reducing foods. They are also lip-smacking good, diet or no diet. Here are some beverage suggestions that will satisfy your taste as well as your thirst, all quick and easy to prepare.

### Orange Juice

In large measure, you can judge the nutritional value of orange juice by its sweetness and natural color. Canned orange juice is your best bet because the oranges used are picked lush ripe, and processed in a matter of hours—whereas fresh oranges you buy are often picked green to last longer, and are not so tasty. To eliminate any "canny" taste, and get the full rich flavor, expose the juice to open air for about 15 minutes.

### Lemonade

Lemon juice is extremely valuable in plain lemonade, in combination fruit punches, and for adding to vegetables (especially greens), sauces, soups and salad dressings. Use lemon juice with any dish it will improve, and treat it with respect as a remedy of value in any sickness characterized by fever. Of even higher vitamin C content than orange juice, it is still potent when diluted.

juice of 1 lemon                     sugar or honey to taste
1 cup cold water

Combine juice and water. Sweeten to taste and serve cold. (Use boiling water for hot lemonade.) Yield: 1 serving.

*Limeade*

Limes contain considerably less Vitamin C than lemons but are still an eminently worthwhile source. They are well-suited to making "ades," non-alcoholic drinks and salad dressings when an aromatic, sour flavor is desired.

juice of ½ lime                      1 cup cold water
juice of ½ lemon                     sugar or honey to taste

Combine juices and water and sweeten to taste. Garnish with mint or maraschino cherry. Yield: 1 serving.

*Grapefruit Juice*

Grapefruit is not a cross between lemons and oranges, as some people think. It is a true citrus fruit in its own right, and one of the best sources of Vitamin C among fruits. A half-grapefruit makes a splendid first course for any meal, and it is a wise selection as a dessert for any heavy or rich meal. The grapefruit is "tops" for people who wish to stay slim. Many people who do not tolerate orange juice well may drink grapefruit juice without fear of upset stomach. All citrus-fruit juices are converted by body chemistry into acid-neutralizing carbonate salts which swell the body's alkaline reserves. There is no better way to alkalinize than with grapefruit juice.

*Pineapple Juice*

Pineapple is a high catabolic, fat breaking, speed reducing food. For centuries, tropical people used the fruit in dozens of ways medicinally. It was an unfailing worm remedy for children. It healed common sore throat, and helped to allay fever. Modern science has demonstrated why fresh pineapple possesses these virtues. It not only has a generous quantity of Vitamin C, but in addition it contains, when fresh, a chemical called bromelin, which is a powerful digestant. Bromelin actually destroys many types of intestinal parasites, yet it is entirely agreeable to the human body. It also helps in the digestion of protein (egg, cheese and meat) dishes. Fresh or canned unsweetened pineapple juice is especially helpful to sufferers from gastric ulcers, who may not like orange or grapefruit juice.

*Tomato Juice*

For reducers, tomato juice is an escape from the ever-inviting but fattening hors d'oeuvres or cream soups which introduce so many meals. As a between-meal beverage for children, or for adults with that "letdown feeling," the refreshing qualities of tomato juice are unequalled.

*Apple-Grape Juice*

Apple juice is a good alkalinizer and an excellent source of food minerals. It is very helpful to the digestive system, because apple pulp contains a great deal of pectin, which is soothing in various digestive inflammations. While not particularly catabolic (speed reducing), it can be mixed with orange, lemon, lime, grapefruit or grape juice—all of which are catabolic, speed reducing foods.

½ cup chilled apple juice          ⅓ cup water
⅓ cup chilled grape juice          1 tablespoon lemon juice

Combine apple juice, grape juice and water. Add lemon juice and sugar syrup to taste and mix well. Yield: 1 serving.

*Grape Juice Punch*

Grape juice is particularly valuable because it contains acid potassium tartrate which is readily converted by body chemistry into splendid acid-neutralizing salts. In addition, it is a gentle stimulant to digestive action and kidney function. In large amounts, it ceases to be catabolic and becomes fattening, but this can be minimized by mixing it with other juices.

1 pint chilled grape juice          1 quart chilled gingerale
juice of 1 lemon

Add gingerale to combined fruit juices just before serving. Garnish with lemon slices. Yield: 8 servings.

## Canapés and Sandwiches

Canapés, in contrast to sandwiches, require only one slice of bread or toast, which is covered with any suitable vegetable, fruit, egg, cheese, fish or meat spread. For normal persons, who usually eat more than enough carbohydrate foods anyway, canapés are preferable to sandwiches for use at lunch or supper. Always slice bread thin, and spread mixture so that it is twice as thick as bread slice. This makes a better-tasting canapé, besides increasing its protective quality. All canapé and sandwich recipes yield approximately 1¼ cups spread—enough for 6 large (24 tiny) canapés or 6 sandwiches. Use whole wheat, rye, or high fiber bread, as desired. High fiber has ½ the calories, but is often more palatable toasted. Unless mixture to be used is very moist, spread first with a thin covering of your favorite diet dressing.

### Cheese-Egg Canapés

¾ cup American cheese
2 hard-cooked eggs
½ small onion
1 pimiento
¼ teaspoon salt

1 teaspoon paprika
3 tablespoons diet
   Mayonnaise
6 slices high fiber bread
   (toasted)
3 tablespoons diet margarine

Put cheese, eggs, onion and pimiento through meat grinder, using finest blade. Mix and season with salt and paprika. Moisten with Mayonnaise and spread mixture on buttered bread.

### Egg-Celery Canapés

4 hard-cooked eggs, chopped
¼ cup minced celery
2 tablespoons minced parsley
2 teaspoons onion juice

3 tablespoons diet
   Mayonnaise (approximate)
6 slices high fiber bread
   (toasted)
3 tablespoons diet margarine

Combine chopped eggs, celery and parsley. Season with onion juice and moisten with Mayonnaise. Spread mixture on buttered bread. Garnish with small sprinkling of minced parsley in center.

*Liver Canapés*

| | |
|---|---|
| 1 cup finely chopped cooked beef liver (or chicken livers) | 3 tablespoons diet Mayonnaise (or chili sauce) |
| 3 hard-cooked egg yolks | salt and pepper to taste |
| ¼ cup chopped watercress | 6 slices high fiber bread (toasted) |
| 1 tablespoon onion juice | ½ cup diet margarine |

Combine all ingredients but bread and butter. Mix well. Chill. Toast and butter one side of bread, and spread mixture on untoasted side. Lemon butter (see page 69) may be used to add flavor.

*Chicken Canapés*

| | |
|---|---|
| 1 cup minced cooked chicken | 3 tablespoons diet Mayonnaise (approximate) |
| 2 tablespoons minced pimiento (or parsley) | 1 teaspoon lemon juice |
| 1 small onion, minced | 6 slices high fiber bread (toasted) |
| ¼ cup minced celery | ½ cup diet margarine |

Combine chicken, pimiento (or parsley), onion and celery. Moisten with lemon juice and Mayonnaise to taste. Spread mixture on buttered bread. (Flaked cooked or canned lobster meat, or crab meat, may replace chicken.) If used as sandwich filling, cover chicken with lettuce leaf and another slice of bread.

## Sandwiches

On a speed reducing diet, you are limited to one slice of bread per meal, 2 slices if high fiber bread is used—in which case a sandwich may be eaten, without using up your entire quota for the day (one sandwich per meal, preferably, your limit for the day being 3 sandwiches). Sandwiches are just canapés with a second slice of bread to cover the filling. All canapé spreads may be used as sandwich fillings. Use sandwiches for lunch or supper, balanced with salad (or a light soup, fruit juice or vegetable juice), fruit dessert and milk. Spread bread with diet margarine, flavored with lemon juice, mustard, minced parsley (or watercress or pimiento).

*Lettuce-Tomato Sandwich*

12 slices high fiber bread
  (toasted)
 3 tablespoons diet margarine
18 slices of medium-sized,
  ripe tomatoes

12 lettuce leaves
salt and pepper
2 tablespoons diet
  Mayonnaise (optional)

Butter 6 slices of bread. Cover each with crisp lettuce leaves and sliced tomatoes. Season tomatoes lightly and cover with remaining lettuce leaves. Spread remaining bread with Mayonnaise (or margarine) and cover sandwiches Serves 6.

*Tongue Sandwiches*

¾ cup ground cold boiled
  tongue
½ cup finely diced celery
2 sweet pickles, minced

3 tablespoons diet
  Mayonnaise
½ cup diet margarine
12 slices high fiber bread

Put cold tongue through meat grinder, using finest blade, and mix with celery and pickles. Moisten with Mayonnaise. Butter bread and spread 6 slices with tongue mixture. Cover with remaining slices of bread. The addition of lettuce leaves and sliced tomatoes makes this a very filling sandwich.

## Eggs and Cheese

Eggs and cheese are not speed reducing, in the sense that they are not fat destroying. But we need them for a balanced diet. Eggs provide Class A protein, and are rich in every vitamin (except C) and all the important minerals. They rank as milk's equal in the human diet, and every child and adult should eat at least 2 or 3 eggs per week.

Reducers may eat plain egg dishes freely, but should avoid those made with much butter (unless diet margarine is used), cream sauces, or Mayonnaise (unless diet Mayonnaise is used). High fiber toast may be used, and bacon, too, if used sparingly. Fried eggs are inadvisable for most people, especially anyone with weak digestion or gall bladder trouble. Stuffed eggs are also not recommended for anyone with digestive difficulties. Coddled and poached eggs are among the most easily digested of all forms of eggs.

Fortification of eggs with parsley, milk, pimiento, cheese, etc., always increases the protective value of the dish. Egg-cheese combinations provide an especially good form of protein, and should be used occasionally in place of meat. Eggs begin to coagulate quickly as heat increases. Because of this, they should always be cooked slowly, without high heat; otherwise, they will be tough, leathery and not easily digested. Thus, water in which eggs are coddled or poached should never boil. The water is best at 185° F. Oven temperatures (for baking eggs) may be as high as 300° F. Use cooking thermometer for best results.

*Poached Eggs*

1 quart boiling water                    6 eggs
¼ teaspoon lemon juice                 6 slices high fiber toast
2 teaspoons salt

Heat water to boiling point in large skillet. Add lemon juice and salt. Turn heat very low. Break each egg carefully into a cup or saucer and carefully slip into the water; or place eggs in greased muffin rings or an egg poacher (to help preserve their shape) and place containers in the water. Be sure water covers eggs.

Cook eggs just until whites are set or firm, and a white film forms over the yolks. Do not overcook. While eggs are cooking prepare toast. Use skimmer to remove eggs as soon as set, and serve at once on hot, buttered toast (using diet margarine) to taste. May be served with cheese sauce, if desired.

*Coddled Eggs (soft, medium or hard-boiled)*

6 eggs                                6 cups boiling water

Use spoon or tongs to slip eggs into boiling water; cover pan and remove it from heat at once. Let stand in warm place 6 to 8 minutes for soft-cooked eggs and about 10 minutes for medium-cooked eggs. For hard-cooked eggs, do not remove pan from heat, but as soon as water boils, reduce heat as low as possible and slip eggs gently into water. Cover pan but do not permit water to boil again. Eggs will be hard-cooked in 20 to 25 minutes. Then remove eggs, place in cold water to cover for a few minutes, and crack shells to permit liberation of sulphur. Placing eggs in cold water makes shell removal easier. (If eggs are to be used as garnish, place them in ice water until thoroughly chilled; this prevents crumbling of yolk or breaking of whites when sliced.)

*Soft-Cooked Eggs* (Double Boiler Method)—Fill lower part of double boiler ⅓ full of boiling water. Fill upper part of double boiler ½ full of boiling water. Place both parts over direct heat and let water boil rapidly. Then place upper part into lower container and turn off heat. Use spoon or tongs to place eggs in upper part. Cover tightly. Eggs will be soft-cooked in 5 minutes. Lift each egg from water and carefully crack shell, removing one-half of it; then, with small spatula, remove egg whole. It will be soft and creamy throughout.

*Scrambled Eggs*

| | |
|---|---|
| 6 eggs | ½ cup skimmed milk |
| 1 teaspoon salt | 3 tablespoons diet margarine |
| ⅛ teaspoon pepper | |

Break eggs into bowl. Beat slightly, and add seasoning and milk. Melt margarine in heavy skillet. Reduce heat and pour in egg mixture. As soon as mixture begins to thicken, stir it with steel fork slowly and constantly over low heat, scraping eggs from bottom of pan as they cook to prevent their becoming dry and hard. A further precaution is to turn off heat (or, if necessary, to remove pan from heat) before eggs are entirely cooked, as pan retains sufficient heat to complete the cooking. Cook just until eggs have a creamy, fluffy consistency. Serve at once.

*Continental Scrambled Eggs*—Add 2 tablespoons minced parsley, 1 tablespoon minced chives, or ¼ cup minced pimiento to egg-milk mixture before it is cooked, and then proceed as in basic recipe.

*Scrambled Eggs with Sautéed Vegetables*—Sauté 2 tablespoons chopped onions, 2 tablespoons minced green peppers and ½ cup sliced mushrooms in diet margarine about 3 minutes. Then add egg-milk mixture and proceed as in basic recipe.

*Deviled Eggs*

| | |
|---|---|
| 6 hard-cooked eggs | 2 tablespoons diet |
| 1 teaspoon diet margarine | Mayonnaise (approximate) |
| ½ teaspoon salt | few drops lemon juice (or |
| ⅛ teaspoon pepper | cider vinegar) |
| ¼ teaspoon dry mustard | ⅛ teaspoon paprika |

Prepare hard-cooked eggs as directed on page 114. Cut into halves crosswise or lengthwise. Use a small spoon to remove yolks to a small bowl, being careful not to break the whites. Force yolks through a sieve or ricer. Add margarine, seasoning and Mayonnaise. Mix until creamy smooth. Add a few drops of lemon juice or vinegar for a more piquant flavor. Refill whites with yolk mixture and sprinkle lightly with paprika for color. Chill before serving. If desired, mix minced onions, pimiento, parsley, chives or watercress to taste with the mashed egg yolks.

*Foamy Omelet*

6 eggs, separated                    dash of pepper
6 tablespoons water                  2 tablespoons diet margarine
½ teaspoon salt

Separate eggs; beat whites until they stand in peaks. Beat yolks with water and seasoning until foamy. Fold in stiffly beaten whites. Melt margarine in heavy skillet. Reduce heat, add eggs and cook over low heat, cutting omelet as it cooks. Use spatula to lift edges of omelet as it cooks and gently push cooked eggs to center of pan, letting uncooked egg liquid run to outer edge of pan to cook. When all the egg mixture is partly cooked to a soft consistency and bottom is lightly browned, place about 3 inches from preheated broiler heat, and cook about 1 minute, just until top is dry and delicately browned. Cut part way through center. Fold and serve immediately on hot platter.

If you have a special omelet pan, just butter both halves of it, place egg mixture in one half of pan, cover tightly with remaining half and cook over low heat about 8 to 10 minutes. Do not open cover (thus letting steam escape) for at least 7 minutes. Omelet will be cooked when it has risen to top of cover and is delicately browned. Serve at once.

*French Omelet*

6 eggs                               dash of pepper
6 tablespoons skimmed milk           3 tablespoons diet margarine
½ teaspoon salt

Beat eggs slightly; add milk and seasoning. Melt butter in heavy skillet and pour in egg mixture. Cook over low heat about 10 minutes. Cut omelet with a spatula as egg on bottom of pan cooks; this cutting process is to permit uncooked egg liquid to run through cut to bottom of pan to cook. The success of this dish depends upon constant watching, cutting cooked portion and lifting of edges of omelet. When cooked, omelet should have a delicate crust, and be of a soft, creamy consistency, not dry or tough. To remove, hold a warm platter over omelet and carefully turn pan upside down, keeping plate close to omelet.

*French Cheese Soufflé*

| | |
|---|---|
| 1 cup milk | 1 cup grated cheese |
| 3 tablespoons quick-cooking | ¼ teaspoon dry mustard |
| tapioca | 3 egg yolks, well beaten |
| 1 teaspoon salt | 3 egg whites, stiffly beaten |

Combine tapioca and milk in top part of double boiler, and cook over hot water, stirring frequently, until mixture is thick and clear (about 8-10 minutes). Remove from heat, add cheese and seasonings, and stir until well blended. Add small amount of tapioca-cheese mixture to well-beaten egg yolks, stirring constantly. Add egg yolk mixture to remaining tapioca mixture, stirring constantly. Fold in stiffly beaten egg whites. Pour into casserole and bake in moderately hot oven (425° F.) about 25 minutes.

*Corn and Tomato Soufflé*

| | |
|---|---|
| 1 tablespoon diet margarine | 1 cup (¼ pound) shredded |
| 1 small onion, minced | American cheese |
| 4 tablespoons minced pepper | 2 cups canned or cooked |
| ½ cup tomato paste | yellow whole kernel corn |
| ½ teaspoon salt | 3 eggs, separated |

Melt butter in heavy skillet. Add onion and green pepper, and sauté until onions are yellow, about 3 minutes, stirring occasionally. Add salt, tomato paste and cheese. Stir constantly until cheese melts, then stir in corn. Remove from heat and cool slightly. Meanwhile, separate eggs; beat yolks until creamy and beat whites until stiff enough to stand in peaks. Stir yolks into corn mixture and mix thoroughly. Fold in stiffly beaten egg whites. Pour into buttered casserole and set in pan of hot water. Bake in moderate oven (350° F.) about 40 to 50 minutes or until firm in center. Serve at once.

## Cheese

Cheese is made up of Class A protein—largely casein from milk. When made from whole milk, it is rich in Vitamin A and high in fat content. Cheese made with rennet (a coagulating substance) is a fine source of calcium. Cottage and pot cheese are poor in this mineral because they are coagulated with acid instead of rennet, and most of their calcium escapes into whey.

Cheese is a concentrated, high-protein, high-fat food, and should be treated as one. Use as meat substitute, or blend into sauces and add to foods which need its flavor or food value. High fat cheeses are not recommended—in large quantity—for anyone who is overweight or has digestive difficulties. These include American, Camembert, Cheddar, Cream, Edam, Gorgonzola, Liederkranz, Limberger, Muenster, Neufcahtel, Norwegian, Pimiento, Roquefort, Swiss. They can, however, be eaten in moderate amounts, combined in high catabolic (fat-burning) vegetable salads, or in a cheese soufflé. Pot cheese is original cheese produced from curds of skim milk to which lactic acid has been added (or from sour milk). If sweet cream is added, the result is cottage cheese. But cottage cheese made of skim milk, and pot cheese, are very low in fat, and highly recommended. High fat cheese should not be used as a between-meal or bedtime snack, or at the end of a rich meal. This gives rise to indigestion. Fatty cheeses are most easily digested when eaten with salads or other bulky foods, which make for thorough chewing.

### Meat, Cheese, and Fish Salads

Because of protein content, cheese, fish and meat (including poultry) salads are really main dishes, not salads in the usual sense of that word. They should be served at lunch or supper (or light dinner) with tomato or fruit juice, a starchy food such as bread, and a simple fruit dessert. If heavier dinner is desired, balance with a soup, and include a more filling dessert. These protein salads provide excellent dinner dishes during the hot weather, when the body needs light foods only.

The Chicken Salad recipe is basic for all leftover meats, such as chicken, or veal, and for seafood, such as lobster and shrimp. Both chicken and fish salad may be used to stuff large tomatoes (centers of tomatoes should be chopped with salad). This is an attractive and popular main-dish salad for special summertime luncheons.

*Chicken Salad (Basic Meat Salad Recipe)*

2 cups cooked, diced chicken
salt and pepper
1 cup diced celery
1 tablespoon minced onion
1 tablespoon minced parsley
½ cup French dressing (or

diet French dressing)
1 small head lettuce (or other salad green)
½ pimiento
½ cup Mayonnaise (or diet Mayonnaise)

Chicken should be free from fat, skin and cartilage. Sprinkle diced pieces with salt and pepper, and add celery, onion, parsley and

French dressing. Chill for ½ hour or longer. Arrange on lettuce leaves; garnish with pimiento. Serve Mayonnaise separately (or put some on each plate).

*Jellied Chicken Salad*—Soften 1 tablespoon granulated gelatin in cold water; dissolve in 1½ cups boiling chicken stock. Add ¼ teaspoon salt, stir until dissolved, stir in 2 tablespoons lemon juice and place in refrigerator to chill. When mixture begins to set, add 1 cup cooked, diced chicken, ¼ cup diced celery, 2 tablespoons each chopped green pepper and chopped pimiento. Turn into 1-quart mold or individual molds and chill until set. Turn out on bed of lettuce or shredded lettuce; serve with Mayonnaise.

*Cottage Cheese Salad*

| | |
|---|---|
| 1 pound cottage cheese | paprika |
| 1 teaspoon salt | 6 to 12 lettuce leaves (or 1½ |
| 2 tablespoons minced onion | cups shredded cabbage) |
| (or chopped chives) | ¼ cup French dressing (or |
| 3 tablespoons minced parsley | diet French dressing) |

Mix cottage cheese with salt, onion or chives, and parsley. If cheese is dry, moisten with sweet or sour cream. Pack in small bowl and chill half an hour or more. Unmold on large plate, sprinkle with paprika and surround with lettuce which has been sprinkled with French dressing. Mounds of sliced cucumbers and radishes may be arranged on the lettuce.

*Cottage Cheese and Pepper Salad*

| | |
|---|---|
| 1 cup cottage cheese | 2 tablespoons milk (or more) |
| 2 green peppers | 1 small head lettuce (or other |
| ¼ cup thinly sliced scallions | salad green) |
| (or 1 teaspoon minced | 2 tablespoons Mayonnaise (or |
| chives) | diet Mayonnaise) |
| ¼ cup thinly sliced radishes | paprika |
| ½ teaspoon salt | |

Cut tops from peppers, remove seeds, and wash. Cut into 6 ½-inch rings and mince remaining pepper. Add minced pepper to cheese with scallions, radishes and salt. Moisten with milk and use steel fork to mix ingredients well. Place pepper rings on shredded lettuce and fill with cheese mixture; garnish with Mayonnaise, a sprinkling of paprika and a few additional radish slices.

*Shrimp Salad*

2 cups cooked or canned
  shrimp
½ cup finely chopped celery
¼ cup minced pimiento
1 small onion, minced or
  grated
½ cup diced cucumber

¼ cup minced green pepper
3 tablespoons lemon juice
2 tablespoons minced parsley
salt and pepper to taste
½ pimiento, cut into strips

Drain fish, reserving liquor, and separate into flakes with a fork.
Combine with celery, minced pimiento, onion, cucumber and green
pepper. Use fork to toss together lightly. Add lemon juice, parsley
and seasoning to 4 tablespoons of reserved fish liquor and mix
thoroughly. Combine with fish and vegetables and chill at least 30
minutes before serving. Place on large platter, garnish with pimiento strips and surround with salad greens, tomato slices, etc.

# 6

## Devil Fat Is Defeated!

"Because this diet has almost 90 per cent catabolic efficiency, the three pounds of food it permits you to eat each day should make moderate overweights lose about a pound of fat per day," said Dr. Lindlahr. "Heavyweights lose a pound-and-a-half or so daily. . . . That fatty OIL under your skin is going to disappear."

### SPEEDY WEIGHT LOSS GUARANTEED!

Few people clearly understand the meaning of the word *calorie*. It is an obscure term representing the amount of heat a food produces if burned—not stored—in the body. It is absolutely meaningless to the average overweight, since the food he eats is largely stored—not burned—and he is concerned with *fat*, which is what unburned fuel becomes.

An easier way of understanding calories is to regard them as fuel in food, which may be burned or stored, and to use the word *calorie* as a unit of measurement of how much fuel a food contains, like gallons of gasoline. The less calories of fuel a food contains, the less fattening it is. Lack of fuel guarantees loss of weight. It forces the body to turn to its own fuel reserve for energy. But it does not guarantee speedy weight loss.

## REVERSE CALORIES BURN FAT!

*Speedy weight loss* results when a food not only lacks fuel, but is *difficult to burn*. Weight loss is accelerated! The foods Dr. Lindlahr recommends have all these benefits. They not only lack fuel, they are difficult to burn. These foods require much more fuel to burn than they contain. As a result, you lose weight faster! They are speed reducing foods!

To a much greater degree than ordinary thinning foods, speed reducing foods force the body to burn its own fat—in record speed. They don't merely *let* the body lose its own weight. They actually *take weight from the body*. That's why Dr. Lindlahr called them *minus* foods. They contain what I call *reverse calories* that are *never stored*, never turned to fat, for all practical purposes. To burn them, the body needs *extra* energy from its own fuel reserve, or from other fattening foods you've eaten. They make these other foods *less fattening*, by using up their fuel before it can be stored. They can even *neutralize* the effect of fattening foods, if eaten in large quantities. In Dr. Lindlahr's case, he could eat fattening foods, without gaining weight, if 65 per cent of the meal contained speed reducing foods, which require lots more energy to digest than they provide.

## EVEN SOME FATTENING FOODS
## HAVE REVERSE CALORIES!

Oddly enough, some fattening foods have reducing qualities, even though we don't normally think of them as thinning foods—while other foods are just plain fattening. It all depends on how much inert, non-caloric material a food contains. This may be fiber, water, vitamins, minerals or protein.

The more of these a food contains, the less fattening it is—even if it contains plenty of carbohydrates—because they make the food more difficult to burn. They *cost* the body an abnormal amount of heat and energy to get at the fuel part (the carbohydrates).

If you will remember that the calories contained in food are made less formidable by the cost to the body of digesting that food, you can fool Devil Fat! Two and three-quarters ounces of potatoes have the same caloric value as one ounce of bread, yet two and three-quarters ounces of potatoes *cannot be made into the same amount of fat* as that one ounce of bread will provide.

The potato calories are harder to get at, or, as we would put it, they have a greater digestive cost. Potatoes are more catabolic (thinning) than is bread. Yet high fiber bread is only ½ as fattening as regular bread (white, rye, whole wheat). Incidentally, potatoes are really an excellent food. Not as thinning as some foods, but not nearly as fattening as many suppose.

*Remember that just as some foods are more or less fattening*, so others *are more or less thinning*, Dr. Lindlahr declared. A pint is a pint, but a pint of whiskey is more potent that a pint of beer! Fried eggs are higher in calories than boiled eggs. Ice cream, cake and candy turn into fat with almost 100 per cent efficiency—they are *too easy* to digest. Yet plain ice cream is less fattening than flavored ice cream. And fruit ice cream is even less fattening, since the little wedges of fruit displace the full amount of ice cream you'd normally get, and are catabolic (fat burning). Cakes with icing, layer cakes, nut cakes are fattening, since they require almost no energy to digest. Yet pound cake, sponge cake, and angel food cake are less fattening than the richer varieties (with large air pockets) and fruit cake is even better. Caramels and soft candies are highly fattening. Yet hard candies are less fattening. *Knowing your foods is more important than sheer number of calories, said Dr. Lindlahr!*

## OTHER FACTORS MAKE FOODS MORE THINNING!

Cooking reduces the calorie value of vegetables sharply, partly because water replaces the solid matter of the food, and partly because the starch and sugar of vegetables and fruits are soluble. Note especially that the calorie value of cooked foods such as spaghetti and macaroni is astonishingly lower than that of the raw pastes. Practically all the calorie value of vegetables could be destroyed by repeated cooking and washing. However, the health-giving vitamins and minerals would also be destroyed. Vegetables must be quick-cooked, and their valuable pot liquors saved and used (improves flavor, too).

Calorie values often vary slightly with the food itself.

Perhaps you will find that the calorie values of certain foods as given on our lists will vary from those given in other lists. Especially in the Meat Substitution Lists (15, 16, 17) you will find calorie values quoted lower than the average. This is because these calorie estimates are for lean meat with all the extra fat removed.

## THE SPEED REDUCING DIET
## DOES NOT DEHYDRATE!

Once in a while a dieter does not lose weight the first day. There is a reason. It has to do with water balance in the body. When fat is oxidized or burned in the body, water is formed. Ordinarily this is eliminated through the skin, the breath, the kidneys, or the intestines. Sometimes it is temporarily held by the tissues. Thus, while the dieter really has burned fat, his loss does not show on the scales. However, it will in a day or two when the water metabolism adjusts itself.

It is even possible apparently to gain weight in this situation. However, such a gain is most temporary. Our body tissues do not get water just from the fluids we drink; they get a considerable amount from the foods we eat. If a person were not eating or drinking, he would make some of the body tissues into water.

## HOW WATER ACCUMULATES
## WITHOUT DRINKING!

Here is a most peculiar chemical fact. A hundred ounces of body fat will yield 107.1 ounces of water. That is because the element of hydrogen in body fat picks oxygen out of the blood to form water. Also, out of 100 ounces of alcohol, the body will get 117.4 ounces of water. That is why people who drink too much alcohol may become waterlogged and flabby. A hundred pounds of fat in a camel's hump will give him 107 pounds of water, and so on.

So you see, it is possible for water to accumulate without drinking. A fellow who exercises and adds muscle to his frame will add four ounces of body weight for every ounce of muscle tissue he builds. The person who eats candy and adds to the sugar stores of the body will add four ounces of weight for every ounce of sugar actually stored. Salt retains four times its weight in water. When a person eats too high a percentage of starches, he becomes waterlogged. That is why people who eat too much starch are apt to have catarrh, swollen nasal membranes, or a flabby condition of the skin.

## WHY SOME REDUCING DIETS ARE DANGEROUS!

Here is a little-known secret. Adding fat to the diet prevents water storage. Some very dangerous reducing diets have been formulated because of this fact. For example, when a person begins to eat a considerable amount of fatty foods in place of starchy foods, he loses water from the tissues (dehydrates). This seems like weight loss—and in a sense it is—but you are not losing fat!

And there are dehydrating diets. Some of them, like the high-protein diets, have been used; not for long, however. Their ill effects were too readily apparent. The unwary victim imagines he has lost weight; he hasn't. He has lost some water and some health, and he soon drinks back the amount of water he has lost. One of the objections to losing weight by exercise is the fact that exercise is dehydrating, giving only apparent weight loss, sometimes as high as 15 pounds in one day!

Dehydration can be responsible for violent toxemias, causes tissues to shrivel and the victim to appear gaunt or haggard, and produces a miserable string of symptoms ranging from headaches to exhaustion. Body fluids are 99 per cent water. The bones, which are the hardest of the tissues, are 40 per cent water. Thus, if some diet or method of reducing drives water from the body and causes dehydration, the result is a definite disease state.

So it is important to avoid dehydration. Any method of reducing which includes this **evil** is dangerous.

## THE SPEED REDUCING DIET DRAINS AWAY POUNDS OF EXCESS FLUID WITHOUT DEHYDRATION!

The speed reducing diet does not dehydrate. The three pounds of solid food you eat, with the exception of the proteins, are from 90 to 96 or 97 per cent water. The greedy, exaggerated, distorted fat and sugar metabolism of fat people is corrected by a high catabolic (a thinning) food intake, but, best of all, the water balance of the body is straightened out, says Dr. Lindlahr.

## HOW THE SPEED REDUCING DIET PREVENTS WATER WEIGHT GAIN!

Most fatties are waterlogged. Jowls that wibble and wobble, hips that billow and surge, abdomens that undulate soon become firm on the speed reducing diet. Watch and see. To a great extent, waterlogging made these portions of the anatomy flabby and floppy. The speed reducing diet changes them to solid, natural flesh, not by dehydration but by making the tissue water balance normal, says Dr. Lindlahr.

## PREVENTS EXCESS ACID!

Body tissues, being mostly protein and fat, leave an acid ash when broken down. Therefore, during the reducing or catabolic process, excess acid may develop. That is the harm of a great many reducing diets. They produce not only acidemia—excess acid—but a virtual acidosis. Acidosis covers very special situations in which the alkaline reserve of the body has been completely diminished, such as in the last stages of diabetes.

The speed reducing diet is carefully calculated to provide such an excess of alkaline or base ash that it will neutralize roughly two pounds of tissue breakdown a day—a guarantee that you cannot suffer from acidemia on the diet, according to Dr. Lindlahr.

## HOW TO "STARVE" THE FAT OFF YOUR BODY—WHILE EATING LIKE A KING!

Small amounts of sugar and starch are needed to "spare" proteins and to burn fats rapidly, and to prevent a chemical state called ketosis. This is amply provided for with adequate fruit in the diet (besides, body fat is made into sugar when there is a need for it). Also enough of the essential fatty acids (linoleic, etc.) are provided, and are found in sufficient quantities in quite a few of the speed reducing foods, according to Dr. Lindlahr.

## HUNGER PAINS CAN BE A THING OF THE PAST!

Since most speed reducing foods are bulky, they help fill the dilated stomach that is characteristic of most fat people. As a result, there can be no hunger pains while the stomach is stretched with food. You need three times as much fattening foods (pastries, sweets, and breads) to provide the same satisfying fullness.

## YOU GET GOOD MILEAGE ON SPEED REDUCING FOODS!

As long as our concepts of energy are determined by our knowledge of mechanical engines, we shall never be able to comprehend the miracle of body energy production. A fairly good car can be propelled fifteen miles on one gallon of gasoline, which represents 26,505 food calories. That means such a car needs 1,767 food calories to run one mile. Yet an averaged-sized man of 154 pounds obtains enough energy from 51 food calories to walk a mile, and take care of all regular body processes at the same time.

The human body is like a small, compact economy car. It gets a lot of mileage out of surprisingly little fuel. For instance, that little fist-sized organ which you call your heart pumps a gallon of blood per minute through the body while you are sleeping. It pumps five or six gallons per minute when you're running for the bus. Over 500 voluntary and involuntary muscles, all exquisitely tuned engines in themselves, work at their special tasks. More messages are sent over your millions of nerve fibers each day than all our telegraph companies handle in a year. Your kidneys receive 600 quarts of blood every twenty-four hours. Thousands of other functions are performed by the human body daily.

How many calories does all this take? Just 600 a day—that's all!

## SPEED REDUCING IS STRENGTHENING AND HEALTHFUL!

The speed reducing diet is a diet of protective, fully nutritional foods which are healing, restorative, and health-bringing. Practically the same kind of diet was used successfully to treat certain types of heart trouble, gall bladder crises, and other important ailments. The speed reducing diet is good for you, fat or no fat, says Dr. Lindlahr!

Speed reducing foods are strengthening and healthful. In the first place, you get approximately three pounds of solid food a day, and each one of these foods (except those of the protein group) is literally a mine of minerals and vitamins. This is a far cry from "starvation" diets. The speed reducing diet starves only fat!

## EVERYTHING IS DONE FOR YOU!

Dr. Lindlahr, a trained nutritionist, spent 20 years perfecting the speed reducing diet. It requires a trained nutritionist, plus years of careful study and consideration, to formulate a healthfully balanced reducing diet—providing for almost 40 different elements you need for health!

These include food minerals, various vitamins, essential amino acids, water balance, bulk, and the acid-alkaline ash qualities. Certain minerals and vitamins must definitely be provided to carry on rapid fat destruction without harm. Careful protein balance must be maintained to prevent destruction of tissues other than fat. It has all been done for you in the speed reducing diet.

# 7

## How to Follow the Diet!

The speed reducing diet is easy to follow. In many cases, it's no-cook cooking all the way—no muss, no fuss, no bother. It gives you day-by-day menus to follow for 7 days. If you wish, you may continue beyond 7 days—or use it every other week, until your weight is normal. Some people have followed it for weeks and months, practically without change! As long as there is surplus fat in your body, you can afford to eat fat-dissolving, speed reducing foods.

### YOU NEVER HAVE TO EAT THE SAME FOOD TWICE!

The day-by-day menus do not have to be followed exactly. The food substitution lists give you an endless variety to choose from. You never have to eat the same food twice. The variety and endless combinations make it a pleasant, easy diet to follow. You'll never feel "bored" or cheated, because you'll discover many delicious speed reducing foods you never knew existed!

Of all the menus listed for 7 days, some people settle on three daily menus which they particularly like and use over and over again. The only caution necessary to give about such a plan is that at least one of these menus should include a glandular meat. Many, many people, of course, have given enough study to the principles involved in reducing to plan their own menus, using as a basis the general program outlined here.

## THERE ARE MANY SURPRISES!

Essentially, the principle of the diet is one of food substitution. You are substituting low-caloried, catabolic, protective foods for fattening foods. As you are probably aware, most people have no great decided food preferences—they desire only to be "filled up" three times a day. The speed reducing diet is filling—try it and see. Many people complain there's just too much to eat. But you must eat large amounts of speed reducing foods to lose weight fast!

You will enjoy some agreeable surprises. You'll be so delighted and impressed by the speed of the decided drop in your weight when you step on the scale each morning—yes, each morning—it changes that fast, you won't mind it at all! Every single day you'll be sure you're reducing, starting the very first day, in most cases!

With absolute, medically proved safety, you may lose as much as 15 pounds the first week alone on this quick-action diet. With the speed-reducing diet, there's no guessing. This method has been proved in thousands of cases! It will work for you, too—swiftly, pleasantly, surely—says Dr. Lindlahr!

There's no hunger, no headache, no frayed nerves, no regaining lost weight! Because if you ever do, it's a simple matter to speed reduce again, and drop those pounds, often in as little as one day! This unique feature of the plan will help you once and for all, to take off poundage fast and stay slim forever, no matter how many times you have failed before. Starting today, you can lose pounds and inches quickly, and have a slimmer, more attractive figure in a hurry!

## YOU ARE GUARANTEED TO LOSE UP TO 2 POUNDS A DAY IF YOU FOLLOW THESE RULES!

During your speed reducing, use only speed reducing foods. Guard, above all things, the table salt intake. Make no mistake: small amounts of salt are necessary to body health; we must not cut salt intake entirely. But salt demands a very definite percentage of water to be retained in the body. An excess, through its involvement with water balance, actually helps you to remain fat. So hold down the salt.

Drink no water during the meals. Drink it half an hour before or half an hour after, and drink all you please between meals. If hungry between meals or before bedtime, chew celery. No other food or drink, not even fruit juice, is permitted. Remember, it's no great sacrifice: it'll be over before you know it.

Make absolutely certain of a complete bowel elimination every day. Actually, your entire weight loss is going to be gauged by the type, quantity, and degree of this elimination. Here, too, is a long and involved story. Briefly, any consideration of body nutrition must be linked with the question of waste riddance. The digestive system is not only the larder of the body; it is also the chief channel through which unwanted food residues are expressed. Some breakdown tissues and results of catabolic fat destruction going on in the body are also eliminated. If a person becomes constipated while on a diet, he not only fails to lose weight, but also feels exceedingly miserable. Such a situation is not to be tolerated.

You'll never become constipated, if you follow this plan. Drink plenty of water—by that I mean a glass of water 30 minutes before each meal, and one before bed. It's as simple as that. You don't have to guzzle gallons and gallons of water on the speed reducing diet. Many of the foods are over 90 per cent water, and you get water in your tea or coffee, which may be used in place of water, and are not listed on the individual menus.

Dr. Lindlahr did not approve of chemical laxatives. They act by irritation. The use of mineral oil is taboo on the speed reducing diet, because it has a tendency to leach vitamin A from foods, and it interferes with absorption of various food nutrients. Thus, if mineral oil is used, the nutritive value of the diet will be lost and the intricate mineral and nitrogen balance will be upset. Since the diet is swung on very fine balances, we must insist that mineral oil not be used. Any pill or laxative that causes a watery or diarrhea stool (dehydration) is strictly forbidden. It will upset the delicate water balance which has been taken into careful consideration, and which the diet is so deliberately balanced to maintain.

Hydrogels are fine, as an aid to elimination, and the use of them is approved—and even urged—by Dr. Lindlahr. A hydrogel added to the diet provides a gentle stimulus to the movements of the digestive system. They are composed of vegetable pentosans. You might ask your doctor to recommend one. Use it to guard against irregularity, even if you are not constipated.

The speed reducing diet will not interfere with your daily activities. As a matter of fact, exercise and work will encourage the destruction of fat in your body. Obviously, the more active you are, the more weight you will lose. Many of those who went on the "test" diet aided fat destruction by taking a daily walk, of at least half a mile.

It is easier to reduce in summer, when the skin pores are more active and the heat loss from the body is greater than in colder weather. Two-hundred pound John Smith, who can lose ten pounds in ten August days on the speed reducing diet, would probably lose only eight and three-quarters pounds in winter, and nine pounds in the spring or fall.

Because perspiration carries a considerable amount of salt from the body, summer dieters might take a pinch of salt once in a while. This is not a bad plan for any fat person who perspires freely, whether he is on the diet or not, because salt depletion in the body causes most uncomfortable symptoms.

Winter dieters can compensate somewhat for their lack of summer-heat losses by taking, daily, a hot sitting bath. The bath technique is as follows: Run enough hot water into the tub to cover the hips; lean back and rest. Heat will escape from the body, the body thermostat will move up, and your metabolism rate will increase.

When swirling currents of air strike the nude skin, the body metabolism increases amazingly. If you will devote twenty minutes in the morning or evening to lolling without clothes in your bedroom (window shades down, of course), you will increase your metabolism noticeably and so help your weight reduction.

If you are allergic in any degree whatsoever to any food suggested on the speed reducing diet, do not use that food. Substitute another. According to Dr. Lindlahr, when the question of food intolerance is involved, the formal diet *must* be modified to suit the individual. So, to repeat, if you are intolerant of any food, if it does not "sit well," if you have a logical or illogical aversion to it, omit it from the diet.

Lack of physical well-being while on the diet may mean that you are allergic to one or another of the foods given. Your good sense and good judgment must avoid the pitfalls of allergy. If you meet up with any special difficulty, avail yourself of a physician's tests to determine the offending food.

## FINAL DIRECTIONS

Immediately following these directions, you will find menus for seven days outlined for you. These are the original seven-day speed reducing menus which were given over the air, during Dr. Lindlahr's famous reducing party.

On pages 146-149 there are twenty substitution lists. Each one of these contains foods which may be substituted safely, one for the other. There are numerous reasons why these allowable substitutions were selected—chiefly because important vitamin and mineral values were taken into consideration.

It would be best, although it is not absolutely necessary, to preserve as nearly as possible the allowed calorie values. In other words, if you wish to substitute some other vegetable for one listed in a given day's lunch, you would turn to Substitute List 11. By eating more or less of a substitute food, you'll be assured of a correct calorie count. Strict calorie counting is not necessary, however, because these are *speed reducing foods*, and if one has more calories than another, the increased energy (burned calories) it takes to digest it makes up, in some degree, for the higher calorie value, according to Dr. Lindlahr.

A pure celery salt may be used in place of ordinary salt for seasoning, or salt substitutes can be purchased at a drug store. The latter are now commonly used, for a salt-free diet is quite often prescribed by doctors in cases of high blood pressure, hardened arteries, kidney disease, allergy, and so on.

Any and all foods suggested can be used either canned or fresh; fresh, of course, are preferable. However, modern canning methods take such exceptional notice of delicate vitamin values that no fear need be felt in using a canned instead of a fresh food. In fact, canned vegetables often have better nutritional values than those purchased in the market, according to Dr. Lindlahr, for canneries demand that their produce be lush ripe. Frozen foods may also be used, as they are even closer to fresh.

May we remind you that the seven-day diet is really only a spearhead thrust against Devil Fat? It is only relatively important to take off eight pounds in seven days, as can most certainly be expected on this diet, says Dr. Lindlahr. The big gain is that you learn how to use the speed reducing foods. You get the feel of your weapons against fat.

You can settle back—after your initial speedy weight loss—for a more or less easy-going war on the enemy. You will have Devil Fat on the defensive—or, let us say, where he has you now.

Whenever canned fruits are prepared for any meal on the diet, please wash off all the syrup. Water-packed fruits can be purchased— these are canned without sugar. However, it is more convenient to drain the syrup from those you use and let the rest of the family benefit by the syrup that is left.

A few people have reported that they felt "woozy"—"not good" —for a day or two while on the diet. This may be due to the fact that certain stimulants like coffee, tea, or alcohol are missed. The abrupt withdrawal of these produces headache in some people. According to Dr. Lindlahr, the speed reducer should stick to water, skim milk, or 100 per cent natural fruit juices on the diet. However, I have not found this to be necessary in my own experience, and certainly not on any maintenance diet afterwards. Check with your doctor and follow his advice.

A baker who stayed on the job while following the diet developed feelings of faintness. Dr. Lindlahr suggested that, because he perspired so heavily, his condition might be due to a salt depletion. The guess proved to be right. A pinch of salt followed by a glass of water did away with the symptom.

Some people have a very low sugar content in the blood (technically called hypoglycemia). For example, diabetics taking insulin may use too much and develop a hypoglycemia. Some reducing diets produce such a state.

Under ordinary circumstances, this cannot happen with the speed reducing diet, according to Dr. Lindlahr, because it is rich in fruit and vegetable sugars. However, it is possible that some people with hypoglycemia might have it aggravated by this low starch diet, with symptoms of fatigue. No problem here. According to Dr. Lindlahr, a lump of sugar would restore them.

Remember that while the speed reducing diet is very low in calories, its catabolic feature is what causes rapid weight reduction. For example, if you tried to reduce by eating six pieces of bread a day (a very low-caloried diet), you would have very little success, says Dr. Lindlahr.

When you are watching your calories, always remember that it is more important to eat a catabolic (fat-burning) food to reduce than simply to eat few calories. It is the catabolic feature that counts, Dr. Lindlahr emphasizes.

# 8

## The Most Powerful
## Fat-Dissolving Foods
## Known to Science!

Although much more liberal variations follow in the next chapters, it is best to follow the same standard breakfast, every day, on this particular version of the speed reducing diet. The point is, the speed reducing diet will often break weight deadlocks—long periods of time, in which no loss occurs, for some people on standard diets. To do this effectively, and minimize the chances of a "standstill" or no-loss days, the high catabolic action of certain foods is needed.

This breakfast is only a suggestion. Instead of toast and coffee, Dr. Lindlahr recommends the following:

juice or whole of 1 small orange .............,,...., 4 oz.   50 cal.
2 halves Bartlett pears (fresh)................. 4 oz.   50 cal.
1 cup coffee (no sugar) ...................... 8 oz.    0 cal.
or ½ cup skim milk......................... 4 oz.   50 cal.

It is the standard breakfast used in Dr. Lindlahr's original radio reducing party. It need not be a hardship, for the short time involved— 7, 10 or 14 days, rarely more than a month. *Your reward? Over a pound a day lost!* Many people are used to a small breakfast anyway. This is especially true of overweights who—strangely enough—eat far less breakfast than their slim friends.

You may substitute milk for coffee (as indicated), or use tea, or a coffee substitute. For orange juice, you may substitute any fruit juice in Substitute List 2. Any fruit in Substitute Lists 1 or 4 may be eaten instead of pear.

Even though it has been your habit to drink only coffee, with perhaps not even a roll or a piece of toast, you *must* eat some sort of fruit, and eat at least 150 calories, on the speed reducing diet. In the first place, we want the catabolic action of these fruits, and, equally important, the vitamin and mineral values of fruits as well as their alkaline ash. So plan your own breakfast, if you please (along these lines), but eat it religiously.

### MONDAY, THE FIRST DAY*

Good morning. Digestive hygiene, before or after breakfast. How about an air bath? Weigh yourself, after elimination. Remember to watch your salt intake. Drink no water at your meals.

*Standard Breakfast*

Don't skip it—remember you have to eat to reduce.

| Substitution list | *Luncheon* | | |
|---|---|---|---|
| 6,7,8 | tomato and lettuce salad<br>1 small tomato<br>2 ounces lettuce<br>diet dressing (see page 149) | 6 oz. | 32 cal. |

---

*Throughout the diet, the calories given for fruit are for the fresh kind. Canned varieties have slightly high calorie values unless washed or water-packed.

| 10,11 | 1 cup mashed turnips | 8 oz. | 60 cal. |
|---|---|---|---|
| 9,12 | ⅔ cup string beans | 4 oz. | 20 cal. |
| 1,4 | 2 peach halves | 6 oz. | 45 cal. |
| | Total . . . . . . . . . . . . . . . . . . . | 24 oz. | 157 cal. |

*Substitution*          *Dinner*
list

| 7,8 | watercress and onion salad<br>½ cup watercress<br>4 small scallions<br>dressing | 4½ oz. | 36 cal. |
|---|---|---|---|
| 13,14,15 | 1 lean mutton chop | 4 oz. | 150 cal. |
| 10,12 | 6 asparagus stalks (6"),<br>dressing | 4 oz. | 20 cal. |
| 1,2,4 | ⅔ cup pineapple | 4 oz. | 45 cal. |
| | Total . . . . . . . . . . . . . . . . . . | 16½ oz. | 251 cal. |

*Total calories for day—558*
*Total amount of food for day—3 lbs., 4½ oz.*

## TUESDAY, THE SECOND DAY

Good morning. Again, digestive hygiene? Weigh yourself afterward. An air bath will clear your head. It would be silly to cheat today or to forget about salt and water drinking at meals. Today you will notice a marked increase in energy.

*Standard Breakfast*

It will set you back if you don't eat it.

*Substitution*          *Luncheon*
list

| 6,8 | cabbage and pimiento salad<br>1 cup cabbage<br>2 slices pimiento<br>1 tablespoon parsley | 7 oz. | 45 cal. |
|---|---|---|---|

| 16,18,19 | 1 sliced hard-boiled egg | 1½ oz. | 75 cal. |
|---|---|---|---|
| 7,10,11 | ½ cup carrots | 2½ oz. | 25 cal. |
| 1,2,4 | 4 apricot halves | 1½ oz. | 30 cal. |
| | Total .................... | 12½ oz. | 175 cal. |

| Substitution list | *Dinner* | | |
|---|---|---|---|
| 6,8 | shredded radish salad<br>3 ounces radish<br>3 ounces lettuce<br>diet dressing | 6 oz. | 25 cal. |
| 13,14 | codfish steak filet | 4 oz. | 110 cal. |
| 10,12 | ⅔ cup spinach | 5 oz. | 18 cal. |
| 11,12 | 1 cup squash | 6 oz. | 27 cal. |
| 3,5 | ¾ cup strawberries | 3 oz. | 35 cal. |
| | Total .................... | 24 oz. | 215 cal. |

*Total calories for day—540*
*Total amount of food for day—3 lbs., ½ oz.*

## WEDNESDAY, THE THIRD DAY

Good morning. Again, how about digestive hygiene? Weigh yourself afterward. Then take your air bath. The diet will be much easier going today. Remember, though, watch your salt intake and drink *no* water at mealtimes.

*Standard Breakfast*

Your fruit breakfast helps to alkalinize.

| Substitution list | *Luncheon* | | |
|---|---|---|---|
| 6,8 | cucumber salad<br>1 cucumber (4 x 2½″)<br>1 ounce shredded cabbage<br>1 scallion<br>dressing | 6 oz. | 34 cal. |

| | | | |
|---|---|---|---|
| 18,19 | cottage cheese and chives | 1 oz. | 86 cal. |
| 3,4,5 | ½ cup apple sauce—no sugar | 4 oz. | 60 cal. |
| | Total . . . . . . . . . . . . . . . . . . | 13 oz. | 180 cal. |

Substitution list

### Dinner

| | | | |
|---|---|---|---|
| 6,7,8 | romaine salad<br>10 leaves romaine<br>dressing | 3½ oz. | 20 cal. |
| 10,11 | ½ cup boiled onions | 2 oz. | 22 cal. |
| 16,19 | beef liver | 4 oz. | 155 cal. |
| 9,12 | ⅔ cup wax beans | 4 oz. | 20 cal. |
| 3,5 | ½ cup Queen Anne cherries<br>(canned, washed) | 3 oz. | 35 cal. |
| | Total . . . . . . . . . . . . . . . . . . | 16½ oz. | 252 cal. |

### Before Retiring

| | | |
|---|---|---|
| ½ grapefruit (3½″ wide) | 4 oz. | 40 cal. |

*Total calories for day—622*
*Total amount of food for day—2 lbs., 13½ oz.*

## THURSDAY, THE FOURTH DAY

Good morning. Daily hygiene? Don't you like your air baths? Now what do the scales say? Swell! Drink no water at your meals.

### Standard Breakfast

Don't skip it—remember you have to eat to reduce.

Substitution list

### Luncheon

| | | | |
|---|---|---|---|
| 6,7,8 | celery stuffed with cottage cheese<br>3 stalks celery<br>1½ ounces cheese | 4 oz. | 66 cal. |

| | | | |
|---|---|---|---|
| 9,10 | ⅔ cup broiled oyster plant | 4 oz. | 45 cal. |
| 10,12 | ½ cup red cabbage | 2 oz. | 20 cal. |
| 1,2,4 | ½ grapefruit (3½" wide) | 4 oz. | 40 cal. |
| | Total ................... | 14 oz. | 171 cal. |

| | | | |
|---|---|---|---|
| Substitution list | *Dinner* | | |
| 6,7,8 | escarole salad<br>6 leaves escarole<br>1 tablespoon dressing | 2 oz. | 15 cal. |
| 10,12 | ⅓ cup broccoli | 3 oz. | 24 cal. |
| 9,11,12 | ⅔ cup sauerkraut | 4 oz. | 30 cal. |
| 15,17 | broiled lean round steak or<br>roast beef | 4 oz. | 170 cal. |
| 3,5 | ½ cup cherries (canned,<br>washed) | 3 oz. | 35 cal. |
| | Total ................... | 16 oz. | 274 cal. |

*Before Retiring*

| | | |
|---|---|---|
| ½ grapefruit (3½" wide) | 4 oz. | 40 cal. |

*Total calories for day—635*
*Total amount of food for day—2 lbs., 14 oz.*

## FRIDAY, THE FIFTH DAY

Good morning. Digestive hygiene should be like clockwork by now, the air bath a welcome freedom. So you didn't think it possible to lose weight so fast and pleasantly? You know, too, that you can get along without so much salt. We won't even remind you not to cheat. Do your water drinking between meals, and steer clear of anabolic (fat-producing) foods!

*Standard Breakfast*

Don't skip it—remember you have to eat to reduce.

| Substitution list | Luncheon | | |
|---|---|---|---|
| 6,7 | asparagus salad<br>4 stalks asparagus<br>1 lettuce leaf<br>1 scallion<br>diet dressing | 3 oz. | 22 cal. |
| 11 | 1 cup baked cauliflower | 4 oz. | 20 cal. |
| 9,12 | ½ cup young peas | 4 oz. | 60 cal. |
| 9,11 | ½ cup carrots | 3 oz. | 30 cal. |
| 1,2 | ½ grapefruit | 4 oz. | 40 cal |
| | Total .................... | 18 oz. | 172 cal. |

| Substitution list | Dinner | | |
|---|---|---|---|
| 6,7,8 | tomato stuffed with celery<br>diet dressing | 5 oz. | 30 cal. |
| 9,11 | ½ cup turnips | 4½ oz. | 30 cal. |
| 13,14 | filet of haddock, broiled | 4 oz. | 100 cal. |
| 10,12 | ¾ cup red cabbage | 3 oz. | 30 cal. |
| 1,4,5 | 4 apricot halves | 1½ oz. | 30 cal. |
| | Total .................... | 18 oz. | 220 cal. |

*Total calories for day—542*
*Total amount of food for day—3 lbs.*

## SATURDAY, THE SIXTH DAY

Good morning. Do you appreciate now how important digestive hygiene is? Where do you get all that pep? Well, for one thing, your body is being "charged" with magic minerals and vitamins. You look so much firmer this morning because the water metabolism has by this time adjusted itself. The compliments of friends are pleasing, aren't they? Salt and water intake are still important.

*Standard Breakfast*

Don't skip it—remember you have to eat to reduce.

| Substitution list | *Luncheon* | | |
|---|---|---|---|
| 1,2,4 | celery and apple salad<br>3 stalks celery (6″)<br>½ small apple<br>1 lettuce leaf | 5 oz. | 44 cal. |
| 10,12 | ¾ cup mixed beets and leaves | 6 oz. | 45 cal. |
| 11,12 | 1 cup cooked mushrooms | 6 oz. | 7 cal. |
| 3,4,5 | 2 peach halves | 6 oz. | 45 cal. |
| | Total .................. | 23 oz. | 141 cal. |

| Substitution list | *Dinner* | | |
|---|---|---|---|
| 6,8 | raw shredded turnip on lettuce<br>½ cup turnip<br>1 lettuce leaf<br>dressing | 4 oz. | 33 cal. |
| 9,11 | okra and tomatoes<br>⅓ cup okra<br>⅓ cup tomatoes | 6 oz. | 27 cal. |
| 15,16 | roast leg of veal | 4 oz. | 145 cal. |
| 1,4 | ⅔ cup pineapple | 4 oz. | 45 cal. |
| | Total .................. | 18 oz. | 250 cal. |

*Total calories for day—541*
*Total amount of food for day—3 lbs., 5 oz.*

## SUNDAY, THE SEVENTH DAY

Good morning. The last day—so are you pleased? Your body cells and your long-abused fat metabolism are, too. Do you appreciate now why 500,000 copies of the speed reducing diet were purchased? More pounds to annihilate? Stay on the diet a few days longer. Start with Monday's meals tomorrow. Rout Devil Fat completely.

*Standard Breakfast*

Don't skip it—remember you have to eat to reduce.

| Substitution list | *Luncheon* | | |
|---|---|---|---|
| 6,7,8 | tomato and lettuce, diet dressing | 4 oz. | 35 cal. |
| 10,12 | 1 cup mushrooms | 6 oz. | 7 cal. |
| 9,11 | ½ cup turnips | 4½ oz. | 30 cal. |
| 13,16,17 | broiled chicken breast | 4 oz. | 155 cal. |
| 3,5 | ¾ cup strawberries | 3 oz. | 35 cal. |
| | Total .................. | 21½ oz. | 262 cal. |

| Substitution list | *Supper* | | |
|---|---|---|---|
| 18,19 | scrambled egg with asparagus<br>1 egg<br>3 stalks asparagus | 4 oz. | 90 cal. |
| 10,12 | 1 cup mixed greens | 4 oz. | 25 cal. |
| 1,2,4 | 1 small orange, sliced | 4 oz. | 50 cal. |
| | Total .................. | 12 oz. | 165 cal. |

*Before Retiring*

| ½ grapefruit (3½" wide) | 4 oz. | 40 cal. |
|---|---|---|

*Total calories for day—617*
*Total amount of food for day—3 lbs., 1½ oz.*

*Raw Fruit Substitution Lists*

(Calorie values per 4-ounce serving.)

### (1)

| | |
|---|---|
| Cantaloupe | 29 |
| Honeydew | 33 |
| Muskmelon | 46 |
| Papaya | 58 |
| Watermelon | 35 |

### (2)

| | |
|---|---|
| Grapefruit | 57 |
| Lemons | 51 |
| Limes | 60 |
| Oranges | 60 |
| Rhubarb | 27 |
| Tangerines | 57 |

### (3)

| | |
|---|---|
| Blackberries | 68 |
| Blueberries | 80 |
| Cranberries | 44 |
| Huckleberries | 84 |
| Raspberries | 57 |
| Strawberries | 45 |

### (4)

| | |
|---|---|
| Apples | 72 |
| Apricots | 85 |
| Nectarines | 84 |
| Peaches | 47 |
| Pears | 48 |
| Pineapple | 50 |

### (5)

| | |
|---|---|
| Cherries | 91 |
| Grapes | 85 |
| Kumquats | 87 |
| Plums | 48 |
| Prunes | 69 |

*Raw Salad and Vegetable Substitution Lists*

(Calorie values per 4-ounce serving.)

### (6)

| | |
|---|---|
| Asparagus | 26 |
| Cabbage | 28 |
| Cauliflower | 35 |
| Celery | 21 |
| Celery cabbage | 16 |
| Cucumbers | 20 |
| Radishes | 26 |

### (7)

| | |
|---|---|
| Beets | 54 |
| Carrots | 53 |
| Onions | 48 |
| Pimiento (red pepper) | 55 |
| Tomatoes | 26 |

### (8)

| | |
|---|---|
| Chicory | 30 |
| Chives | 56 |
| Endive | 24 |
| Leeks | 30 |
| Lettuce | 14 |
| Parsley | 0 |
| Watercress | 36 |

*Cooked Vegetable Substitution Lists*

(Calorie values per 4-ounce serving.)

(Please note how cooking diminishes calorie value.)

**(9)**

Beans:
  green, canned . . . . . . . . . 27
  string . . . . . . . . . . . . . . . 23
  string, canned . . . . . . . . . 23
  wax, canned. . . . . . . . . . 19
Okra. . . . . . . . . . . . . . . . . . 20
Pepper, green, sweet . . . . . . 23

**(10)**

Beets . . . . . . . . . . . . . . . . . 48
Beet greens . . . . . . . . . . . . 26
Broccoli. . . . . . . . . . . . . . . . 34
Carrot tops. . . . . . . . . . . . . 52
Celeriac, cooked . . . . . . . . 40
Chard. . . . . . . . . . . . . . . . . 28
Collards. . . . . . . . . . . . . . . 48
Dandelion greens . . . . . . . . 69
Kale. . . . . . . . . . . . . . . . . . 29
Sorrel . . . . . . . . . . . . . . . . 10
Spinach . . . . . . . . . . . . . . . 14

**(11)**

Beets . . . . . . . . . . . . . . . . . 48
Carrots . . . . . . . . . . . . . . . . 36

Cauliflower . . . . . . . . . . . . 17
Eggplant . . . . . . . . . . . . . . 32
Kohlrabi. . . . . . . . . . . . . . . 17
Onions . . . . . . . . . . . . . . . . 47
Oyster plant. . . . . . . . . . . . 50
Parsnips, boiled. . . . . . . . . 57
Potatoes, white, boiled . . . 113
Pumpkin . . . . . . . . . . . . . . 38
Tomatoes . . . . . . . . . . . . . . 26
Turnips. . . . . . . . . . . . . . . . 27

**(12)**

Asparagus . . . . . . . . . . . . . 21
Cabbage:
  red . . . . . . . . . . . . . . . . . 26
  white . . . . . . . . . . . . . . . 19
Celery . . . . . . . . . . . . . . . . 6
Chervil, leaves . . . . . . . . . . 79
Cucumbers . . . . . . . . . . . . 4
Lettuce. . . . . . . . . . . . . . . . 6
Mushrooms . . . . . . . . . . . . 2
Radishes, raw . . . . . . . . . . 26
Salsify . . . . . . . . . . . . . . . . 52
Sauerkraut . . . . . . . . . . . . . 28
Squash, average . . . . . . . . . 23

*Fish Substitution Lists*

(Calorie values per 4-ounce serving.)

**(13)**

Clams. . . . . . . . . . . . . . . . . 100
Crabmeat. . . . . . . . . . . . . . 93
Lobster . . . . . . . . . . . . . . . 98
Mussels . . . . . . . . . . . . . . . 77
Oysters . . . . . . . . . . . . . . . 57
Shrimp . . . . . . . . . . . . . . . 116

**(14)**

Abalone . . . . . . . . . . . . . . . 120
Bass . . . . . . . . . . . . . . . . . 105
Buffalo. . . . . . . . . . . . . . . . 110
Cod . . . . . . . . . . . . . . . . . . 105
Flounder . . . . . . . . . . . . . . 77
Frogs legs . . . . . . . . . . . . . 75
Terrapin . . . . . . . . . . . . . . . 135

## Meat Substitution Lists

(Calorie values per 4-ounce serving.)

### (15) *Muscle*

Beef:
    boiled . . . . . . . . . . 255
    chopped . . . . . . . . 165
    roast . . . . . . . . . . . 185
    steak . . . . . . . . . . . 175
Ham, baked . . . . . . . . 175
Mutton chop, lean . . . 155
Veal:
    chop, lean . . . . . . . 172
    roast leg
    (fat removed) . . . . . 145

### (16) *Glandular*

Beef liver . . . . . . . . . . 155
Mutton kidneys . . . . . 110
Sweetbreads . . . . . . . . 220

### (17) *Fowl*

Chicken:
    broiled . . . . . . . . . . . . . . 156
    white meat . . . . . . . . . . . 167
    roast . . . . . . . . . . . . . . . 210
Guinea hen breast . . . . . . . 170
Quail . . . . . . . . . . . . . . . . 170
Turkey, roast . . . . . . . . . . . 195

## Protein Substitution Lists *(for Vegetarians)*

(Calorie values per 4-ounce serving.)

### (18) *Muscle Meat and Fish Substitutes*

Beans:
    baked . . . . . . . . . . . . . . . 150
    kidney . . . . . . . . . . . . . . 122
    lima, green . . . . . . . . . . 152
    lima, yellow . . . . . . . . . 160
    soy (average) . . . . . . . . 170
Peas . . . . . . . . . . . . . . . . . 145

### (19) *Glandular Meat Substitutes*

Cottage cheese . . . . . . . . . . 191
Hen eggs . . . . . . . . . . . . . . 180
Soy beans (average) . . . . . 170

*Cheaters' and Procrastinators' Substitution Lists*

(Calorie values per 4-ounce serving.)

(20)

*Instead of midnight suppers*

Beef consommé ......... 30
Bouillon ............... 19

*Instead of dumplings*

Dill pickles ............. 12
Sour pickles ........... 5

*Instead of beer*

Lemonade .............. 36
Limeade ............... 36

*Instead of highballs*

Grapefruit juice ......... 50
Plain soda ............. 0

*Instead of cocktails*

Orange juice ........... 45
Pineapple juice ......... 69

*Instead of whiskey*

Black coffee ........... 0

*Instead of puddings*

Gelatin with fruit ....... 178

*Instead of candy*

Ginger ................ 68

*Instead of between-meal nibbles*

Skim milk ............. 47

*Instead of seasonings*
Seasoning quantity

Chili sauce (1 T.) ....... 25
Garlic ................. 0
Onion ................. 0
Parsley ............... 0

## A SUGGESTED DIET DRESSING!

Rub a little garlic around the bowl which is to be used. Combine skim milk and lemon juice in proportion for taste desired. To prevent curdling of the milk, add a bit of salt before stirring in the lemon juice. Paprika may be added for color and flavor.

*Catabolic Foods Best Eaten Raw!*

| | | |
|---|---|---|
| apples | cucumbers | pears |
| apricots | dandelion greens | peppers, green or red |
| berries | endive | (pimiento) |
| cabbage, white | grapes | pineapple |
| carrots | leeks | plums |
| celery | lettuce | prunes |
| celery cabbage | melons | radishes |
| cherries | onions | sauerkraut |
| chives | parsley | tomatoes |
| citrus fruits | peaches | watercress |

*Catabolic Foods Best Eaten Cooked!*

| | | |
|---|---|---|
| asparagus | chard | oyster plant |
| beans, string or wax | chervil | parsnips |
| beet greens | chicory | pumpkin |
| beets | collards | rhubarb |
| broccoli | eggplant | salsify |
| cabbage, red | kale | sorrel |
| carrot tops | kohlrabi | spinach |
| cauliflower | mushrooms | squash |
| celeriac | okra | turnips |

*Weights and Measures*

| *Dry* | *Liquid* |
|---|---|
| 2 teaspoons .... 1 tablespoon | 1 fluid oz ....... 2 tablespoons |
| 4 tablespoons ... ¼ cup | 2 pints ......... 1 quart |
| 8 tablespoons ... ½ cup | 4 quarts ........ 1 gallon |
| 16 tablespoons ... 1 cup | ½ pint jar ....... 1 cup |
| | 1 quart jar ...... 4 cups |
| | 1 cup (glass) .... 236 cc |
| | 1 quart ......... 1000 cc |

| *Grams—Ounces* | *Grams—Calories* |
|---|---|
| 1 ounce ...... 30 (28.4) grams | 1 gram carbohydrate ... 4.1 cal. |
| 3.5 ounces ........ 100 grams | 1 gram protein ........ 4.1 cal. |
| 16 ounces ........ 460 grams | 1 gram fat ........... 9.3 cal. |
| 2.2 pounds ....... 1 kilogram | 1 gram alcohol ....... 7.0 cal. |

We have now given you the reducing diet, the very same one which 26,000 radio listeners followed in April 1936. I have not dared to make any modification of it, for some people will insist that no other diet could cause them to lose weight.

Of course, that is not true. The catabolic principle involved is what does the reducing. Actually, dozens and dozens of seven-day regimens could be formulated which would cause the average overweight individual to lose a pound or more a day. The substitution lists were compiled with a purpose. We have, in reality, listed the foods enabling you to work out a catabolic diet best suited to your own taste and needs.

# 9

## How to Break Weight Deadlocks!

About the same time Dr. Lindlahr was developing the speed reducing diet, another expert, working along the same lines, reached many similar conclusions. In her book, *Optimum Health* (1935), famed nutritionist Adelle Davis announced a rapid reducing diet that worked for many of her patients. Her major conclusions were as follows:

**"Although the popular opinion exists that rapid reduction is harmful, there is no scientific evidence to support this belief .... The best scientifically controlled reducing has been done just as rapidly as the patients wished [and is not harmful].**

"There is much evidence, however, that an improvement in health follows to the point of ideal weight .... A good reducing diet must fulfill manifold requirements. It must, first of all, give you so much to eat that you will never be hungry. It must prevent wrinkles and haggard faces. It must keep you free from acidosis. The foods must be easy to prepare, inexpensive, palatable, and attractive. The diet must prevent 'cravings' by providing you with every need of your body .... The success of a reducing diet is not measured by the number of pounds lost, but by the length of time those pounds stay off ...."

## TO PREVENT CRAVINGS!

Quick weight-loss, said Ms. Davis, is preferable to reducing "so slowly that you will become discouraged before reaching your ideal weight .... It is, I feel, more important to reduce rapidly," she said. On a speed reducing diet, every requirement of the body should be satisfied, to prevent "cravings," said Ms. Davis. Her first requirement was a quart of skim milk daily, because of its vitamin and mineral content—and also because it solidifies in the stomach (the only liquid that does this). "You cannot have hunger pains as long as there is solid food in your stomach," said Ms. Davis. There is another, more fascinating reason, for including milk.

## TO PREVENT WRINKLES!

Milk is extremely rich in Vitamin G—the anti-wrinkle vitamin— said Ms. Davis: "Vitamin G preserves the characteristics of youth to a very late age ... skin free from wrinkles, blotches, and irritations .... A wealthy woman once called me for advice concerning her diet. She had collected from faddists much misinformation about foods which were 'harmful.' Moreover, she was convinced that many good foods did not agree with her. For years she had kept herself on a most restricted diet, from which she had eliminated all the vitamin G bearing foods ....

**"Her skin was blotched with dark spots resembling sunburn, and her forearms and other parts of her body were broken out with a severe rash or dermatitis. A physician who was called made the diagnosis of pellagra. An adequate diet rich in vitamin G was given her, and her condition cleared up."**

Other good sources of vitamin G, besides milk, are cheese, brewer's yeast, liver, kidneys, egg and lean meat. But these cannot be eaten in quantities large enough for an adequate daily supply, since they are too filling. Therefore, milk actually becomes the richest source of this vitamin. One quart a day can easily be taken—and should be—by anyone wishing to avoid the kind of wrinkled or haggard appearance associated with dieting. (Incidentally, the more common name for this vitamin is B-2 or riboflavin.)

## YOU MUST EAT FREQUENTLY BETWEEN MEALS!

Ms. Davis recommended large quantities of catabolic foods. On her Rapid Reducing diet, you get 500 to 650 calories daily. But you must eat frequently between meals—preferably every 2 to 3 hours—on this particular diet. As Ms. Davis explained it:

**"These midmeals are extremely important. They prevent acidosis, keep you from getting hungry, and kill your appetite for the next meal to such an extent that you are not likely to overeat .... It is so important to eat frequently during the period you are on the (rapid reducing) diet, you should always carry hard candy .... You may even be saying, 'I can't eat so much.'"**

"This diet," said Ms. Davis, "is not difficult to follow and may be safely continued for several weeks, if one is eager to lose weight rapidly. I recall a patient who was extremely obese, and because of a heart condition, needed to reduce as quickly as possible. She stayed on this diet ... for three months, losing 58 pounds." An average of 20 pounds a month!

If desired, a more generous diet may be followed after 3 days. This diet gives you between 1000 and 1400 calories a day. In either case, said Ms. Davis, "There is plenty of food to eat without breaking the diet."

## TURNS UGLY FAT INTO HARMLESS WATER!

This second, more generous diet can be used to break weight deadlocks—long periods of time, in which no loss occurs—due to water accumulation. It does this by giving the water a chance to drain away. Most people don't realize that water accumulation *means* that *fat is burning rapidly*. When fat is burned, carbon dioxide and water are formed. The carbon dioxide is carried off by the lungs, but the water needs a little extra time to drain away. A 5-pound gain, on a reducing diet, means *you are losing at a terrific rate*—faster than the body can rid itself of the water being formed. But the water is *always eliminated* after a few days—if you have not become so discouraged that your willpower snapped.

The more generous diet lets the water drain away—in the absence of continued rapid fat burning (which would only add more)—and, while this is going on *keeps you satisfied with more delicious foods*. It sounds too good to be true, but it *IS* true! On the rapid reducing diet, you lose pounds of fat! On the more generous diet, you lose pounds of excess water (left over from fat-burning). This cannot harm you— cannot dehydrate—in any way, because it is only excess water you don't need, from melted fat you didn't want!

You'll see how speed reducing turns ugly fat into harmless water—floats fat right out of your body. As Dr. Lindlahr said: "Some forms of body fat are a little tougher than others, but even the hardiest can be turned into water, some carbonic acids, and gases very easily by putting certain body chemical processes in motion."

## BREAKS WEIGHT DEADLOCK!

By way of illustration, Ms. Davis says: "Recently a woman to whom I had given a diet reduced from 153 to 112 pounds in a short time. For two full weeks her weight stayed at 133, despite the fact that she was carefully observing a strict reducing diet. Of course she became discouraged. I recommended a liberal reducing diet for a week in the way of a rest from the restricted diet she had chosen for herself. During this one week, while she was eating more food than before, her weight dropped from 133 to 125. She had been burning fat rapidly; water had been stored temporarily in her body, for it had formed too quickly for the body to carry it away. Water formed in this way is always eliminated ... and then the scales show the long-waited for reward."

## YOU CAN GO OFF YOUR DIET WITHOUT GAINING!

This second, more generous diet has two more big advantages—1) you are not conscious of being on a diet. Your foods are those so generally used that it is easy to forget you are actually on a reducing plan. 2) It gives you a rest or a "breather" from the more restrictive diet, and can be used for a week or on alternate weeks, without ruining your plan. In fact, it satisfies your emotional need for "going off a diet." By the time you have reached your ideal weight, you will have "gone off your diet" several times, without affecting weight loss in any way, and as a matter of fact still losing!

## LOSE UP TO 6 POUNDS IMMEDIATELY!

On both diets, you will lose a combination of fat and water. On the Rapid Reducing diet, you'll lose up to 2 pounds a day—6 pounds immediately, until water begins to accumulate. Whenever this happens, you may switch to the more generous diet, and lose over a pound a day, as seen in Ms. Davis' example. Many have enjoyed spectacular weight-loss with this secret—switching diets—one diet more generous than the next, yet each one sparking off a new weight loss!

## I. THE RAPID REDUCING DIET!

On the Rapid Reducing Diet, you must have a quart of milk daily—as mentioned before. In addition, you must have daily two cups (16 oz.) of tomato juice or one cup (8 oz.) of either orange juice or grapefruit juice, or the equivalent in the fresh fruits themselves. The whole fruit will fill you up more than the juice, but the juice has the advantage of being measured more accurately. Tomato juice contains few calories, even when twice as much is taken; however, both orange and grapefruit juice offer a higher content of Vitamin C, the vitamin that builds healthy connective tissue and prevents you from bruising and your gums from bleeding. For the sake of avoiding monotony, most people prefer to eat one small grapefruit, three small juice oranges, and about six ounces of tomato juice or canned tomatoes or a raw tomato salad. *Do not eat or drink anything to which you are allergic*, even if it means skipping the diet.

You may have black coffee and clear tea in moderation, bouillon made from bouillon cubes, or clear, fat-free chicken, beef, and lamb broth.

In order that every requirement of your body can be met, you must have some form of fish-liver oil. Halibut-liver-oil and cod-liver oil concentrates are the best sources of vitamin A, and can be purchased in tasteless capsules at every health food store. These are not fattening. There are 3500 calories in a pound of fat. One capsule contains about two calories. You would have to take 1700 of them before you could gain one pound.

Buy fish-liver-oil capsules which contain no Viosterol, unless advised otherwise by your physician or dentist. Take two or three of them daily. They may all be taken at one time, for they are not medicine.

The milk, orange, grapefruit, or tomato juice and the fish-liver-oil capsules take care of all the body needs except one, namely, Vitamin B. This vitamin makes for normal digestion by controlling the health of the nerves. The only appreciable source of Vitamin B in most diets is whole-grain breads and cereals, which are not permitted on this diet. Sufficient amounts of Vitamin B, at best, are difficult to obtain from ordinary foods. However, two excellent sources which you can use are brewer's yeast tablets and wheat germ, available at any health food store.

You should take at least 6 brewer's yeast tablets daily—and preferably 8 to 12—said Ms. Davis. These can all be taken at the same time, she said, for they are not medicine. Some people have difficulty swallowing tablets, she noted, but we have all swallowed pieces of steak for years which are many times larger.

If you choose wheat germ as your source of B vitamins, cook it a few minutes and eat it with skim milk as a hot cereal, said Ms. Davis. You may eat it as a cold cereal if you like, or in orange juice or milk. Take 2 or 3 level tablespoonfuls daily, she advised.

Brewer's yeast is more expensive, but contains fewer calories than wheat germ. Both brewer's yeast and wheat germ are somewhat laxative. Since there is little bulk on this diet, do not expect a bowel movement more often than every two or three days, said Ms. Davis. Remember that constipation means, not a small nor an infrequent stool, but a hard stool, she said. Do not take cathartics at this time, or at any other time for that matter, as they push the food through the body before the vitamins and minerals are properly absorbed, said Ms. Davis.

If you wish to stay on this diet longer than three days, modify it by adding two servings of leafy vegetables and one serving of fat-free meat or one egg. Choose your meats and vegetables from those allowed on the more generous reducing diet. With these simple additions, the program is not difficult to follow and may be safely continued for several weeks if one is eager to lose weight rapidly.

During this time you must eat something every two or three hours. Your daily schedule might be somewhat as follows:

**8 a.m.**

> 2 tablespoonfuls of wheat germ with a half cup of milk; or 6 to
>     10 yeast tablets
> 2 or 3 fish-liver-oil capsules
> half a grapefruit
> 1 or 2 cups of black coffee; more if it is weak

**10 a.m.**

> 1 small juice orange

**12 a.m.**

> 1 cup of broth
> 1 glass of milk
> Beginning on the 4th day, add a vegetable to this meal from the
>     permitted list on page 161

**2 p.m.**

> 4 ounces of tomato juice

**4 p.m.**

> tea, if desired
> 1 glass of milk

**6 p.m.**

> bouillon
> 4 ounces of tomato juice
> Beginning the 4th day, add one serving of fat-free meat or one
>     egg to this meal, and a vegetable—from the permitted
>     lists on pages 161-162.
> 1 glass of milk
> 1 small orange

**Before retiring**

> remainder of quart of milk

With the possible exception of iron and protein, this diet is far superior to that eaten by the average person who is not even trying to reduce, for it furnishes the needs of the body more adequately. It will not hurt the health. It will probably improve the health, said Ms. Davis.

Let us summarize and check this diet. You must have daily:

1 quart of skim milk . . . . . . . . . . . . . . . calcium, phosphorus,
                                             protein, vitamin G

1 cup of orange or grapefruit juice or 2
    cups of tomato juice . . . . . . . . . . . . vitamin C

2 or 3 fish-liver-oil capsules . . . . . . . . . vitamins A and D

6 to 10 yeast tablets . . . . . . . . . . . . . . . vitamins B and G
    or

2 to 3 tablespoonfuls of wheat germ . . . vitamins B and E

black coffee, clear tea, bouillon, broth . to satisfy appetite

Beginning the 4th day, add:

1 egg or 1 serving of meat . . . . . . . . . . protein, iron, phos-
                                             phorus, vitamin G

2 servings of leafy vegetables . . . . . . . . bulk, iron, vitamin A, al-
                                             kaline minerals

However, if you cannot follow all the rules of this diet, pass it by and go directly to the more generous diet.

There are two disadvantages to staying on this Rapid Reducing Diet for any length of time: first, you are conscious of being on a diet; second, you are not retraining your food habits. Compared to these disadvantages, the advantages are many: you are reducing rapidly; you are becoming accustomed to a slight pressure in your stomach; you are building your health. Best of all, you are learning that the less you eat, the less you care to eat.

## II. THE MORE GENEROUS DIET!

On this diet, you eat to satisfy your taste as well as your hunger. "If we are to enjoy our meals, we want them to be attractively served, luscious to the taste, and sufficient in amount for us to leave the table feeling completely satisfied," said Ms. Davis.

An interesting experiment was carried out in a hospital where the patients were totally unaware that they were being observed. One day, very rich, concentrated foods were served, so rich that the total daily intake of each person was between 5000 and 6000 calories. On the following day, bulky nonfattening foods were served, resulting in an average total intake of 1000 calories per person. On each day it was found that each person ate a certain bulk or volume of food which gave him a feeling of fullness at the end of the meal. Not only were the patients unaware that they were observed, but they were even unaware that the diets on the two days differed. Since there are 3500 calories in a pound of fat, each patient could have gained over a pound the first day; on the second day, each could have lost one-half pound. On both days the patients were equally happy because the foods were tasty, well-cooked and sufficient in amount to make them feel satisfied at the end of the meal.

Throughout your reducing program eat well-cooked, well-served, delicious food in quantities large enough to keep you satisfied, said Ms. Davis. Eat foods that are low in calories, but try to forget their caloric content.

The foods prescribed on Diet I—the Rapid Reducing Diet—must be continued throughout your reducing program; in fact, you should continue them throughout life, said Ms. Davis. These foods form the essential foundation of your diet by furnishing your normal daily vitamin, mineral, carbohydrate, and protein requirements.

Besides these foods, you may have small servings of certain fruits. However, vegetables should be largely substituted for fruits on Diet II—the more generous diet. Have about two raw salads daily, said Ms. Davis. In addition, have two or three vegetables at each meal if you want them. (You will note that the following foods are exactly the same as those Dr. Lindlahr recommended.)

*Foods Permitted in the Reducing Diet*

*Vegetables, generous amounts:*

| | | |
|---|---|---|
| artichokes | escarole | okra |
| asparagus | green peppers | parsley |
| broccoli | greens | radishes |
| Brussels sprouts | Italian squash | spinach |
| celery | kale | summer squash |
| chard | leeks | tomatoes |
| cucumbers | lettuce | vegetable oysters |
| eggplant | mushrooms | watercress |

*Vegetables, smaller amounts:*

| | | |
|---|---|---|
| beets | celery root | parsnips |
| cabbage | cream squash | rutabaga |
| carrots | Danish squash | string beans |
| cauliflower | onions | turnips |

*Fruits, small amounts:*

| | | |
|---|---|---|
| blackberries | lemons | raspberries |
| cantaloupe | oranges | rhubarb |
| casaba melon | Persian melon | strawberries |
| grapefruit | pineapple, fresh | watermelon |

*Fruits, sparingly:*

| | | |
|---|---|---|
| apples | cherries | peaches |
| apricots | grapefruit juice | plums |
| canned fruits | grapes | prunes, fresh |
| (pour off syrup) | orange juice | tangerines |

*Meats, generous amounts if fat free:*

| | | |
|---|---|---|
| bacon, crisp | liver | tongue |
| drained | mutton | turkey |
| chicken | rabbit | veal |
| chops | roast beef | venison |
| kidney | squab | liverwurst |
| lamb | steak | wieners |

*Fish, generous amounts if fat free:*

| | | |
|---|---|---|
| abalone | lobster | shrimps |
| halibut | oysters | trout |
| herring | mussels | tuna, washed |

*Eggs and cheese, moderate amounts if fat free:*

| | | |
|---|---|---|
| boiled eggs | omelet | coddled eggs |
| poached eggs | scrambled eggs in | baked eggs |
| soufflé | milk | dry cottage cheese |

*Soups, generous amounts if fat free:*

| | | |
|---|---|---|
| barley soup, | bouillon | noodle soup, |
| strained | chicken soup | strained |
| bean soup, | chowder | tomato soup, |
| strained | lamb broth | home-made |
| beef broth | milk vegetable | vegetable soup |
| beef tea | soup | |

*Milk:* skimmed milk, buttermilk (strained)

*Richest Sources of Body Requirements Allowed*

| | | |
|---|---|---|
| **Vitamin A:** | liver | oysters |
| fish-liver-oil capsules | lettuce | green vegetables |
| colored fruits | spinach | egg yolk |
| liver | **Vitamin G:** | **Copper:** |
| kidney | milk | |
| **Vitamin B:** | cottage cheese | oysters |
| yeast | meat | liver |
| wheat germ | liver | spinach |
| | egg | green vegetables |
| **Vitamin C:** | **Calcium:** | egg yolk |
| tomato juice | milk, buttermilk | **Protein:** |
| green peppers | cottage cheese | milk |
| grapefruit | | cottage cheese |
| oranges | **Phosphorus:** | meat |
| cabbage | milk | fish |
| **Vitamin D:** | meats | eggs |
| fish-liver-oil capsules | cottage cheese | **Bulk:** |
| sunshine | fish | vegetables |
| **Vitamin E:** | eggs | fruits |
| wheat germ | **Iron:** | milk (by increasing |
| | liver | bacteria in intestines) |

If you are to enjoy your salads, you must have good salad dressings. However, do not use mineral-oil dressings. Mineral oil causes a loss of vitamins and minerals through diarrhea. Moreover, since it is a fat, it dissolves the fat-soluble vitamins A, D, and E from the intestinal tract, thus preventing their absorption by the body.

Make a boiled dressing of skim milk, egg yolks, seasonings, and a small amount of flour or cornstarch; thin it with lemon juice to any consistency you prefer. Use any boiled dressing recipe and omit the fat. Lemon, vinegar, or wine vinegar, together with seasoning, makes a palatable substitute for French dressing. To the plain boiled dressing you can add chopped pickle, making a tartar sauce which is delicious on head lettuce. You may add tomato catsup, chopped pickle, hard-boiled egg, green pepper, pimiento, celery, onion, and a bit of garlic if you choose, making thousand island dressing.

You may have fat-free soups in any amounts you want. Make your own soups, so that you know what goes into them. Always buy a soup bone with enough meat on it to give the soup a delicious flavor. Let the soup stand until cold and skim off all the fat. As with your salad dressings, the secret of good soups is the seasoning. Get acquainted with spices and use them.

Fortunately the protein foods (milk, eggs, meats, fish, and cheese) cannot make you gain if they are eaten fat-free. These foods "stick to your ribs" and keep you from getting hungry. Dry cottage cheese can be added to combination vegetable salads, moistened with skim milk or salad dressing. If you have only a few pounds to lose, buy the usual cottage cheese to which cream is added. You can have Monterey jack cheese if it is made from skim milk, but be sure you are not buying the whole-milk jack cheese.

You may have meat or fish twice daily if you like. Meats can be dry pan-broiled, broiled before the open fire, or roasted. Roasts can be placed on a mesh cake-cooler so that the fat may drain to the bottom, cool, and be removed, and the meat juices used for unthickened gravies and soups or for seasoning vegetables. Fish canned in oil such as tuna can be placed in a wire strainer and held under the hot-water faucet until all the oil is removed; then it may be chilled and used for salads. Baked fish, stuffed with tomatoes, green peppers, onion, eggplant, and other vegetables, is delicious.

You may have one and sometimes two eggs daily. Hard-cooked eggs stay in your stomach longer than soft-cooked eggs; hence, they keep you satisfied longer. If you prefer a soft texture, add enough skim milk to your omelets or scrambled eggs to make a soft consistency; yet cook them well over a low fire. Pour a little milk in the pan before adding the eggs for an omelet or for scrambling, and use no fat. Fresh tomatoes, mushrooms, green peppers, asparagus tips, spinach, egg-plant, artichoke hearts, or other vegetables, dry cottage cheese, or jack cheese may be added to scrambled eggs and omelets to improve the flavor and increase the bulk.

If you serve enough vegetables, meat, milk, and other foods, you will not need a dessert, although fruit is allowed. It is best, however, to break the dessert habit, on this particular diet, said Ms. Davis.

Four food habits are largely responsible for all unwanted pounds, said Ms. Davis: the dessert habit; the bread-and-butter habit; the cream-and-sugar-in-coffee habit, and the habit of adding fats to vegetables. Break these for a lifetime and your weight problem will be solved.

Foods not mentioned on the diet lists are definitely barred from Ms. Davis' diet. This includes pork, ham, sausages, fish canned in oil; candies and sweet desserts; fried foods, gravies, cream, butter, olive oil, nuts, and cheeses other than cottage cheese; starchy vegetables, cereals, and breads. If you have only a few pounds to lose, eat these forbidden foods sparingly. Soda fountain beverages and alcoholic drinks must be omitted if you sincerely want to reduce. Let us see what alcohol would do to an otherwise reducing diet:

*Caloric Values of Liquors*

| | Weight in ounces | Calories |
|---|---|---|
| **Distilled Liquors:** | | |
| California brandy | ⅔ | 65 |
| Cherry brandy | ⅔ | 62 |
| French brandy, cognac | ⅔ | 73 |
| Cocktail, dry Martini | 2⅓ | 131 |
| Gin | 1⅔ | 116 |
| | | |
| **Liqueurs:** | | |
| Benedictine | ⅔ | 88 |
| Chartreuse | ⅔ | 87 |
| Curacao | ⅔ | 82 |
| Kummel | 2½ | 61 |
| Rum | 2½ | 153 |
| Rum, Jamaica | 2½ | 245 |
| Whiskey, American | 2½ | 152 |
| Whiskey, European | 2½ | 137 |
| | | |
| **American Wines:** | | |
| California red | 4 | 95 |
| California | 4 | 89 |
| | | |
| **Sweet Wines:** | | |
| Catawba | 1 | 30 |
| Champagne | 4½ | 132 |
| Port, California | 1 | 53 |
| Sherry, California | 1 | 38 |
| Tokay | 1 | 39 |

American Malt Liquors:

| | | |
|---|---|---|
| Ale............................................ | 8⅓ | 153 |
| Lager Beer, bottled.......................... | 8⅓ | 130 |
| Lager beer, draft............................ | 8⅓ | 120 |
| Porter....................................... | 8⅓ | 140 |

European Malt Liquors:

| | | |
|---|---|---|
| Ale............................................ | 8⅓ | 145 |
| Bock beer ................................... | 8⅓ | 154 |
| Export beer ................................. | 8⅓ | 140 |
| Light beer ...........................  ...... | 8⅓ | 120 |
| Munich, heavy ......................  ...... | 8⅓ | 180 |
| Pilsen, export .............................. | 8⅓ | 123 |
| Porter, stout................................ | 8⅓ | 172 |
| Weissbeer ................................... | 8⅓ | 103 |

In interpreting these figures, remember that there are 3500 calories in a pound of fat. On the Rapid Reducing Diet you get about 500 to 650 calories daily; and on the more generous reducing diet, between 1000 to 1400. If you carefully follow the rules of the diet, it is difficult to eat more than 1200 calories of the foods allowed you. Add a few ounces of Jamaica rum to your diet, and that diet ceases to make you lose.

However, there is plenty of food to eat without breaking the diet. You may even be saying, "I can't eat so much!" You need not eat everything suggested here unless you desire. You may eat just as little as you choose as long as you get the essentials given on the Rapid Reducing Diet, and as long as you eat frequently, said Ms. Davis.

The success of this diet depends to a very large extent on your desire or ability to cook well and on your willingness to make the little extra effort in planning your meals, said Ms. Davis. Everyone likes well-cooked and attractively served foods. Everyone wants enough food not to be hungry. Aside from these things, the average person cares little about vitamin and mineral content of food—but these things are important on a reducing diet.

Watch for variety in preparing salads, soups, meats, eggs, and vegetables. Make any mixture or combination of foods given on the diet which appeals to you. It requires talent to make luscious salads and salad dressings, and to season bouillon so tastefully that your husband will like it in spite of the fact that it is not his favorite and very fattening cream soup. To prepare delicious meals is your supreme test. You can pass this test if your desire to have a healthy, attractive, normal body is sufficiently strong.

Choose well, cook well, and season well. It means the difference between success and failure in your reducing program, said Ms. Davis.

## WHY YOU MUST EAT FREQUENTLY BETWEEN MEALS!

Even on the more generous diet, you must eat between meals, preferably about 10:30 a.m. and 4:30 p.m. These midmeals are extremely important. They prevent acidosis, keep you from getting hungry, and kill your appetite for the next meal, said Ms. Davis.

But the factor which must be watched most carefully on this particular diet is acetone acidosis. This is what makes people irritable on a poorly planned diet. An hour after eating, the person becomes calm again.

Here's what happens. Sugar is not stored in the body as such except in small amounts—if an excess is taken at any one time, it is turned into fat. Fat, which is to furnish you with heat and energy while you reduce, cannot be burned completely without the aid of sugar. In the absence of sugar, the fat is burned only partially, leaving a residue of certain acids in the body. In large amounts, this causes a condition known as acetone acidosis.

The symptoms of acidosis are unusual weariness, nervousness, headache, dizziness, bad breath (acetone), and even nausea and vomiting. Fortunately all of these symptoms disappear as soon as you have eaten anything which contains sugar. On a reducing diet, acidosis to the point of nausea or vomiting rarely happens. But tiredness, nervousness, dizziness, headaches, irritability, and bad breath are common among careless dieters.

It is absolutely needless to get even the slightest touch of acidosis—on this diet—if you follow directions.

Acidosis can be prevented by eating at frequent intervals something which contains sugar. Almost all foods on Ms. Davis' diet contain sugar in *small amounts* (skim milk, tomato juice, wheat germ, vegetables). You must eat frequently to *replenish* these amounts for fat burning, or the fat will be burned incompletely, resulting in fatigue.

You have learned that every body requirement must be met if all cravings for food are to be prevented. Now we add another body requirement, sugar. Whenever exercise is taken, sugar is used. Every normal body function requires sugar. All these activities may use up the small amount of sugar you eat on Ms. Davis' diet. The amount of sugar in the blood decreases, and you suddenly crave sugar. Unless your will power is unusually strong, you will eat the first thing in sight—like chocolate cake. A craving for sugar (on this particular diet) can be avoided by eating frequently.

On Ms. Davis' diet, you must eat frequently, during the entire program—for you are eating foods which contain little sugar. Unless the mid-meal snacks are included, acidosis, fatigue, and extreme irritability will result, not to mention a strong craving for sugar.

"I recall a patient who, when referred to me, weighed 80 pounds more than she should," said Ms. Davis. "She was told that eating between meals was an essential part of the reducing program. At the end of the week, when she had not reported, I called her on the telephone.

" 'Your diet is no good,' she fairly shrieked at me.

" 'Why not?' I asked.

" 'I've never had such a headache in all my life!' she retorted.

" 'Did you eat between meals?'

" 'Of course not,' she replied. 'I'm not such a glutton that I have to eat six times a day!'

"I tried to explain why she had a headache, but she was not interested. Her desire to reduce was gone. So will yours if you do not eat frequently."

On the Rapid Reducing Diet (Diet I), especially, if you take any strenuous exercise which will cause the supply of body sugar to be depleted quickly, it is best to eat something every hour. If you are very obese, a two-hour schedule is better in your case than a three-hour schedule throughout this reducing program, for the more overweight you are, the easier it is for you to have acidosis.

It is so important to eat frequently, during the period you are on the Rapid Reducing Diet, that you should always carry hard candy, such as small lemon, cinnamon, or peppermint drops, with you in case it is impossible to get to the foods on your diet, said Ms. Davis. In this case, eat one small candy every hour.

## SUGGESTED MENUS (DIET II)

If any member of a family deviates from his ideal weight, everyone immediately assumes that special cooking must be done for him or her. This is entirely wrong, said Ms. Davis. Food should *always* be prepared for the overweight member of the family—*to the same foods, the others can make additions* such as butter, cream, mayonnaise, cheese, nuts, cereals, breads and sweets.

No special dishes need be prepared. The person of normal weight may add or subtract as many fattening foods as his weight demands. These menus do not have to be used in any particular order, as long as an entire day's menu is followed.

---

MENU #1

Breakfast

    fish-liver-oil capsules
    orange juice, 4 ounces
    cantaloupe, half small
    crisp drained broiled bacon, 2 slices
    wheat-germ muffin, small
    clear coffee or tea

10:30

    skim milk, 8 ounces

Luncheon

    scrambled egg with green peppers, 5 tablespoonfuls
    okra, 4 tablespoonfuls
    diced beets, 3 tablespoonfuls
    stuffed tomato salad with 1 tablespoonful of boiled dressing;
        ingredients: celery, cucumber, string beans, lettuce
    skim milk, 8 ounces

4:40

    tomato juice with lemon, 8 ounces

Dinner

    fat-free chicken broth, 8 ounces
    white meat of chicken, 1 breast
    new peas, 1 tablespoonful
    Brussels sprouts, 6 tablespoonfuls
    watercress and escarole salad with lemon-juice dressing
    strawberries served unstemmed, half cup

9:30

    skim milk, 8 ounces

---

MENU #2

Breakfast

    fish-liver-oil capsules
    tomato juice with clove, 8 ounces
    grapefruit, half large
    wheat germ, 2 tablespoonfuls, with 6 ounces of skim milk
    clear coffee or tea

10:30

    orange, small

Luncheon

    stuffed eggplant, 6 tablespoonfuls; ingredients: par-boiled eggplant
        stuffed with tomatoes, green peppers, onions and covered with
        jack cheese
    cabbage and pineapple salad, three-fourths cup, with boiled
        dressing
    skim milk, 8 ounces
    Persian melon, small slice

4:30

    skim milk, 8 ounces

Dinner

    tomato aspic, half cup
    broiled liver, 2 large slices
    smothered onions, 2 tablespoonfuls
    mashed Danish squash with parsley, 3 tablespoonfuls
    artichoke, large, with 2 tablespoonfuls of boiled dressing
    skim milk, 8 ounces

9:30

    orange, small

---

MENU #3

Breakfast

>   fish-liver-oil capsules
>   grapefruit juice, 4 ounces
>   casaba melon, medium serving
>   egg, hard-boiled
>   wheat germ, 2 tablespoonfuls, with half cup of milk
>   clear coffee or tea

10:30

>   orange, medium

Luncheon

>   broiled frankfurters, 2
>   sauerkraut, 4 tablespoonfuls
>   carrots, 4 small
>   string beans, 4 tablespoonfuls
>   head-lettuce with cottage cheese
>   skim-milk, 8 ounces
>   ice tea

4:30

>   skim milk, 8 ounces

Dinner

>   baked trout, 3 inches square
>   Spanish sauce, 3 tablespoonfuls
>   spinach, 4 tablespoonfuls
>   asparagus, 10 stalks
>   green pepper, celery, and escarole salad, 6 tablespoonfuls
>   skim milk, 8 ounces

9:30

>   tomato juice, 8 ounces

MENU #4

Breakfast

> fish-liver-oil capsules
> tomato juice cocktail, 8 ounces; add Worcestershire sauce, horse-
>     radish, and mustard
> scrambled eggs with green peppers, 2 tablespoonfuls
> clear coffee or tea

10:30

> skim milk, 8 ounces

Luncheon

> baked tomato, small, covered with jack cheese
> cauliflower, 4 tablespoonfuls
> summer squash, 5 tablespoonfuls
> baked rutabaga, 1 small
> wheat-germ muffin, medium-size
> skim milk, 8 ounces
> fresh pineapple, 2 slices

4:30

> raw tomatoes with salt, 2 medium

Dinner

> broiled meat balls, 2, with mushrooms
> Brussels sprouts, 3 heaping tablespoonfuls
> steamed eggplant cooked with tomatoes, 5 tablespoonfuls
> beet and cucumber salad, 6 tablespoonfuls, with boiled dressing
> skim milk, 8 ounces

9:30

> skim milk, 8 ounces

---

MENU #5

Breakfast

> fish-liver-oil capsules
> sliced grapefruit, large
> wheat germ, 2 tablespoonfuls, with 8 ounces of skim milk
> poached egg
> clear coffee or tea

10:30

> tomato juice, 8 ounces

Luncheon

> baked spinach with egg, 6 tablespoonfuls; run spinach through food
>> chopper, season with salt, pepper, chopped onion; bake in
>> individual ramekins, cover with egg and garnish with pimiento
> diced beets, 2 tablespoonfuls
> Italian squash, 4 tablespoonfuls
> head-lettuce salad with tartar sauce made of boiled dressing
> skim milk, 8 ounces
> raspberries, half cup

4:30

> orange, medium

Dinner

> baked white fish, medium serving
> string beans, 3 tablespoonfuls
> broccoli, 4 tablespoonfuls
> vegetable salad molded in gelatin, 1 serving
> skim milk, 8 ounces
> watermelon, small serving

9:30

> skim milk, 8 ounces

---

MENU #6

Breakfast

> fish-liver-oil capsules
> tomato juice with lemon, 8 ounces
> cantaloupe, half medium
> Spanish omelet, 5 tablespoonfuls
> wheat-germ hotcake, 1; make entirely of wheat germ, and bake on a
>> dry griddle
> clear coffee or tea

10:30

> skim milk, 8 ounces

Luncheon

> liverwurst, 5 thin slices
> cooked celery, 6 tablespoonfuls
> shredded carrot, apple, and lettuce salad, 8 tablespoonfuls, with 2
>     tablespoonfuls of boiled dressing
> skim milk, 8 ounces

4:30

> orange, medium

Dinner:

> jellied consommé, 1 cup
> broiled chicken, half small
> beet greens, 5 tablespoonfuls
> baked carrots, 4 small
> combination vegetable salad, 6 tablespoonfuls, with lemon juice
>     dressing; ingredients: celery, cucumbers, radishes, green
>         onions, lettuce, watercress; rub salad bowl with clove of garlic
> skim milk, 8 ounces
> grapefruit, half medium

9:30

> skim milk, 8 ounces

---

MENU #7

Breakfast

> fish-liver-oil capsules
> tomato juice, 8 ounces
> raspberries, 1 cup
> wheat-germ cereal, 2 tablespoonfuls, with half cup of skim milk
> clear coffee or tea

10:30

> orange, medium

Luncheon

> fat-free vegetable soup, 8 ounces

    vegetable salad, 2 cups; ingredients: half head of lettuce, water-
        cress, green onions, hard-boiled egg
    skim milk, 8 ounces
    unstemmed strawberries

## 4:30

    raw tomatoes, 2 large

## Dinner

    fruit cocktail, half cup, unsweetened
    lobster, half large
    string beans, 5 tablespoonfuls
    broccoli, 5 tablespoonfuls
    apricot, lettuce, and cottage cheese salad, small serving, with 1
        tablespoonful of boiled dressing
    skim milk
    canned pineapple, 1 slice, no juice

## 9:30

    skim milk, 8 ounces

---

## MENU #8

## Breakfast

    fish-liver-oil capsules
    tomato juice cocktail, 8 ounces
    sliced orange, medium
    wheat-germ cereal with half cup of skim milk
    poached egg
    clear coffee or tea

## 10:30

    heart of celery

## Luncheon

    consommé, fat-free, 8 ounces
    cottage cheese, 3 tablespoonfuls
    summer squash, 5 tablespoonfuls
    asparagus, 10 stalks, with half head of lettuce and boiled dressing
    skim milk, 8 ounces
    fresh blackberries, half cup

4:30

skim milk, 8 ounces

Dinner

half grapefruit
roast beef, fat-free, 2 thick slices
cauliflower, 4 tablespoonfuls
baked tomato, 1 large
vegetable salad of artichoke heart, baby beets, onion, lettuce
skim milk, 8 ounces
fresh peach, medium

9:30

orange, medium

---

MENU #9

Breakfast

fish-liver-oil capsules
tomato juice, 8 ounces, with lemon
Persian melon, small serving
scrambled eggs with ground spinach, 3 tablespoonfuls
wheat-germ waffle, half of one
clear coffee or tea

10:30

skim milk, 8 ounces

Luncheon

clam chowder, fat-free, 1 cup
vegetable salad, 2 to 3 cups; ingredients: lettuce, cauliflower, green
    pepper, green onions, celery
stewed tomatoes, 1 cup
skim milk, 8 ounces

4:30

raw carrots, 3 small, with salt

Dinner

> oysters, 6 large, with tomato catsup
> spinach, 5 tablespoonfuls
> celery, cottage cheese, and lettuce salad, large serving
> steamed turnips, 3 tablespoonfuls
> skim milk, 8 ounces
> watermelon, small serving

9:30

> orange, large

---

MENU #10

Breakfast

> fish-liver-oil capsules
> sliced orange sprinkled with nutmeg
> wheat-germ cereal, 2 tablespoonfuls, with half cup skim milk
> clear coffee or tea

10:30

> apple, small

Luncheon

> broiled lamb chops, fat removed before cooking, 3 medium
> fresh peas, 2 tablespoonfuls
> tomato and cantaloupe salad; add onion juice and 1 tablespoonful of
>   boiled dressing
> skim milk, 8 ounces
> honey dew melon, medium serving

4:30

> orange, medium

Dinner

> shrimp cocktail, 3 tablespoonfuls, with tomato catsup
> broiled liver, 2 large slices
> Italian squash, 5 tablespoonfuls
> steamed carrots, 4 medium
> artichoke hearts and lettuce, large serving

skim milk, 8 ounces
fresh apricot

9:30

skim milk, 8 ounces

---

"A strict reducing diet," said Ms. Davis, "can be superior to that eaten by the average person today. A generous reducing diet can be made to build and improve health. A normal diet, which includes all of the foods given on a reducing diet, together with a few foods which offer body requirements but must be omitted from a reducing diet, is by far the best diet of all. The normal diet you can eat, if you will only reduce to your ideal weight."

In the list on pages 161-163, you will note that the foods are exactly the same as those Dr. Lindlahr recommended. They are speed reducing foods. Here are some personal experiences that I have heard about over the years, with the use of amazing speed reducing foods:

*Janet B. weighed 140 pounds, instead of her ideal weight of 120. She wanted to slim down fast, for her class reunion. With these speed reducing foods, she lost 20 pounds in one week! Here's her record:

> Day 1 ...... 6 lbs
> Day 2 ...... 3 lbs
> Day 3 ...... 2½ lbs
> Day 4 ...... 1½ lbs
> Day 5 ...... 3 lbs
> Day 6 ...... 2½ lbs
> Day 7 ...... 1½ lbs
>
> Total ....... 20 lbs

*D.R. was grossly fat at 205 pounds, instead of his ideal weight of 135. He was single, and lonely, and craved companionship, but— ashamed of his huge bulk—he kept to himself. Locked in the vicious circle of eating to relieve loneliness, he could never reduce and stay reduced—until he heard how speed reducing foods guaranteed speedy weight loss, while eating frequently between meals! He tried it and lost 15 pounds the first week, 11 pounds the second week—70 pounds in 2 months, permanently! Afterwards, he could continue eating most of his favorite fattening foods, without gaining an ounce (and so can you)! Here's D.R.'s record:

| 1st week | Weekly Record | |
|---|---|---|
| Day 1 .. 5 lbs | 1st Week ... 15½ lbs | 1st Month .. 41½ lbs |
| Day 2 .. 2½ lbs | 2nd Week .. 11 lbs | 2nd Month .. 28½ lbs |
| Day 3 .. 1½ lbs | 3rd Week .. 7 lbs | _____ |
| Day 4 .. 1½ lbs | 4th Week... 8 lbs | |
| Day 5 .. 2 lbs | 5th Week... 5 lbs | Total ....... 70 lbs |
| Day 6 .. 1½ lbs | 6th Week... 5½ lbs | |
| Day 7 .. 1½ lbs | 7th Week... 11 lbs | |
| 15½ Tot. | 8th Week... 7 lbs | |

# 10

## Eat Your Cake and Have It!

I discovered this variation of Dr. Lindlahr's speed reducing diet years ago, at a time when I was grossly overweight. At 5'7", I tipped the scales at 185, about 50 lbs. overweight. What fascinated me most about Dr. Lindlahr's method was that speed reducing foods not only destroyed fat, but countered the effect of fattening foods!

**With speed reducing foods, I felt it should be possible to eat your cake and have it, even though Dr. Lindlahr recommended no bread or pastry, on the actual speed reducing phase of the plan. At this point, my doctor modified the Lindlahr diet for me, so that it contained a mixture of fattening and non-fattening foods. And it still worked! The results were spectacular!**

And I can tell you, I needed it. I looked like a mushroom. My hips fleshed out, my belly bulged, my buttons seemed to pop every time I stretched, and none of my clothes fit. I was embarrassed to go out, and I'd skulk around and hide. All I could see when I looked in a mirror were my double chins. I delved deeply into the literature on dieting, and discovered Dr. Lindlahr's work. Armed with the facts, I asked my doctor if what I hoped for was possible. He said, "Of course!" and suggested this amazing new method.

## TWENTY POUNDS MELT AWAY IN ONE MONTH!

With nothing to lose (except my blubber), I tried it. To my astonishment, I dropped twenty pounds the first month, fifteen pounds the next month, and kept making new notches in my belt, until I reached 135! Some days I dropped five pounds overnight! My double chin was gone. I lost not just pounds, but specifically, the bulges I wanted to get rid of—all in the right places. I lost fifty pounds in five months, and took off another seven for good measure.

When I reached 128 (at 5'7" my ideal weight is 135), I bought a new suit. My waist was so slender the haberdasher didn't have a decent-looking belt that size, so I bought suspenders. Between Labor Day and Christmas, 1962, I lost 40 pounds. By Lincoln's birthday, I was 128! *What I did, you can do!*

## HOW TO EAT THE THINGS YOU LOVE—AND STILL LOSE WEIGHT!

This method suited me to a "T" because I got to eat anything I wanted—absolutely anything (see the next chapter)—and still reduce and stay reduced! It's absolutely true! And today I can still eat anything and never worry about gaining weight! And I expect to be able to eat this way the rest of my life! I believe it is the naturally skinny eating secret!

**Notice, I didn't say diet. I hate diets. I can't stay on one. On regular diets, I feel cheated and miserable all the time. I hate counting calories. I don't want to count carbohydrates. I don't like ONE food all the time. I think these methods are inconsiderate torture regimens—and with the naturally skinny eating secret, I don't have to put up with them. Ever.**

With this diet, you are guaranteed to lose up to 2 pounds a day. Some have reached their goal in only a week! Others have lost as much as twenty-five pounds the first month! Every person who has ever tried it has had the same fast results! You will not find this diet anywhere else, but I can tell you it works, even in the most stubborn cases. It is a high fiber diet, rich in magic minerals!

## HOW TO EAT YOUR CAKE AND HAVE IT ON THE SPEED REDUCING DIET!

This amazing speed reducing diet is like no other diet you have ever seen before. It is a magic combination of several diets—the most powerful fat-dissolving foods known to science—that gives you an endless variety of delicious meals and snacks to pick from each day. The major feature of this diet is that it is extremely well-rounded, giving you large, generous portions of food every day—food of all kinds—so that you never miss out on anything, as well as delicious gourmet snacks between meals. The basic diet I followed had fruit, cake and candy every day!

BREAKFAST:

An orange or grapefruit (grapefruit may be sweetened with a little honey).
Two slices of buttered toast, using high fiber bread and diet margarine.
Tea or coffee, sweetened with milk.

LUNCH:

A hamburger (chopped sirloin), with ketchup, onions, relish, anything you like (no roll), or
A piece of broiled chicken (legs, breasts, wings) or
Tuna fish salad (one or two portions), mixed with a dash of Mayonnaise or diet Mayonnaise—if desired—onion and bits of celery.
A large, heaping vegetable salad, prepared same way.
A small piece of fruit—a plum, an apple, ½ orange, a pear, or half a cantaloupe. (Pick one.)
One piece of candy, or
Several low caloried candies, or
Small slice of plain cake of any kind, or

One or two small cookies, or crackers.
Tea or coffee, sweetened with milk, or any 100%
natural fruit juice.

SUPPER:

A leafy green salad, prepared as above or with vinegar
or diet dressing (as many portions as you want).
One or two vegetables (one portion each).
One portion of steak or chicken or fish.
A small piece of fruit—see lunch—or
One piece of candy, or
Several low calorie candies, or
Small slice of plain cake of any kind, or
One or two small cookies, or crackers, or
Jello (regular or low-calorie, any flavor).
Tea or coffee, sweetened with milk.

Have an additional portion of meat, fish, poultry, salad or
vegetable—at any meal—if desired. Concentrate on green, leafy
vegetables, cabbage, green beans, spinach, kale, Brussels sprouts,
broccoli—and you may even use butter on them for flavor, if your
doctor permits. Margarine is even better because it is a soft fat, and diet
margarine contains fewer calories. Steer clear of baked beans, lima
beans, and, to some extent, potatoes. In the fruit category, try to avoid
bananas, as these are high in starch and calories. However, once or
twice a week it is permissible to sneak these things in a lunch or supper,
no harm done. For salads, use lots of tomatoes, green peppers, lettuce,
celery and carrots. One slice of bread is permitted at any meal, two
slices if made from high fiber bread, in which case sandwiches are
permitted (your quota is one sandwich per meal, more on slower
versions of this diet).

## ADDITIONAL POINTS TO REMEMBER!

In the fishes, the best fish to use is codfish or halibut, because
they are lower in calories. Filet of flounder won't hurt you (assuming
fried foods agree with you). Pork and lamb are the only meats I
avoided. They slowed down the weight loss. And I always took two
multi-vitamin tablets in a yeast base daily, to guard against stress.
Once or twice a week, you can have a bit of rice (½ cup) or
spaghetti or French fries (½ cup each). Mushrooms may be eaten by the

can, or mixed with rice or vegetables—they are very low in calories. Most normal condiments, such as ketchup, mustard or horseradish, are fine. Relish and pickles are a little high in salt, but fine in moderation. Sauerkraut is very low in calories, has a reputation for breaking up fat, and is perfect in almost any amount.

## BETWEEN MEAL SNACKS!

Between lunch and supper, and after supper, typical snacks might include Jello, one or two handfuls of soybeans or sunflower seeds, a fruit—in other words, one or two of the desserts you did not pick for lunch or supper. Don't overdo it. Have one or two short snacks and stop. Of course, you have to cut your fluid intake—you can't drink gallons and gallons of different things—but you can fill up, between meals, on pure fruit juice in moderation. Technically, you should have six glasses of water a day, but few people can drink that much. You get water in your coffee or tea, and you get water in your foods, as well. If unsweetened coffee or tea are not to your taste, you may use honey as a sweetener (see Chapter 15) and skimmed milk (avoid whole milk, cream and sugar on this speed reducing diet, although in other versions they are acceptable).

## WORKS IN CASE AFTER CASE!

There are people who swear that this speed reducing diet melts off pounds faster than anything else in the world. Among them:

*Gertrude B., a typist. Weight: 140. For her, this was 20 pounds overweight. She complained of headaches, high blood pressure, a bloated feeling. She tried other diets—but they took so long, and she felt so cheated and miserable all the time, she gave up. Then she tried this speed reducing diet, which satisfied her taste as well as her hunger. Result: 20 lbs. lost in a month! All her symptoms vanished, and she retained the weight loss!

*Lawrence O., 25, a shipping clerk. Weight 255. Quite active. Though he watched calories, he remained overweight. He tried everything—as soon as he stopped, he'd gain it all back. Then he tried this speed reducing diet. Result: 70 lbs. lost in 6 months. Not a hunger pang along the way.

*Catherine D., 28, said she had a large frame, and put on weight quite easily. Height: 5'10". Weight: 195 lbs. She was accustomed to big meals and many snacks throughout the day. Then she tried this speed reducing diet, that gave her cake, candy and sweet snacks, and found she could still lose weight: 15 lbs. the first week! Also, these were no-fuss foods. Result: in 5 months, she lost 50 lbs.

*Raymond E., 39, a garage mechanic, 5'8" tall, 175 lbs. His main concern was a large "beer belly" that protruded over his belt. With this amazing speed reducing diet, he'd have breakfast as usual, lunch and snack at work, snacks at home. Result: 38 lbs. lost in 3 months—and a slim and dashing new figure!

## HEAVY THIGHS NOW SLIM AND SHAPELY!

Mrs. M.B. complained about her heavy thighs. They were enormously fat, all lumpy and bulging—from hips to knees. She was told how the speed reducing diet cleanses the entire system, forcing out poisons and excess fluids, with all-natural foods (not drugs); how it can even help clean out lumpy veins and arteries—get rid of sludgy, gum-like deposits of cholesterol. She was told how these foods metabolize nicely, leaving a minimum of poisonous residue in your body. She tried it, and in a few months, she looked absolutely stunning in a new bathing suit. The fat thighs had been transformed, and were now slim and shapely. Gone were the lumpy bulges. Her skin was firm and young-looking!

## OTHER COMPLAINTS VANISH!

Thighs, hips, buttocks, neck—all hard-to-reduce areas—seem to "slenderize" on the speed reducing diet. It's so easy and painless, it's unbelievable, but true. I have never seen a case of flabby skin or new wrinkles with this method. If anything, skin on face, throat and arms seems to become taut, smooth, and young-looking. Creases, lines, wrinkles, and crow's feet around the eyes, forehead, nose, and mouth seem to fade away. One woman who had all these complaints is so pleased now with her image in the mirror, that she looks and acts like a young woman again. She's 62. Her flabby double chin has given way to an incredibly youthful silhouette.

Another woman commented that this diet actually seemed to make her feet "smaller." She wore a size 7-D shoe, and now takes a C width.

Other symptoms of poor or failing health also seem to go "by the boards" as body weight is lightened. Ulcers have completely healed, as X-rays proved. One man who had a hiatal hernia (a diaphragmatic hernia worsened by increased weight on internal organs) tried this diet, and says it saved him from an operation. A middle-aged executive, he had developed what doctors call "big man's fat gut fatigue" (splanchnic neurasthenia). His problem, simply, was that he overate and never got any exercise. Along with symptoms of indigestion, eventually, came the hernia, with an incredibly full or bloated feeling most of the time, especially during meals. He could never eat a decent meal without "suffocating" half-way through, and having to leave the table to stretch out somewhere, or walk it off. His doctor gave him an antispasmodic drug, told him to place the head of his bed on four-inch blocks (which does help), and get that excess weight off. But every diet had failed. He seemed a hopeless case, until he tried the speed reducing diet. Result: 43 pounds gone, in about 4 months. Without realizing it, the hiatal hernia symptoms had vanished, too. Gone were the spasms and seizures, the "bloating" and suffocating feeling.

## HOW A MAN LOST 20 POUNDS IN 12 DAYS!

Recently, a national newspaper told how a famous actor, John L., uses speed reducing foods to lose weight quickly. "I can lose a pound-and-a-half a day," he says, or about 10 pounds a week! While making a movie, he had to lose 20 pounds and did it in 12 days with this amazing speed reducing diet!

Breakfast—a glass of juice (orange or grapefruit), one piece of dry toast and a cup of black coffee.

Lunch—a large salad of endive and lettuce smothered in oil and vinegar and loaded with garlic. Or grated celery or carrots (raw), covered with garlic dressing.

Dinner—a healthy portion of meat, sliced tomatoes doused with garlic dressing, an occasional baked potato and a glass of wine.

This diet illustrates how speed reducing foods can be mixed with fattening foods (toast, potato, wine), and still produce quick weight loss. A consulting dietician said this diet is medically safe, but suggested adding more bread! There are much more liberal variations on the speed reducing diet.


## HOW TO EAT ALL YOU WANT AND STILL LOSE WEIGHT

Maimonides, the renowned 12th century physician, prescribed a diet based on this simple principle: eat lots of filling speed reducing foods first. In this spectacular 800-year-old diet, you fill up first on salads and lean meat, then move on to the potatoes and fattening foods—if you have room.

**And this can include French fries, ice cream, angel food cake, cookies, and even beer! Maimonides said that fruits and other easy-to-digest foods should always be eaten first, and this would include a large salad (any dressing), fruit cocktail, and steak or other lean meat, in that order. The French fries, ice cream and beer would come last, when you are already fairly full!**

The scholar who discovered this secret says it works like magic! And he used it himself to effortlessly lose 40 pounds in only 13 weeks!


## THE SPEED REDUCING FOOD THAT DISSOLVED PEARLS!

Apple cider vinegar contains powerful enzymes that help dissolve clumps of fat, and wash them right out of the system—so powerful, in fact, that meat soaked in apple cider vinegar is tenderized. When you drink it, even in such small quantities as 2 tablespoons in fruit or vegetable juice, moments later it is breaking up accumulated fat in cell tissues, according to Carlson Wade, in *The New Enzyme Catalyst Diet* (Parker Publishing Co., 1976). He states:

**"The powerful fat-dissolving action of apple cider vinegar is mentioned by Pliny, the early Roman author and naturalist. He told how Cleopatra won a bet when she dissolved pearls in vinegar. Since pearls are lipidlike (fatty) tumescent exudations that have solidified, layer by layer, it appears obvious that the enzymes can dissolve solid fat in the body."**

You can make your own apple-cider vinegar by putting apple peelings, cores and slices in a jar. Fill with water to cover, cover with a lid, store in a warm place, and watch. You can "see" the enzymes in the form of a slowly thickening substance that accumulates at the top, notes Mr. Wade. This is a prime source of fermented enzymes, containing the bacteria, *Acetobacter*, he says. When it tastes strong enough, strain it, bottle and cork it and use regularly. Sauerkraut is another such food, he says.

### A Reported Case:

> *John O. was a typical "meat and potatoes" man. As a factory worker, he was raised on heavy meals. Years of such eating had put a "spare tire" around his waist. The company doctor told him he was 44 pounds overweight. He noticed the foreman in the factory was slim, and he ate the same foods John did, so John asked for the secret. The secret was to take 2 tablespoons of apple cider vinegar in a glass of any beverage, before a meal. Or just sprinkle it over raw salad. John O. followed this simple program. Every day, he found that his appetite was controlled. But more important, even if he ate his luscious roasts or stews, the heavy feeling was gone, and his waistline started to melt. Within six weeks, John O. had melted down 50 pounds!

# 11

## Eat Anything You Like!

Here is a new method of reducing weight which calls for no self-denial, and allows you to eat anything and as much as you like, while enjoying your meals far more than before. It is a scientifically proven method of eating which enables anyone to eat well without gaining; to increase eating pleasure; to prolong life twenty years or more.

### NO MORE AGONIZING SELF-DENIAL!

Hippocrates, the father of medicine, knew 2,000 years ago that fat persons were particularly prone to acute diseases. In one of his books, he gives directions for ''those who wish to get thin.'' Among these are sleeping on a hard bed; strenuous bodily exercises, preferably in the morning, on an empty stomach; vegetable foods, especially greens; lots of activity, in good weather or bad; abstaining from hot baths; and drinking diluted wine. Needless to say, this method will never win any popularity prizes.

No doubt, at that time, and during all the succeeding centuries, individuals who wished to reduce complained, as they do today, that everything they liked was forbidden. Banting declared that he did not eat too much; but his favorite and daily diet consisted of bread, milk, butter, beer, sugar, and potatoes—all of which cannot be eaten on standard low calorie diets. They were the things which, to Banting's great disgust, Doctor Harvey promptly forbade him to eat and drink. But that was before the naturally skinny eating secret!

## AN IMPORTANT DISCOVERY!

The Germans have given much attention to the question of reducing, for obvious reasons. Visitors to Germany are often amazed at the amount of food consumed. Important books on reducing have been written in Germany, consisting largely of the discovery that *verboten* is not necessarily the best motto for overweights. Professor Ebstein, instead of forbidding fattening foods, prescribed them. His main reason for doing so was to satisfy his patients' taste buds!

As a result, other doctors began permitting pastry and candy, nuts and ice cream, at mealtime (but not between meals), in moderate amounts. Scientists began taking a second look at previously forbidden foods, such as milk, cream, cheese, pork, ham, olive oil, bacon, butter, corn, wheat, buckwheat, rice, oats, bread, macaroni, sugar, stick candy, potatoes, figs, bananas, grapes, chestnuts, walnuts, raisins, etc.

Amazingly, it was discovered that not all these foods are necessarily fattening, unless eaten in large quantities—we do need *some* fat to run the body chemistry. *All of them can be indulged in in moderation!* A dozen of the above named foods are, moreover, so rich in essential nutrients that it is wise not to discard them entirely.

Therein lies the secret! There is no reason in the world why you should give up all fattening foods. Today, most doctors agree, you may eat anything you like, provided you eat wisely and not too much of certain things. Naturally, if you eat fat beyond the body's needs, it is deposited in other parts of the body—around the heart and kidneys—where it may do a tremendous amount of harm. But a certain amount of fat is necessary for health—about an ounce a day!

That gives you your chance! Give up, for instance, butter, bacon, and olive oil? *On the contrary*! You may not have all three of them on the same day, but you can have either olive oil with your salad dressing, or a strip or two of bacon with your breakfast eggs, or you can have butter with your whole wheat toast, or with your vegetables to make them more tasty!

It is cruel to forbid milk and cheese with their fabulous wealth of calcium, vitamin A, and amino acids (the building blocks of life). Likewise, potatoes, cereals, and raisins should not be avoided. Instead of two potatoes, eat *one*, and so on. Try to cut your consumption of carbohydrates by one-half. *Replace* the fattening portions you've eliminated with speed reducing foods, which are so filling and tasty that 600 *reverse* calories seem like 6,000! Religiously adhered to, this should reduce your weight fifteen pounds a month!

And yet you have been eating anything you liked!

## FORGET ABOUT COUNTING CALORIES!

Some years ago an individual who was apparently fond of arithmetic invented a horrid thing which he called a calorie. He ought to have been publicly whipped, for his invention soon became as great a nuisance in the food world as mosquitoes are to lovers!

A calorie is a sort of yardstick with which to measure the fuel value of foods. Foods, you will remember, are burned in the body, as coal and wood are burned in a stove. The amount of heat required to raise the temperature of a quart of water 1 degree Centigrade, is called a calorie.

Those who invented this name used an apparatus called a bomb calorimeter in which all sorts of fuels—turnips and butter as well as kerosene and wood—were burned and the resulting heat was measured. It was found that food oxidized in the body yields about the same amount of heat or energy as when burned in this apparatus, so the word calorie was introduced in the food world, where it was received with a yell of fiendish joy as a new fad.

Poor men, women, and even children were pounced upon and informed that they *must* count calories. Multiplication, division, and subtraction were supplied and the poor victims of overweight were told just how many calories there were in a mouthful of mush or melon or meat or marmalade, and so on to the end of the list. These calories were then to be added together till they reached the exact number which the doctor or dietician, guessing and bluffing, assigned to you.

In 19th century England, prisoners were forced to sit all day grinding a machine, so devised that it had resistance gears inside, which made the handle very difficult to turn. Each complete turn of the handle registered one point on a meter. To earn his breakfast, the poor devil had to register, say 1,000 revolutions, lunch 2,000, supper 4,000.

In one form or another, this medieval torture method has persisted down to the present day—under various guises (calories, grams, carbohydrates, etc.). It is no way to live!

A doctor once suggested that I should start counting calories, weighing and analyzing and compounding and calculating everything I ate. I politely but firmly informed him that in college I had helped to make a bonfire of all books on arithmetic, algebra, geometry, trigonometry, and calculus, and that I was not going to have any mathematical hocus-pocus at *my* supper table.

There is no need whatever of mathematics at meals. The speed reducing method—even on a maintenance diet, such as I am suggesting here—is essentially one of substitution. If you find yourself gaining weight, it is not necessary to count calories or cut your meals in half, or deny yourself in any way. Just lean a little heavier on speed reducing foods, until you find those excess pounds slipping away. By all means, eat some of everything you like. Forget about starvation. But *use* speed reducing foods to counter the effect of fattening foods.

It is the kind, not the quantity, of foods you eat that counts!

# 12

## Mineral Salts as Reducers!

Dr. William Banting, enormously fat, reduced himself by cutting down on starches and fats. He lived practically on meat alone. He took off pounds all right—but he eventually killed himself with his unbalanced diet. *To survive, we need a rich supply of minerals, found mainly in speed reducing foods!*

Today, there is a vague understanding of the fact that fat persons may owe their condition to disease—the fat "diathesis" the doctors call it—and not necessarily to the absence of a will strong enough to prevent them from eating too much.

In the light of modern science we may go even farther and excuse real gluttony in many cases, looking on it as a *result of starvation!* A funny paradox this seems—but it is easily explained. A glutton in very many cases is simply an unfortunate individual who eats a great deal because that is *the only way he has found instinctively, for getting into his system sufficient quantities of the various mineral salts he absolutely needs for health.*

What are these mineral salts that are so essential to health and that can come to the rescue of those who persistently eat too much, to miraculously slim them down? Some, like iron and calcium, you read about a good deal in newspapers and magazines. Others include iron, potassium, phosphorus, magnesium, manganese, sulphur, silicon, sodium, fluorine, chlorine, and iodine.

Take iron, for example. Iron enables the blood to absorb oxygen and carry it throughout the body to renew tissues and burn up waste matter. If there is only half enough iron in your blood you do not die right away, but you do grow pale and sickly and wonder if life is worth living. Nor is it in the blood only that iron is needed. It is also needed in the digestive juices: the saliva in the mouth, the gastric juice in the stomach, the bile in the liver, and the fluid in the pancreatic gland which helps burn up sugar, to furnish body energy, and to maintain the right temperature.

A shortage of iron in any of these parts of the body leads to anemia and general loss of vigor and vitality. It has been estimated that the amount of iron in a man's body would just suffice to make a small nail—yet without this small quantity our tissues would collapse.

You now understand why a fat man on the wrong diet keeps on eating, *instinctively* and *pardonably*, because he feels he hasn't had enough iron. He doesn't *know* this, but his body tells him he needs more food!

## IODINE HELPS YOU LOSE WEIGHT!

If you are desperately trying to lose weight or keep your weight constant, look to iodine from a natural source, like garlic or kelp. Iodine is the magic mineral salt that activates the thyroid. The thyroid gland regulates body metabolism—the rate at which you burn your food. A deficiency in iodine causes thyroid trouble. The thyroid gland enlarges, the rate of metabolism slows down, you become sluggish, glassy-eyed, chubby and lazy.

What can an iodine deficiency mean to you? You are cold when other people are comfortable; your hands are clammy; your feet are so cold at night that you cannot get to sleep. You are mentally and physically sluggish. You gain weight easily, forever trying to reduce and forever staying too fat. A little iodine in the diet may relieve all these symptoms.

Garlic, one of the cheapest vegetables in the market, may be that source for you—or garlic powder, which may be used as seasoning by those on salt-restricted diets. Iodine is not readily absorbed without vitamin E. However, the foods with which garlic is usually eaten— salads and green, leafy vegetables, for example, are rich in vitamin E.

## POTASSIUM DRAINS OFF POUNDS OF WATER!

Potassium is another magic mineral salt. It is pushed out of the body by sodium chloride (table salt), resulting in water-weight gain. What happens is that, normally, potassium remains largely in the cells. When sodium (salt) is added to food at mealtime, it upsets a balance— sodium passes into the cells, bringing with it so much fluid that tissues become waterlogged.

The potassium passes out in the urine. The remaining salt holds pounds of water. Persons suffering a loss of potassium appear bloated— and frequently follow extremely low calorie diets, yet the scales do not budge.

In extreme cases, known as dropsy or edema, the water retention may be so extensive—starting with puffy eyes and swollen ankles— that an emaciated person appears overweight. Adequate potassium intake releases this fluid! You get the correct balance of potassium and sodium from speed reducing foods, which is why nutritionists advise against *adding* table salt at mealtime, or eating commercially packaged foods which are heavily salted.

## CALCIUM STARVATION!

The reason animals flourish on meat is that they also lap the blood and gnaw the bones, which are full of calcium. Some years ago, it was found at a London zoo that the lion cubs were deformed, bow-legged, club-footed, dwarfed, and always died young. A doctor, on being consulted, asked about their food. He was told they were fed the very best meats. He suggested the feeding of bones and bone meal. His advice was followed, and the trouble soon disappeared.

Is there in these facts a lesson for human beings? What happens when we do not get enough calcium in our food? A number of very undesirable things. Bone disease has been increasing rapidly, thanks to "refined" foods, the fast-food items that we snack on, like ice cream, cake and candy. Rheumatism and many other diseases plague those who eat meat to excess without also getting the calcium that saves the bone-eating animals from disease and premature death.

When there isn't enough calcium in your daily food you come down with a bad case of "nerves"—and you cannot outwit *these* nerves except by eating plenty of calcium. Every dentist knows that unless there is sufficient calcium in the food we eat, our teeth decay prematurely. In the case of serious wounds, it is the calcium in the body which prevents the injured person from bleeding to death. A muscle deprived of calcium quivers and twitches unpleasantly.

Calcium is necessary for the strength of the bones, for the firmness of the muscles, for the tone of the nerves, for the coagulation of the blood on demand, for every pulsation of the heart, for the digestion of food, for the functioning of the kidneys and other vital organs, for the health of the body! You find it in abundance in those speed reducing, magic mineral foods!

## A NATURAL REDUCING AID!

Is it any wonder that a fat man on a demineralized diet—as most Americans are—keeps on eating and eating because his body tells him he *needs more* of something, he knows not what?

Animals know—by instinct. If you place two slices of bread, one white (demineralized), the other whole wheat, where a mouse can find them, it will invariably eat the whole wheat. Dogs know they must have bones as well as meat. It has been found that chickens and livestock do best if allowed to choose their own food in separate hoppers. If allowed to do this, selecting just what they feel they need, they also eat less!

Will we ever catch up with the animals?

Dr. John Harvey Kellog, in his 933-page volume, *The New Dietetics*, stated that "a point which has heretofore been neglected in all (reducing) diets ... a serious oversight which has unquestionably been a most prolific cause of failure and has often resulted in ... ill health (is the need for mineral salts). It is a frequent observation on the part of (reducers) that while they feel lighter ... they recognize at the same time a notable loss of energy, endurance ... often so pronounced as to lead the individual to prefer ... obesity."

## MIRACULOUS EFFECTS OF FOOD MINERALS!

The most important thing to remember is that reducing weight is *not* a matter of calories and what proportion of proteins, carbohydrates and fats you are eating, but *are there enough mineral salts in the foods you eat?*

If your food is deficient in *sodium*, for example, the elimination of body wastes and poisons is interfered with. The same is true of *iodine*, which is the active principle of the poison-destroying thyroid gland. *Potassium* is the enemy of joint inflammation, and makes tissues soft and pliable. *Fluorine* is needed for the pupils of the eye, and for tooth enamel. Wild animals are never bald because they have in their food all the *silicon* and *sulphur* needed for luxuriant hair. If meat is minced and soaked a few hours in distilled water it loses its *potassium*, *magnesium*, and *calcium* salts; also, its flavor. If fed to animals they soon refuse to take more.

When you know these facts as to the simply enormous importance of mineral salts to health and life itself, you can understand the rage and anger of some observers, like Alfred McCann many years ago, who wrote: "All the scientists are talking about calories. The dieticians base all their tables and formulas upon these calories. Every hospital and sanitarium in the country talks glibly of calories .... The government publishes bulletins on calories .... Even restaurants have fallen under the spell," in spite of the fact that *"it is the easiest thing in the world to condemn a man to death while stuffing him with the fattest calories found in the grocery store."*

Many scientific tests have proven that animals sicken and die if fed only fats, carbohydrates, and proteins from which the mineral salts have been removed. But they are immediately restored to health if food such as greens, which have no caloric value at all but are full of food minerals, are added to the diet. This actually happened to the officers and crew of a German raider who were living on demineralized foods—foods such as most of us eat all the time—taken from captured ships. They were so crippled by acidosis that they had to head for home, where they were quickly cured with large doses of foods rich in mineral salts.

*Calories were killing them. Mineral salts saved them.*


## HOW TO GET THE MINERAL SALTS YOU NEED!

The best source of organic minerals is Mother Nature. Her plants absorb these minerals from the soil, and metabolize them in a way that cannot be reproduced in the drug store or laboratory. It is to the garden, therefore, that you must go for those food minerals which will so surprisingly and inevitably reduce your abnormal appetite and with it your weight!

It is in garden vegetables that food minerals are found in richest abundance. Make them your principal food and you can choose your own waist measurement, regulating it to an inch, almost automatically!

In a later chapter the all-important subject of vegetables and their helpful mineral salts will be considered in detail. Here, let me simply give you a short list of Magic Mineral Foods which contain particularly great amounts of all twelve mineral salts, especially calcium and iron: almonds and other nuts, Boston brown bread, bran, chard, dandelion greens, dock greens, egg yolk, endive, dry figs, pure gluten, lentils, maple syrup, genuine molasses, mustard greens, olives, red root, savita, spinach, turnip tops, lettuce.

A government booklet, *Food Values*, shows how important food minerals are. Fruits and vegetables are listed first, and the main feature of this Bulletin is a series of diagrams or charts which show at a glance the mineral values of fifty important reducing foods. The protein (body building) and fuel values are also given, thus enhancing the value of these charts for overweights, whose duty it is to keep out fuel foods (sweets, starches, fats) while shoveling in minerals.

In eating spinach, for instance, we see how very much less you get of fattening fuel (energy) than of calcium, phosphorus, and iron. The following chart shows the proportions of these elements needed per day furnished by one pound of spinach:

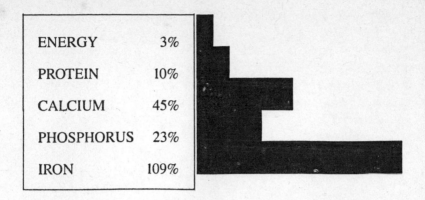

| ENERGY | 3% |
|--------|-----|
| PROTEIN | 10% |
| CALCIUM | 45% |
| PHOSPHORUS | 23% |
| IRON | 109% |

## TABLE SALT INCREASES YOUR WEIGHT!

Strange things happen in this world. While twelve food salts good and true are praised and sanctified in this chapter, the thirteenth—unlucky number—poor, pitiable table salt, the only food salt most mortals know anything about, is to be cast out into the garbage can, or at any rate shorn of its locks—so far, at least, as overweights are concerned!

What's the matter with table salt? What's the matter, indeed! For every ounce of salt, one hundred to one hundred and twenty ounces of water will be retained in the body. This means that six or seven pounds are added to your weight because you eat too much salt! To be sure, this extra weight is water, not fat. All the same, it adds to one's bulk, and from the point of view of personal appearances—which we all cherish—it is objectionable.

Lemon juice and other wholesome juices will help you overcome your morbid and dangerous craving for salt. You may eat a little sweet butter daily, but salt butter? Never! It is your enemy. In all probability, you owe a good deal of your excess weight to your habit of using salt at every meal. Most people eat five times as much salt as they need. Use garlic powder or kelp, instead.

Salt eating is merely a habit, like coffee or whiskey drinking. The American Indians did not use it. And Eskimos detest salt. It's like a narcotic. It's as hard to break off its use as it is to stop smoking. But after you have been a month or two without salt, you cease to long for it. In fact, the taste of meat boiled in salt water becomes very disagreeable.

There is an old saying that ''salt is that which, if you don't put it in the soup, spoils it.'' Well, you may put a little—very little—into some things, like soups or potatoes. But most foods have in them naturally all the salt you need.

What you can hardly have too much of are the twelve mineral salts extolled in this chapter. These you must have if you want to be slender and well and live long. And there is another thing you need quite as much as mineral salts—so important, in fact, that a whole chapter must be devoted to it. And that is fiber, or bulk, or cellulose, as it is variously called.

# 13

## Bran, Blueberries, and Regularity!

To most people, eating less is the one sure way to lose weight. But is it the best? We have just seen that one reason many people are "hearty" eaters is that the kind of food they choose does not supply them with the mineral salts they need; so they eat on and on. If they ate less, they would have fewer still of these salts and be worse off than before.

But give them all the necessary food salts and they will still be wretched unless they also get bran and blueberries—using these as representatives of the whole class of foods that supply cellulose (or bulk, or roughage, or whatever you choose to call it) for regular bowel action.

## ELIMINATE MORE THAN FAT!

When Seneca wrote, nearly two thousand years ago, that "man does not die, he kills himself," he was talking about *autointoxication*. What is autointoxication? It is infinitely worse than alcoholic intoxication. The Greek word *toxikon* means poison, and autointoxication is nothing less than slow self-poisoning.

An incredible number of diseases arise from poisonous matter in the intestines. Out of a hundred and sixty different species of bacteria living in the alimentary canal, more than thirty percent give off poisons, some of which resemble the venom of snakes, and many of which are capable of producing the most distressing symptoms.

It makes one dizzy merely to pronounce the names of some of these miserable microscopic imps—for instance, parahydroxyl-phenilethylamine.

The decaying food in the colon harbors not only billions, but trillions of these bacteria. Is it any wonder that the large intestine becomes, if neglected or maltreated—as it is by nine persons out of ten—a veritable Pandora's box of ailments?

## LIKE THE ROOTS OF TREES

When the food we eat or drink leaves the stomach through the pylorus gate, it enters the small intestine, which, measuring about twenty-three feet in length, is provided with millions of villi, which absorb the liquefied food just as the million rootlets of a tree absorb the moisture from the soil.

At the lower end of the small intestine where it joins the colon, or large intestine, there is another gate, called the colon gate, or ileocecal valve. This valve, of which not one person in a thousand even knows the name, is the most important anatomical structure in the whole human body; so much so that to say, "How's your ileocecal valve?" is like saying, "How's your health?"

Why? Because as long as this muscular valve is in order the poisonous contents of the colon cannot pass back into the small intestine, to be absorbed there by the million rootlets just referred to and carried with the blood throughout the body, poisoning every organ.

The colon itself, fortunately, has normally few absorbent villi. As long as the mucous membrane which forms its inside lining is sound no special harm results from intestinal stagnation (constipation). But as we get older, such stagnation and hardening irritate the mucous membrane, producing congestion and inflammation (colitis). Then the mischief begins. The poisonous bacteria are absorbed and carried to all parts of the body; and thus the colon becomes a breeding place of miseries and maladies almost too numerous to mention.

What are some of the diseases resulting from a crippled ileocecal valve, or from the catarrhal irritation and congestion of the mucous membrane of the colon, known as colitis, and causing autointoxication?

## A NICE BATCH OF DISEASES

Among the diseases and symptoms caused by autointoxication are: degeneration of blood vessels and high blood pressure; constant fatigue; rheumatoid arthritis and joint inflammation; hives and other skin troubles; myocardial and other heart troubles; diarrhea; irritability; foul breath; gout, rheumatism, crippling arthritis; wasting of the muscles; diseases peculiar to women; headache; epilepsy; goitre; enlarged glands; pyorrhea; asthma; baldness; various diseases of the eyes and ears.

Metchnikoff summed up the whole matter in this sentence: "The micro-organisms inhabiting our bodies have set going there a poison factory which shortens our existence, and by secreting poisons which penetrate all our tissues, injures our most precious organs, our arteries, brain, liver, and kidneys."

At famous European health spas, doctors report that fully three-quarters of the patients owe their troubles to sluggish intestines. Fortunately, this autointoxication can be cured in practically all cases, often with astonishing rapidity.

There are four ways of avoiding intestinal poisons: (1) cutting out the intestines; (2) bullying them with drugs; (3) exchanging good bacteria for bad ones; (4) accelerating the food movements.

Drugs and surgery offer no real solution, and often do more harm than good. Sooner or later, frequent use of laxatives produces colitis and spastic conditions that leave the patient worse than in the beginning. Why whip a sick horse when he can be made more vigorous by gentler methods?

Changing the intestinal flora is one of these gentler methods. Metchnikoff noticed that in Bulgaria, people drank a great deal of sour milk, and that many of them lived more than a hundred years. In their milk he found a bacillus which is violently hostile to the colon bacilli of putrefaction; with this he soured the milk he drank daily. Unfortunately, this bacillus is usually digested and absorbed before it reaches the intestines. It has therefore been combined with other bacilli, which help to keep it alive; and in this combination millions have used it in various commercial forms. It is called lactobacillus acidophilus, and is found in acidophilus yogurt.

The famous grape cure, and other fruit cures, used in European health spas are effective chiefly because of the change they bring about in the intestinal flora, substituting good bacilli for those which breed disease and hasten senility. Carrots work just as well. Potatoes and dates have also been found particularly antitoxic. In many cases, the transformation of a patient from a sluggish, overweight invalid to a lean, healthy, forceful person is often so rapid as to seem almost miraculous.

## AN AUTOMATIC WEIGHT REGULATOR!

High fiber foods are automatic weight regulators. Normally, even if you are not on a reducing diet, the simple addition of high fiber foods will tend to normalize your weight, and help you lose pounds and inches if you are too heavy.

High fiber foods also help rid the body of poisons. When food passes through the body in twenty-four hours—as it does if there are three bowel movements a day—there is no time for the contents to putrify and poison the body. If there are only two movements, the conditions are less favorable, while one movement a day (or less) can lead to constipation and autointoxication. And oddly enough, mushy foods breed constipation by causing a general slackening of the muscles of the intestines. With frequent constipation, not only do poisons accumulate in the system, but the hard stool itself irritates the intestinal wall, stretching delicate membranes (diverticulitis), causing open sores (ulcers), and if the irritation is constant, even cancer.

High fiber foods, consisting of bulk or roughage, increase peristaltic action, greatly accelerating the movement of each meal, and reducing the total time needed for elimination from two days or longer to less than one day, thus preventing the colon from being a sewer.

The use of high fiber foods for roughage is becoming widely accepted by the medical profession. While useful as a harmless laxative, they have the further advantage of being rich in iron, calcium and other mineral salts. In fact, the magic mineral salt diet *is* a high fiber diet.

Among the best high fiber foods is bran. The time will come—for many it has already come—when bran will be on the table all the time to be mixed by the spoonful with cereals, soups, fruit sauces and other dishes.

It is a tremendous boon to have at hand so conveniently a cheap food which, besides being one-third cellulose, contains a perfect mine of health salts. A pound of bran, for example, contains 119 grains of potassium carbonate, compared with only 12 grains in the flour of which white bread is made.

According to an English authority, Dr. Ross, this loss of potassium carbonate predisposes to cancer of the colon—may, in fact, be one of its leading causes. And cancer of the colon has been increasing at a startling rate since the habit of taking the bran out of bread began.

I firmly believe that the use of high fiber foods can bring about a complete regeneration of the human race, and the average life span can be increased half a century or more.

## FOODS RICH IN CELLULOSE!

Cellulose is the scientific name for high fiber content—the quality in a food which makes it useful for bulk or roughage. You'll get plenty of roughage if your meals include certain fruits, vegetables and cereals rich in cellulose.

In the vegetable department, this is particularly true of dried peas, green peas, cabbage, parsnips, Brussels sprouts, raw kohlrabi, raw celery, turnip, pumpkin, tomatoes, carrots, beans, lettuce, onion, cucumber, in that order.

Among the fruits useful for roughage—and, like the vegetables named and the cereals to be named, rich in minerals—are blueberries (huckleberries), raspberries, cranberries and blackberries, currants, figs, gooseberries, pears, apricots, cherries, strawberries, oranges, prunes, plums, grapes, raisins, apples, and peaches, in that order.

Among grain or cereal products, bran is far in the lead in roughage value as well as in mineral wealth; it has 200 grains of cellulose to the ounce. Next in cellulose value comes cooked oatmeal, with 44 grains, followed by dried beans, peas, barley, lentils, rye, wheat, corn meal, corn flakes, graham bread, and whole wheat bread.

Naturally, if you are overweight, the vegetable and fruit groups are preferable to the cereals because they are less fattening. Bran is the grand exception. Of that you can eat to your hearts' content, without fear of gaining weight. Among the other cellulose foods just listed, blueberries are tops.

## A HAPPY STOMACH MAKES DIETING A PLEASURE!

Whatever pertains to the colon is of particular importance to the overweight because they are, more than others, liable to constipation. The increasing weight of the abdomen causes it to sag and, by its pressure, to interfere with the free activity of the intestines.

Overweights are particularly given to barking up the wrong tree, accusing the stomach of crimes which in reality are perpetrated in the colon. Experience has taught me the maxim, *"Take care of your colon and your stomach will take care of itself."* With the high fiber diet, eat magic mineral foods, fruits, nuts, vegetables and seeds and you will find your stomach ready to digest almost anything.

I used to swallow tons of soda mints, papaya tablets, and other "life savers," imagined myself a victim of fifty-seven varieties of indigestion, had to give up eating many of my favorite foods, from raw apples to pound cake. You can imagine my joy when, on the high fiber diet, rich in magic mineral foods, I found that my stomach was perfectly normal, as in my youth. Like all the other organs in my body, it had simply been poisoned by the toxins generated in the colon. Colon hygiene soon enabled me once more to eat apples, pound cake, and all the other things I had given up; my happiness was complete!

## HOW THESE AMAZING FOODS SATISFY YOUR HUNGER!

When ordinary mortals talk about a food being digestible, they mean that the stomach has no difficulty in taking care of it. In many official government publications, the word "digestible" is confusingly used as meaning the proportion of this or that food that is completely absorbed in the digestive tract.

This is an absurd way of estimating the value of a food, as all who have read this chapter can see. Bran, which is absolutely the most valuable of all foods, is relegated to the foot of the list by this ridiculous use of the word digestible. While its salts are absorbed, its bulk is *not* digestible; and *that is why it is a life saver*.

By eating bulky foods at the beginning of a meal, overweights can diminish their hunger greatly and thus make it easier for their will to reduce to assert itself.

## WHY YOU MUST EAT MORE TO REDUCE!

Above all things, remember that when you begin to reduce, it is dangerous to eat less than you have been eating, because that diminishes the bulk needed for frequent bowel movements.

What you must do to lose weight is to eat less of the fuel foods, but to make up for that by eating more of the roughage foods you have just read about. These fruits and vegetables can, as we shall see in later chapters, be made so tempting, so completely satisfying, that you will not miss the sweets and starches that have made your body heavy and your life a burden.

# 14

## To Drink or Not to Drink!

Alcohol is a champion fattener. In Munich, that beer drinking city, everybody has a beer paunch. Excess in strong drink has always been as fattening as excess in eating. There is no mystery about it. Alcohol is a splendid fuel. It burns so readily in the body that the fat in the food is spared and stored. That's why drinkers gain weight.

### FRUIT JUICES, TEA AND COFFEE

Fruit juices show the way. They are readily available in supermarkets in amazing variety, and some of them, like loganberry and grape juice, have as fine a bouquet as any wine drinker could crave (although in the case of grape juice the most aromatic varieties of grapes are not generally used).

Nothing is more beneficial for overweights than plenty of weak unsweetened lemonade. To make it more tempting, and for the sake of variety, add to it occasionally a spoonful or two of loganberry or some other highly flavored fruit juice; or mix with orange juice, half and half.

Orange juice alone is more delectable still and needs no blush or sweetening. It is rich in mineral salts. I know a boy of eight whose mother had been told he could hardly drink too much orange juice. Gradually he began drinking the contents of a dozen oranges a day! A bad case of acid stomach resulted. The doctor's first question was, "Was the juice sweetened?" The boy had taken twenty-four teaspoonfuls of cane sugar a day!—a wonder he lived to cry his tale. It was the sugar that gave him the acid stomach, not the orange juice.

Paradoxical as it may seem—and this is a very important thing to know—the effect of orange as well as lemon juice is that of an alkali, *not* an acid. They actually correct acidity. It has been suggested that if lemon and orange juice were universally substituted for tea and coffee it would, indeed, rejuvenate the human race.

Tea and coffee are interesting drinks to talk about, but they are not related to the subject of this book except insofar as many people still mix cream and sugar with them. That makes them fattening, of course, and therefore permissible only in limited amounts; but by sipping a third of a cup of coffee with a *little* cream and sugar in it, you can get a lot of harmless pleasure out of it. In that case the fragrance of the coffee, like the bouquet of wine, is exhilarating in itself. That's worth knowing, too.

## MILK IN THE REDUCING DIET

Drinking a lot of milk and drinking it all day long is one way certain African tribes have of fattening girls for the marriage market in countries where beauty means chubbiness. Should milk be excluded from your diet?

Owing to its richness in mineral salts, which the cow gathers from the grass and herbs it browses on, its richness, also, in all the other elements which make milk the most complete food known, milk should not be withheld entirely from your reducing diet, if it agrees with you. A little goes a long way. Some Eastern holy men exist on one meal a day of sour milk and a little millet. And for overweights, skim milk and the things made of it, like cottage cheese, are ideal. If you find milk difficult to digest, sip it, or *eat it*. All liquids, including soups, fruit juices, tea, and coffee, should be eaten—that is, thoroughly mingled with saliva and never poured down in rapid gulps.

Among the many remedies for obesity, there are several milk cures. One Belgian doctor achieved results by gradually, in four days, omitting all other foods except skim milk. From the fourth day on, nothing but milk—four quarts daily. A sort of hunger cure. There was also a buttermilk cure for obesity. Two quarts a day, supplemented by seven pounds of potatoes! The fact that milk is good for you notwithstanding, diets that consist of one food, and nothing else, over a long period of time, are not recommended.

## WHAT ABOUT WATER?

To drink or not to drink water with meals—that is the question. No one who has any sense will ever take water in his mouth to wash down his food instead of allowing the saliva to lubricate and partly digest it before it goes down. Anyone who does this will soon experience gastronomic burbulence!

On the speed reducing diet, Dr. Lindlahr recommended no water for a half-hour before, and half-hour after meals, and none during the meal—but as much as desired between meals. He pointed out that speed reducing foods themselves contain large amounts of water. Dr. Lindlahr seemed to feel that large amounts of water taken with food dilute the gastric juice in the stomach and thus retard digestion.

But drinking when thirsty *between* meals helps curb hunger, and experiments have shown that frequent water intake perceptibly aids the elimination of fat! It's up to you; no need to force it.

The habit of gulping down ice water with meals has ruined more stomachs than whiskey ever did. If in London or Paris you ask the waiter for a bottle of champagne or red wine on ice, he will look at you disdainfully. Iced drinks are peculiarly American. A small amount of iced water, sipped slowly, does seem to stimulate the appetite, but swallowing a large amount of ice water not warmed in the mouth delays digestion an hour or two and can be harmful. The drinking of tea or coffee very hot can also be harmful. Dr. William Mayo long ago warned that one cause of stomach cancer is the habit of taking extremely hot food and drink into the stomach.

# 15

## Amazing Sugar Substitutes!

Not only does sugar favor, as no other food does, the laying on of super-fat, with all its life-shortening ills and discomforts, but it weakens the body's power to resist such deadly diseases as liver, kidney, lung and heart trouble, and gives rise to diabetes. Our blood, our teeth, our bones suffer. Sour stomach results—since sugar is acid—followed by intestinal upset, ulcers, and other disorders. But don't panic! It is still possible to...

## SATISFY YOUR SWEET TOOTH!

Plan alternatives for sweet treats. For instance, apples, blackberries, blueberries, cherries, cranberries, figs, grapes, honeydew, mangos, nectarines, oranges, peaches, pears, pineapples, plums, prunes, raspberries, strawberries, tangerines, watermelons—are all definitely fat-dissolving foods. Yet they are rich in natural sugars, and will help satisfy your desire for something sweet!

A dessert can be made of unflavored gelatin made with fruit juices, such as orange, grape, or apple. Naturally sweet fruit juices can be refreshing substitutes for fattening soft drinks. A teaspoon or two of sugar or honey can still be used to sweeten tea or coffee, and will not affect your weight in these amounts.

Honey is an amazing sugar substitute. It is one of the few available sources of levulose, the sweetest of all sugars, nearly twice as sweet as cane sugar. It is also the mildest. Yet it is possible to use larger amounts of honey than it would be safe to use cane sugar, because levulose is a slow-absorbing sugar. Levulose and fructose—found in many fruits—are nature's answer to artificial sweets like saccharin. Honey may even be used by diabetics in some cases (ask your doctor). It is among the best, if not the best energy food.

It has an advantage over sugar in that its effects are longer-lasting, it is a natural and gentle laxative, is non-irritating to the stomach, and spares the kidneys. The mineral value of honey is not high, but as slight as it is, it is quite important in cases where honey is used every day as a sweetener. But its vitamin content is much higher than many fruits and vegetables (vitamin C especially). It quickly neutralizes fatigue poisons in the system.

The stickiness and difficulty in pouring it are the chief objections to honey. Both are easily overcome. A small amount of honey should be transferred to a drip-spout pitcher. Then each time before using, let it stand in a bowl or saucepan of warm (not hot) water. Then you will find it will pour in a thin drizzle instead of a heavy stream. When warmed, it tends to liquefy and is much easier to handle. Better still, you can dilute it with water. One-third cup of water to a cup of honey will give it the consistency of maple syrup. One-fifth cup of water to a cup of honey will give it the consistency of corn or cane syrup. Diluted honey will make a more satisfactory sweetener for your morning coffee, cereal, fruit drinks, or waffles. For flavor, mild clover honey is best for coffee, tea or chocolate. Orange-blossom and sage honey are best for fruit drinks, waffles, toast and biscuits. Buckwheat honey is best for buckwheat cakes.

## A HABIT-FORMING DRUG!

Granulated sugar is actually a habit-forming drug and not a food. Yet we eat about twenty million tons a year! Think of the astronomical trillions and quadrillions of cane stalks and beets it takes to produce twenty million *tons!* It is these enormous figures that produce *our* enormous figures.

As sugar eaters, we Americans eat about ten times as much as other nations do and at the present rate it will soon be twenty times as much. We eat about ten times as much sugar as our ancestors ate a century ago. And even they were consuming more than they really needed. As one observer pointed out, we now have three hundred million people in this country condemned to premature death by sugar—in addition to the overweight it causes.

Most amazing of all, the white sugar we use has been deliberately robbed of all the valuable mineral salts that come from sugar cane. The following chart shows the proportions of energy, protein, calcium, phosphorus, and iron needed per man per day furnished by one pound of sugar:

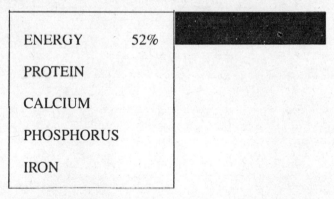

| ENERGY | 52% |
| PROTEIN | |
| CALCIUM | |
| PHOSPHORUS | |
| IRON | |

The fact is that sugar is absolutely valueless as food except for the energy it furnishes. And even that is only one-half of what you need. In other words, to get your daily need of energy you would have to eat two pounds of cane sugar—which would soon end your earthly career.

## CHOCOLATE, MAPLE, HONEY, MOLASSES

Even the humble soda cracker provides more energy than sugar does (54 percent), *with* protein, calcium, phosphorus and iron. Think how much richer in minerals honey is than white sugar: energy, 42 percent; protein, 2; calcium, 3; phosphorus, 7; iron, 21. A pound of lard also has no minerals whatsoever, but its energy value is more than twice that of sugar, being 117. Much more valuable than sugar is chocolate, as it contains in a pound 79 percent of the energy a man needs daily, and plenty of minerals!

Thus, if you should give up sugar for chocolate (commercial chocolate, to be sure, is fattening), you would have not only more energy, but, in addition, valuable protein and mineral salts. And the same is true of the unrefined sweets like honey, maple syrup, and brown cane sugar.

Fortunately it is now possible to get again many of these old-fashioned sweets. Old-fashioned brown sugar is bound to come back, because it appeals to the sense of taste, like white sugar, but also has mineral salts *and flavor*, like honey and maple syrup. Brown sugar is alluring in itself and does not have to be made into expensive candy— that is, sugar flavored with vanilla, wintergreen, spices, nuts, and other ingredients that make it appeal to the sense of smell.

## A GORGEOUS TIME WITHOUT GORGING!

You may ask, "Is it not foolish, in a book for overweights, to try to emphasize the lure of sweets?" Not foolish at all. *Some* sugar we may and should all have, especially if there are mineral salts in it, as in honey, maple and brown sugar and pure cane syrup. And since these also appeal to the sense of smell, they help stimulate the digestive juices. Since you can have but little sugar, make that little as delicious as possible.

A small child I know uses this method. Every morning he puts a spoonful of honey on his plate. Then, with a teaspoon, he takes up on the edge a little of it, the size of a pea, which he keeps in his mouth as long as the flavor lasts; then another, till it's all gone. He never asks for more. In this way, he has a simply gorgeous time without gorging.

Surely, if a child can do this, you can too. The art of eating wisely is really not so difficult as most people imagine. Sugar is bad, principally, because it masks the taste of natural foods and decreases appetite for them. It is a good energizer in itself and the growing child craves it naturally. One wise dietician in an institution gave the children permission to eat candy whenever they wanted to—taking pains to see that they had a well-balanced diet, especially a good mineral supply (which means milk, whole wheat, egg yolk, fruit, and fresh vegetables). Result, the "candy permits" were not often demanded. Provide wholesome sweets at the proper times—such as figs, raisins, plain candies—at the end of the meal, and you will not need heavy sweets.

In such simple ways your "worst enemy" can be made a friend, and there is no need to eliminate sweets from your diet. If you must have coffee or tea, you may sweeten it reasonably, as mentioned previously.

I promised you a method of reducing which calls for no self-denial and allows you to eat anything and as much as you like. I have kept my word. Even of sugar you may eat as much as you want, *after you have learned to savor it*.

## CURBING THE SUGAR MANIA!

Another method of curbing the mania for sugar is to cultivate an enthusiasm for the natural flavors of fruits and cereals. The usual American way is to put spoonfuls of white sugar even on melon, peaches, and pineapples. That ought to be a state-prison offense. For this sugar drowns out the exquisite inherent flavors of these fruits. Get *ripe* fruits and berries and you will soon find plenty of sweetness in them, besides delectable flavor.

# 16

## Bread and Butter, Cereals, Potatoes!

Every human body is a sugar factory. That's another reason why it is foolish to put sugar into so many things we eat. In Huxley's *Physiology* you may read that "all the starch which is eaten as food is converted into sugar in the alimentary canal, and reaches the liver as sugar."

There's a fact of tremendous importance to overweights. Sugar, whether introduced into the body as sugar or starch, has been called "the natural fuel" of the body. Everybody needs *some* of it, to run the machine. In cold weather, we need more of it than in summer. But if we take in more of the starch-and-sugar fuel than our bodies need to get up steam for running the heart and muscles, it is stored up in the body as fat. That's a law of nature and cannot be altered. Sorry. But we can still eat these things and safely lose weight!

## ENJOY BREAD!

Formerly the doctors and dieticians, impressed by these facts, simply placed all the carbohydrates—that is, starch-and-sugar dishes—in the list of things that are *verboten* to the overweight who wants to get thinner. We are more merciful. In this chapter, let me show you how an overweight may indulge in carbohydrate dishes and yet reduce his weight safely.

The fattening element in bread is the starch, which normally constitutes 70 percent of the flour. Bread made of starch alone, or mostly of starch, is therefore to be avoided. That means white bread!

White bread has its use as fuel; but apart from that, its value as food is so slight that life cannot be carried on with it. It has been shown hundreds of times by actual experiments on various animals that if fed on white bread alone they die in a few weeks—*die even sooner than if they are not fed at all!*—whereas if fed on whole-wheat bread they remain in good health.

Why is this so? Because the whole wheat bread has the mineral salts essential to life, which the millers remove when they make white flour by taking out the bran and the oily germs of the wheat. They do this, they say, because women will not buy flour unless it is snow white—which isn't true. Most women never look at the flour they buy, and if they know a thing or two, they ask for the cream-colored brands, which have not been demineralized.

The real reasons for the deathly pallor of white flour are, first, that by bleaching (with dangerous chemicals), the millers can use inferior grades of wheat and make them look like the better grades; secondly, by taking out the oily germ they prevent the flour from deteriorating on the grocer's shelf—which would be all right were it not for the fact that these germs—and the bran, which they also remove—contain the life-sustaining mineral salts.

These salts, along with the germs and hull (bran) are fed to animals (at an extra profit to the millers), while children and adults get the demineralized white bread, useless except as fuel.

Due to the recent great demand for organic foods, some of the largest bakers have reformed, thereby saving the health of thousands.

We are eating in this country nearly forty billion pounds of bread a year. It is worthwhile to make sure that it is as healthful and nutritious as it can be made.

## "OFFSETTING FOODS"

Demineralized bread can only be made up for by "offsetting foods" like eggs, fresh vegetables, fresh fruits, and greens, all of which abound in salts. Even if you are one of those who can afford to pay extra to help make a satisfactory meal out of an empty loaf of white bread, there is abundant reason why you should prefer whole-wheat.

When Thackeray spoke of the delicious pleasure one can get out of a slice of bread with butter, it was whole-wheat bread he referred to. Epicures generally would agree that there is a richer flavor in such bread than in the denatured baked—usually half-baked—flour which is called bread. In eating whole-wheat bread, an overweight gets more flavor as well as more food salts; and, as we have seen, when there is plenty of flavor with an abundance of salts, the appetite is appeased sooner and the tendency to overeat is diminished.

No one who is on a reducing diet need deny himself a slice or two of whole-wheat bread with a little butter, or diet margarine. Toasting still further develops the appetizing flavors while increasing the digestibility. And high fiber bread contains half the calories per slice of regular bread (it's delicious toasted).

## HOW TO SATISFY YOUR TASTE WITHOUT GAINING WEIGHT!

Cereals have become such a universal constituent of American breakfasts, and suppers, too, that it takes some courage not to praise them wholeheartedly. Yet there can be no doubt that for many people, especially those who do not wish to grow fat or fatter, they are objectionable, all the more as they are usually eaten with a lot of sugar, and cream, too.

Eaten very slowly, cereals will, like bread, turn to sugar in the mouth. Learn to do that, savoring the taste with your sense of smell (exhaling slowly through the nose) and you will not crave the added sugar and cream. But if the cereals are demineralized, as most breakfast foods are, it is hardly worthwhile wasting time on them unless you need a lot of cheap fuel, or wish to gain weight.

Please bear in mind that what you are after primarily is pleasure, not nourishment, for you are already overnourished. Hence I am forever dwelling on the pleasure side of wise eating.

Wheat, rye, rice, barley, and other grains have delicious flavors of their own which you can learn to enjoy in small portions. Put a teaspoonful of oatmeal (the most nutritious of all cereals—when not demineralized) into your mouth. Keep it there, guiding the expired air through your nose in sniffs, and all at once the flavor will "dawn on you." That dawn will, by practice, develop into full daylight.

There are in the market some cereal foods, like grapenuts and shredded wheat, which are made with the special aim of subordinating the fattening starch to the vitalizing mineral salts. These may be eaten generously on your high fiber diet, but not to excess.

## ENJOY POTATOES!

Dr. Kellog stated that if the average American would eat four or five times as much potatoes as he now eats, and an equivalent amount of less cereals and cane sugar, the result would be a noticeable lowering of the death rate and a marked increase in physical fitness and freedom from crippling disease.

Potatoes are fattening, too, but they are no longer denied the overweight entirely, at least by the wisest doctors and dieticians, because there are so many good things about them which outweigh their disadvantages.

They are rich in iron, also in soda and potash, which help to overcome a tendency to acidosis which is encouraged by eating cereals. Potash, as science has shown, combats the cancerous tendency.

*The alkaline salts which arrest the hardening of the arteries and rapid aging are more abundant in the potato than in any other staple vegetable food*. The potato furnishes forty times as much of these alkaline elements as do some of the cereals. Mineral salts make up as much as 5 percent of the dry substance of the potato. Tests have proven that these salts are very valuable as an aid in eliminating uric acid and other acid wastes from the body.

Therefore don't deprive yourself of potatoes. Eat them in moderation. It is not so much that the potato is fattening, as what is done to it in cooking. A steamed or baked potato retains all its valuable salts, which are lost in the water when they are boiled, particularly after peeling. And when the mineral salts are lost the potato, instead of being healthfully alkaline, actually leads to harmful acidosis—a fact of tremendous importance in this country, where most families boil their potatoes.

If potatoes are fried it should be done the French way. That is, using the raw slices, in polyunsaturated oil. If the German way, or mashed, they should be steamed—never boiled. One researcher had a patient who lived a whole year in good health on potatoes. *Above all, remember that catabolic (speed reducing) foods—like green, leafy vegetables—when mixed with fattening foods, like potatoes, make them less fattening, by destroying their fat before it can be stored. Turn back to Chapter 4 and note especially all the foods mentioned, which can be used to balance (neutralize) a heavy starch or protein meal. Take parsnips, for example. Reducers can eat them with their potatoes to lower the calorie count of the latter, said Dr. Lindlahr!*

## SATISFY YOUR CRAVING FOR FATS!

We naturally crave a little butter with our potatoes—same as with our bread—and our cereals, too; for cream is simply the material out of which butter is made. This is, therefore, as good a place as any for introducing what overweights should know about butter and other fats.

Perhaps the most surprising thing about fats is that they are not so fattening as starches and sugars. An ounce of fat taken in addition to a full meal increases the weight one ounce, whereas an extra ounce of starch or sugar adds four ounces to your weight.

That's good news for gourmets who happen to be fat. It tells them that if they eat moderately of dishes made of flour and sugar they may allow themselves a reasonable amount of butter (so enticing with bread or with cooked vegetables) and olive oil, without which most salads are a frank failure.

Unfortunately, most olive oil sold in America is a deodorized product that is passed on its way to you through such chemical solvents as carbon bisulphide, benzine, carbon tetrachloride, and trichlorethylene, all of which are used in the resurrection of inedible oils for the American table.

Commercial butter is often quite as bad as chemicalized "olive" oil. Genuine butter, however, is rich in mineral salts. It is an odd fact that many persons who find cream indigestible have no trouble with butter, or with ice cream.

When you eat ice cream, don't let one spoonful chase another. Keep each on the tongue till all the taste and flavor are gone. Then take another small teaspoonful. Enjoy it consciously; don't be absent-minded. That's the way to eat candy, too. And remember that ice cream or candy between meals is more fattening than at meals.

Fats, including oils of all kinds, have, as previously stated, the convenient quality of satiating the appetite quickly. If, nevertheless, you eat them in excess, you have only yourself to blame for their being kept, as fat, in "warm storage" in or on your body. The camel's hump is a storage place of fat. You don't want one.

A funny thing about fat is that if you eat more than the body can use as fuel, it is not only stored in your body, but is stored without any change; pork fat as lard, mutton fat as tallow, beef fat as suet, and so on. You can thus, if you keep at it, make yourself fifty-seven varieties all at once—a crazy quilt of adiposity.

But that isn't a good way to reduce. Fat meat is fattening and to be avoided. Lean meat—see the next chapter.

# 17

## Enjoy
## Your Meat and Potatoes!

Yes, lean meat is not fattening, but—hang it, there is always a "but" for the overweight! Banting's doctor put him on a diet consisting largely of lean meat, and he lost weight rapidly. Was there any objection to that—the meat eating, I mean? Well, we know that Banting lost weight, but we do not know how this affected his health afterward.

What we do know is that the eating of *too much* meat is not good for anybody's health. Dr. Arnold Lorand, in his famous book, *Old Age Deferred*, points out that while meat is more easily digested than most other foods, too much of it can cause fatigue, nervous disorder, weakening of the thyroid gland, severe gout, diabetes, and other diseases. He goes on to say:

"When we study the nature of the diet enjoyed by persons who have lived to and over a hundred, we find, indeed, exceedingly few who are great meat eaters; very many are persons who eat no meat at all; and in many cases, also, the original meat diet was subsequently abandoned in advanced age. According to the report of the Collective Investigation Committee of the British Medical Association, fifty-five centenarians whose cases they examined were, for the most part, small meat-eaters."

## A HIGH PROTEIN DIET IS NOT A CURE-ALL

All the evils of autointoxication, or intestinal self-poisoning, on which I have dwelt at length in Chapter 13, are greatly aggravated by meat eating. Some researchers have shown that a high protein diet— that is, a diet including too much meat, eggs, and cheese—can actually injure your health. Most of us eat two or three times as much protein (tissue-building material) as we need—five or six times as much if we habitually eat in hotels or restaurants, where meals are all built around meat.

The result of such a high-protein diet, which overtaxes the liver and kidneys, is seen in various rheumatic and nervous troubles that vanish when a meatless diet is adopted. From the overweight's point of view these facts—the "but" in the case—are really most annoying, for since lean meat contains no carbohydrates or sugar, it might be eaten in unlimited quantities and to advantage were it not for this excess protein coming in as a trouble maker.

## HOW TO ENJOY MEATS!

But you can still enjoy your meat and potatoes, on a high fiber diet! With high fiber foods, meat has no time to undergo putrefactive changes and poison the body, and need not, therefore, be given up altogether, especially if we eat little of eggs, cheese, and other sources of protein.

Above all, remember the protein-digesting power of such foods as cranberries, cucumbers, and pineapple (see Chapter 4). Cranberries contain a substance which stimulates the flow of digestive juice, aiding digestion. They are helpful in digesting meat! Cucumbers contain an enzyme called *erepsin*, which aids digestion of proteins. The actual protein-digesting power of cucumbers is comparable to that of papaya (papaya is used as a meat tenderizer)! Pineapples, too, are good for digesting meat. They contain an enzyme called *bromelin*, which digests proteins in the same way as does *pepsin*, a substance normally secreted in the human stomach. Pineapple is good in helping to digest meat and egg dishes! And, of course, apple cider vinegar (see Chapter 10), the speed reducing food so powerful that it can digest *pearls*, let alone heavy concentrated foods, like meat and potatoes! And sauerkraut, which is reputed to have similar fat-cutting powers!

By all means, enjoy your steak, chops, ham, bacon, and fish as before—with large quantities of speed reducing, high fiber foods. And savor it! Eat slowly! Again I say, what you need is not nourishment—for you are already overnourished—but pleasure; and for pleasure (need I explain it again?) a little meat eaten slowly goes much further than a plateful gobbled. One slice of smoked bacon lingered over for ten minutes will afford infinitely more delight than five or six slices devoured at a quick-lunch counter.

Use meat for flavoring! In France, this use of meat for flavoring purposes chiefly has long been demonstrated in hundreds of delectable culinary combinations. The number of "tasty" dishes which a good cook can make out of the cheaper cuts of meat, or meat "leftovers," is almost endless.

In addition to eating lean meat, try to avoid the "fat" fishes like salmon, mackerel, sardines, swordfish, or even shad. There are plenty of others, and they are delectable cooked plain, smoked, or in diverse soufflés and salads.

## AND NOW THE GRAVY!

There is no substitute for real meat gravy, French style. Gravy is also fattening, and it is, therefore, among the things forbidden those who are trying to lose weight. But they need not refuse this rich source of flavor if it is made in this French fashion: Bake meat with a little salt and no water until it has browned richly in its own fat, or in butter. Baste with this fat, but add little or no water till the baking is nearly done. When ready to serve, pour the superfluous fat from the pan, add a *little* water, no flour, and scrape the pan thoroughly for every bit of the savory brown substance.

If any is left over, put it in the next soup, to make that more soulful—for after all, flavor is the soul of food.

French cooks, supreme in culinary artistry, make use of the bones as well as the meat. They actually orchestrate flavors just as a composer orchestrates sounds in a symphony. They make the most delectable of all soups *(petite marmite)* out of beef, marrow-bone, chicken giblets, carrots, turnips, leeks, parsnips, onions, cloves, garlic, celery, and brown salt (salt that has not been purified). The bones are crushed, and cooked separately twelve hours. As the saying goes, "You'll hear a symphony in your mouth!"

## AMAZING MEAT SUBSTITUTES!

If you prefer a low-protein or non-meat diet, you should try to include foods that will furnish a full supply of complete protein. Glandular meat furnishes complete proteins. Tongue, brains, liver, kidney and sweetbreads do not appeal to many people, however. A nearly complete supply of proteins (amino acids) can be supplied by milk, eggs, and dairy products.

Just as you can enjoy skimmed milk, you may also enjoy eggs, in moderation. For eggs are such a complete food, and so valuable in making a multitude of dishes, that it would be foolish to forbid them altogether.

Cheese is also wonderfully rich in nutrients. One pound of American cheese can furnish 58 percent of the energy a man needs daily, 131 percent of the protein, 621 percent of the calcium, 235 percent of the phosphorus and 39 percent of the iron. Two or three slices is enough, however, on account of the high fat content.

Cheese is one of the things that help to compensate overweights for eating sparsely. Cheeses are so richly flavored that a little can be made to go a long way. The number of distinctive cheese flavors is much greater than that of meat flavors.

Some cheeses, being full-cream, are fattening; in large quantities they are also constipating; but then, one is not tempted to eat very much of any of them, because they are so filling. An exception may be made of cottage cheese (without added cream); of this you may eat all you want. It's delicious when fresh, or mixed with sweet natural fruit.

## ARE NUTS ALLOWED?

Prominent among protein foods and meat substitutes are nuts. They are supposed to be indigestible. But they are not so when very carefully chewed and eaten by themselves, or with say, greens, or raisins or some other fruit. Eat them with the main meal—in salads especially—rather than as dessert.

It must be remembered that nuts are the most concentrated of all foods. A pound of almonds contains more protein than a pound of meat and nearly as much fat as a pound of butter. Are they, therefore, forbidden?

Not necessarily. You may eat them, in moderation. Nobody, fat or thin, would care to eat a whole pound of walnut meats, for that would be equal in food value to more than four pounds of beef, three pounds of ham, or twenty-two pounds of lobsters.

But sensible overweights who have learned how to savor food may add nut eating to their gastronomic joys. The flavor of three or four almonds, walnuts, or peanuts, reduced slowly to a paste in the mouth, and consciously savored for ten or fifteen minutes, will give more delight than half a pound of them gobbled half chewed; nor will they cause indigestion or an appreciable deposit of fat.

Knowing this, you may eat all you want—you will not want to eat more than a few, since what you are after is not nourishment, but pleasurable flavor.

Candy makers know the immense amount of flavor power in nuts. Most of their sweets are flavored with them; that's one reason why they get rich. It pays to please the buyers. And now we come to the foods which overweights may and should indulge in freely and enthusiastically for quantity (bulk) as well as quality (flavor and minerals).

# 18

## Doctor's Proven, New High Fiber Diet!

The bran diet lets you eat almost anything, as long as you include 9 tablespoons of wheat bran a day. "A high bran diet," says one expert, "will safely take pounds off you and keep them off."

There's no calorie counting on the bran diet, but to lose weight you must eliminate all refined carbohydrates, including sugar, white flour, cakes, cookies, and the like. Otherwise, you can eat anything you like. You just add the bran—a tasteless food fiber, available at health food stores—to any kind of foods you want, from soups to cereals to ground beef.

Reportedly, this diet lets you lose up to 10-12 pounds a month, and once you lose the weight, you may resume your intake of carbohydrates, with a maintenance diet of 9 tablespoons of bran a day. To avoid cramps and diarrhea, it is suggested that you start the diet with one teaspoon 3 times a day, and increase to 3 tablespoons with each meal over a 2-week period, and take a glass of water with each meal, plus one at bedtime.

Experts have stated that the bran diet helps prevent heart disease, colon cancer, gallstones, stomach ailments, hemorrhoids and blood clots. This is due to the swift movement of bran through the body, so that disease-producing elements in food do not have a chance to start working.

## MORE HIGH FIBER FOODS!

You can get the same effect by eating large amounts of salad vegetables—without the cramps and diarrhea—on Dr. Lindlahr's speed reducing diet. Can you imagine a time when fresh fruits and vegetables were a rarity? When tomatoes, rhubarb, cauliflower, eggplants, grapefruits, strawberries, raspberries, head lettuce, okra, and cantaloupes were not to be found at the corner grocery; when oranges and bananas were a luxury of the rich, and none of the finer varieties of grapes, apples, pears, plums, peaches, and quinces were to be had for love or money? Fruits and vegetables have become such old, familiar friends that it is hard to imagine life without them. And yet 150 years ago, they were rare delicacies in many parts of the world, reserved only for the rich.

## EAT ALL YOU WANT AND NEVER GAIN AN OUNCE!

*Obesity, said Dr. Lorand, is seldom found in persons who live chiefly on a vegetarian diet.* Hardening of the arteries and autointoxication from sluggish bowels are rare among vegetarians. His experience and study of the subject led him to conclude that the older we get the less meat we should eat; but he did not believe in an exclusively vegetarian diet.

For overweights, the outstanding fact about vegetables is that they are the most filling, but the least fattening, of all foods. The most filling, because of the abundance in them of cellulose, which provides the necessary bulk for frequent bowel movements. The least fattening, because of their watery make-up.

Green vegetables (such as asparagus, lettuce, cabbage, celery, spinach—also cucumbers, squashes and tomatoes) are made up of 90 to 95 percent water, 2½ to 5 percent carbohydrates, ½ percent protein, ½ percent mineral matter, and a mere trace of fat.

In this compound there is very little nourishment excepting the mineral salts, which, as we have seen, the body works so hard to dig out. That is what makes vegetables catabolic (fat destroying). That is why they require more calories to digest than they themselves contain, as Dr. Lindlahr pointed out.

From the broadest point of view vegetable foods include cereals and nuts, which have already been covered in previous chapters, and fruits, to which we shall come soon. Here we are concerned with what are generally meant when we speak of vegetables; greens (celery, lettuce, etc.), roots and tubers, and legumes (peas, beans, lentils, peanuts).

Of the roots and tubers some (radishes, onions, garlic) are as nonfattening as the greens, while others cannot be eaten quite so freely by those who wish to reduce, although none are tabooed entirely; they include potatoes, sweet potatoes, yams, and the succulent carrots, beets, kohlrabi, turnips, rutabagas, and parsnips.

Of the legumes those that are eaten in fresh form—green peas, lima beans and string beans—are almost as harmless to those who wish to reduce as greens; but dried peas, beans, and lentils must be eaten more moderately; for, while they contain hardly any fat, their fattening carbohydrate content is as high as 66 percent.

## MORE EAT-ALL-YOU-WANT FAVORITES!

Tomato juice contains nearly twice as much iron as cow's milk and more than three times as much calcium as beef. It is also rich in the important potash salts; and those who believe in vitamins will be gratified to know that the tomato is rich in them, especially vitamin C.

A moderate daily portion of carrots will not add appreciably to anybody's weight, and it will do no end of good, for the carrot has extreme nutritive value, due to its richness in mineral salts and a powerful antiseptic quality which makes it curative even externally, when mashed and applied to a sore. Metchnikoff found it valuable as an internal cleansing agent. In France, it is served at every meal, for liver troubles.

In preparing carrots, the simplest way to retain what is valuable in them is steaming. If they are boiled, the water should be saved for soup, for the minerals are dissolved in it. Apart from some French recipes, the most enjoyable way to eat carrots is in a soup with other vegetables.

Spinach, like carrots, is robbed of most of its value by being boiled and the water poured away instead of being saved for soup. Up to 50 percent of its treasure of mineral salts is lost this way. Many who do not like spinach in the plain, American Style, would eat it eagerly as a soufflé, or minced, French style, with plenty of good butter, and with a poached egg dropped on each plate as served.

For overweights, spinach is filling but not fattening, and is an ideal food of which unlimited quantities may be eaten without affecting the weight; and the same is true of celery and of lettuce, with romaine, endive, escarole and other varieties. All are rich in minerals.

Stewed celery is delicious; so are stewed solid heads of lettuce; but raw celery and lettuce are better still. In summer, if you have a garden, be sure to have raw vegetables for breakfast. Carrots, peas, tomatoes, asparagus tips, turnips (preferably yellow) are, like radishes, melons, cucumbers, cabbage, onions, celery and lettuce, even more flavorsome raw than cooked, and eaten that way they are sure to retain all their mineral value and the effectiveness of the cellulose as intestinal roughage.

Salads are the portly person's special foods, unless too much oil is used in the dressing. Lemon, vinegar or diet Mayonnaise gives such a delicious flavor that you won't miss the oil. This is most important.

Vinegar and lemon have long been considered antagonistic to fat. And what a tremendous variety there is of salads! With French artichoke and asparagus tip salads to head the list, I might fill pages with the mere names of all the possible combinations and permutations.

Is a vegetable diet monotonous? Perish the thought! I have mentioned only a few of the thousands of varieties available, all distinctly different! Vegetables afford an endless variety of pleasurable flavors, and may be eaten in almost unlimited quantities.

## THOUSANDS OF NATURAL FLAVORS!

Didn't I exaggerate when I spoke, a moment ago, of "thousands" of varieties of agreeable vegetable flavors? Not in the least; I might have written tens of thousands and more.

When you go to your grocer for potatoes, you ask for "potatoes" and he gives you whatever he happens to have on hand. Seed catalogs are less elementary; they list a dozen or twenty different varieties of these tubers. Actually, there are nearly two hundred known varieties of potatoes, in various parts of the world—and probably many more! They all have their own flavors, known to gourmets.

There are 190 different varieties of peas; 70 varieties of onions; 60 varieties of radishes; 35 varieties of tomatoes; 64 varieties of turnips; 26 varieties of carrots; 114 varieties of lettuce and romaine; 50 varieties of cucumbers; 24 varieties of celery; 27 varieties of beets; 93 varieties of cabbage; over 100 varieties of melons of all kinds; and so on.

Take all the other vegetables, alone or in endless combination in soups and stews, and you will soon reach 10,000 and look around for a higher figure. No one is in a better position to estimate the number of kinds of vegetables, cereals, nuts, and fruits in use as the U.S. Department of Agriculture. Some years ago, they compiled estimates totaling as follows:

| | |
|---|---:|
| Fruits | 600 |
| Vegetables | 300 |
| Nuts | 200 |
| Cereals | 100 |
| | 1,200 Total |

Most of the 900 fruits and vegetables you can eat all you want. Most of the 1,200 plant foods can be cooked in dozens of ways alone, and in thousands of ways in countless combinations with others. The figure 10,000 is, therefore, absurdly low. Let us be modest and make it 100,000; for bear in mind that apples, for example, are listed but once among the 600 fruits, but there are 5,000 varieties of apples, all differing slightly or widely in flavor! Can you imagine it?

## ENDLESS VARIATIONS TO CHOOSE FROM!

The French alone have known the truth. To them we must look for guidance. It has been truly said that where the English and Americans use one vegetable the French use twenty, in delicious combinations (soups and stews) or alone. And you may have second and third helpings—as long as not too much butter is used.

Much of the delicious flavor of French and Italian cooking is due to the skillful combination of onions, leeks, shallots, garlic, chives and herbs—and especially the spicy and iodine-holding parsley.

Tender, succulent, flavorsome vegetables turn ordinary dieting into a gastronomic delight and a joy forever. And all so easily available! (It is understood that fresh vegetables should be used wherever possible. Canned tomatoes, corn, beans, asparagus, are good; but, in general, frozen vegetables are better than canned ones.)

# 19

## Twenty-Five
## Speed Reducing Sweet Snacks!

Tropical fruits! How sweet they are! In Brazil there are more than a hundred kinds of wild oranges, all differing subtly in flavor. Brazilian pineapples are so fragrant where they grow that a field of them saturates the air for a mile around with intoxicating fragrance!

Can pineapples help you lose weight? You can lose 5 pounds immediately with this speed reducing food! A Danish doctor reports using pineapple for fast, permanent weight loss. He says it's safe, simple, and you don't have to count calories. Basically, the diet consists of two days of pineapple and five days of normal eating.

Right away you should lose 4-5 pounds or more, he says. Have one or two slices of pineapple for breakfast, five or six for lunch, two more in the afternoon and the rest for dinner. Don't exceed 3 pineapples or 30 unsweetened canned slices over 2 days. Drink all you want, as long as it doesn't have sugar in it.

Reportedly, the magic ingredient is potassium, which pineapples contain in large quantity. Potassium pushes salt out of the body, and releases large quantities of excess fluid. They also contain lots of water, which makes you feel full. Pineapples are tasty, and contain very few calories.

### Reported Results:

*Over 400 patients lost an average of 10-15 pounds a month on this diet. The doctor who discovered this secret says that patients enjoy the sweet taste and regard pineapples as a treat. He used the diet himself, and lost 45 pounds!

*In a controlled test, another doctor found that one group of patients on a low carbohydrate diet lost only 7 pounds in a month, while those on the pineapple diet lost an average of 11 pounds. Of this method he says: "It's the best I've ever used."

*A young woman in her 20's said she tried everything and nothing worked until she went on the pineapple diet. With this method, she lost an incredible 20 pounds in a matter of weeks.

## MOSTLY WATER, ACIDS AND MINERALS!

Only a few fruits are fattening, like bananas, ripe olives and avocados. The avocado contains over 17 percent oil; in some regions it is known as "butter fruit." Barring these, an overweight may eat all the ripe fruit he wants, while growing beautifully thinner by degrees.

And no wonder, when you look at the composition of fruits. They are mostly water: apples, 82 percent; pears, 83 percent; peaches, 88 percent; cherries, 85 percent; strawberries, 89 percent; oranges, 86 percent; and so on, culminating in watermelons, 92 percent water!

Compared with these figures the carbohydrate, or fuel elements which fatten, are insignificant, varying in the sample fruits just named from peaches, 5 percent, to apples, 12 percent. Grapes go higher (12 to 25 percent) and should therefore not be eaten too freely by those who wish to reduce, otherwise they lose their catabolic effect.

If you look at the mineral content of fruit, you will find small figures. But food minerals are so amazingly potent that only microscopic amounts are needed to produce almost miraculous effects on our tissues. And, as has been repeatedly pointed out in the preceding pages, they are catabolic (fat destroying), because the body works so hard to dig them out. The following raw fruits require more calories to digest than they contain, and this can cause an actual weight loss, according to Dr. Lindlahr.

| | | |
|---|---|---|
| apples | honeydew | pineapples |
| apricots | huckleberries | plums |
| blackberries | lemons | pomegranate |
| blueberries | loganberries | quince |
| cantaloupe | mangoes | raspberries |
| cherries | nectarines | strawberries |
| currants | oranges | tangerines |
| grapefruit | pears | watermelons |
| | peaches | |

Fruits from which the water has been removed are, of course, less desirable for those wishing to reduce their weight. Dried apples have a fuel value of 49 percent; dates, 65 percent; figs, 62 percent; prunes, 66 percent; raisins, 74 percent. In eating dried fruits, therefore, discretion is the better part of valor. But if you eat slowly and savor them, you can still enjoy dried fruits, in moderation. You can have more fun by lingering lovingly over a date or two than by bolting a dozen or two; and you'll increase your life-span a decade or two.

## FRUITS CAN SAVE YOUR LIFE!

Many years ago, in Bolivia and Brazil, thousands of railway laborers died simply because they did not know the food and health value of fruit, or "monkey food," as they derisively called it. They soon developed acidosis, "beri-beri," and tuberculosis, because all the food they ate was of the acid-forming kind—white bread, crackers, refined sugar, tapioca, lard, macaroni and others.

The disease began by a swelling of the limbs, followed by a wasting away of flesh, until nothing remained but skin and bone. The chief engineer was among those stricken. He lost his appetite for bread and meat. He had never before cared for oranges, but now, for the first time in his life, he craved them. When the doctor ordered him away he ate little but oranges all the way across the ocean, and soon recovered.

Oranges and other fruits, abundant in the forest all around those railroad laborers, could have saved their lives. All they needed was some base-forming (alkaline) food elements, such as are found in fruits.

## NATURE'S ANTACID!

Thousands of people believe that fruit eating is likely to produce an acid condition of the stomach, the blood and the tissues, whereas it is just the other way! Fruit acids are oxidized in the body into alkaline carbonates, the deadly enemy of dangerous acids.

Add to this that in fresh fruits the mineral salts are also alkaline, and you see at once why these fruits, and particularly oranges, lemons, grapefruit and grapes, are invaluable in such disorders as acidosis, neuritis, anemia, and especially rheumatism, that baffling disease from which overweights often suffer. As Dr. Kellog explained it, when fruits are eaten, the acids are burned or oxidized, setting free the bases. When absorbed into the blood the acid disappears, leaving behind mineral salts which serve a useful purpose in rheumatism by neutralizing the acid products of tissue wastes which have a tendency to accumulate in this disease.

Melons, he adds, and especially the muskmelon, are particularly valuable in rheumatism, because they tend strongly to alkalize the blood and tissue fluids. The cantaloupe in this respect is more efficient than any other fruit. Potato soup or purée should appear often on the bill of fare of the rheumatic patient, he says, on account of its rich stores of bases which alkalize the tissue fluids. And potatoes and root vegetables should largely take the place of bread and cereals.

## A WONDERFUL AID TO DIGESTION!

Scientists have demonstrated by actual tests that fruit enzymes aid digestion, and that these enzymes can, to a considerable degree, take the place of feeble or insufficient digestive juices. So, eat fruit at all meals, unless you have a particular allergy to something, like strawberries. Overweights who think fruit does not agree with them eaten with other food, should have fruit alone for one daily meal.

Fruit should be eaten before the main meal, to get the full benefit of its digestive enzymes and its luscious, subtle flavor, compared with which the flavors of other more fattening foods will seem rather crude. Fruit is also very filling, and will help curb your appetite.

For dessert—more fruit? Why not? Have an apple or fresh pineapple, and give your teeth a natural brushing, as well.

## FLAVOR GALORE!

It is a proven fact that fruits are the most digestible, beneficial, healthful and weight-reducing of all foods. They are also the most flavorful! Nature created them as a lure to animals, so as to insure the dissemination of the seeds. Let them lure *you* away from sweets, starches and pastries. How can such "dead" food compare with melons, peaches, cherries, apples, pears, plums, and so on down the list of fruit treats?

Savor a strawberry or a slice of pineapple, exhaling the aroma-laden air very slowly through your nose until the nerve endings tremble and thrill with ecstatic joy—joy purely sensual, but also healthful and exhilarating.

## AS SWEET AS CANDY!

If the fruit sellers would only offer the very best, flavorsome, sun-ripened fruit, they'd quadruple their sales because the customers—especially overweights—would gobble up all they could get, entranced by the flavor!

Candy makers know the value of flavor, the lure of which enables them to sell by the carload. The more delicious the flavor, the greater the demand. It is unfortunately true that most fruits are picked green to last longer on the supermarket shelf. For a long time, all attempts to popularize the Japanese persimmon failed because people didn't know that they are not fit to eat till they look like overripe tomatoes—though perfectly sound, healthful, and deliciously sweet. When half-ripe they are sour. Likewise, bananas are sweetest when they are lush ripe, with speckled skin. If more customers would simply refuse the stone-hard pears and peaches that dealers offer, ripe ones would soon appear in their place!

# 20

## Follow the Stars
## to Easy Weight Loss!

It is customary in books on weight control to pepper the pages with menus prescribing exactly what you should eat. While writing this book I have become more and more convinced that it is better to provide readers with clear information which will enable them to make their own menus. In the preceding chapters on mineral salts and roughage, I have endeavored to do this. Reread them, and you will have no difficulty in deciding at any time what to eat.

Get it fixed in your mind that (1) the most fattening foods are those made with sugar, fat, and flour; that (2) you should be on your guard also against foods rich in proteins (meats, eggs, dried legumes) because, while these are not so fattening as sweets and starches, they overwork and clog the organs of waste elimination (liver, kidneys, thyroid), thus soaking the whole body with fatigue poisons, with the result that your will to reduce becomes flabby; that (3) your best friends are vegetables and fruits, of which you may eat almost gluttonously with impunity, and with the advantage that they are needed for bulk or roughage and for plenty of mineral salts.

This method has the advantage of not compelling you to adopt a rigid system of self-denial and overturning all your food habits.

## VARIETY IS THE SPICE OF LIFE!

It's hard to stick to a "blah" diet, one which is monotonous or consists of mainly one or two foods. In addition, many diets do not make allowance for weather, climate, and season. The warmer the weather the easier it is to reduce. Heat raises the metabolism. Thus, on a summer maintenance diet, a few extra sweet snacks may be included, without adding to your weight.

A very special reason for variety is to make sure that we get into our stomachs all the food minerals we need. Some are scarce; and different foods vary greatly, as we have seen, in their mineral content. Therefore, in making your own menus, put in as many different foods—particularly vegetables and fruits—as possible. It is not necessary to have many different things at each meal, provided the desirable variety is included in successive meals.

If I may seem to overemphasize the need of food minerals, it is because most other writers on the subject, while dwelling on the importance of menus in which the other food elements (proteins, carbohydrates, fats) are properly balanced, have ignored the minerals or simply mentioned them as "among those present."

In making your own menus you must, of course, have some way of knowing if you are doing the right thing. A good pair of scales will tell you. Weigh yourself regularly, always at the same hour and making allowance for clothing. And if you are not losing—or if you are gaining on a maintenance diet—put the screws tighter on the sweets, starches, and fats, while eating correspondingly more of the vegetables and fruits. What could be simpler than this method of weight control?

On a maintenance diet, such as I am suggesting here, there's no hurry. If you gain a few pounds, you can take them off easily—often in as little as one day—on the speed reducing diet. More than likely, your weight will not fluctuate too much, and if you wish to lose gradually, simply emphasize the speed reducing foods, and you may still enjoy many of your favorites. If you lose a pound a week, that makes fifty-two in a year, which is probably more than enough.

Remember that flavor and mineral salts are by far the most important things for you. These you want in profusion, all other things in moderation—except bran and other cellulose. This "bran new" doctrine is really one that is ahead of its time; it is the doctrine of the immediate future. It will rid the world of obesity and all the ills that go with it.

## A SATISFYING BREAKFAST!

The average American breakfast menu is made up almost entirely of fattening foods; one would think it had been planned especially for emaciated persons who wish to get stout quickly. It begins usually with a cereal to which cream or milk is added, and several spoonfuls of sugar. Then come bacon and eggs, likewise fattening. Then griddle cakes, with butter and syrup. Potatoes go with the bacon or ham; bread and butter are never absent, and the coffee, too, is made fattening with cream and sugar. It's enough to make you laugh—or weep. Advice to overweights about to eat that kind of breakfast: *Don't*.

Why not? Haven't I approved of every one of those items, allowing you to eat anything you like? Yes—but in moderation. You may have *some* cereal with trimmings; or *some* bacon (two or three thin slices and one egg); or two thin griddle cakes, with a *little* syrup; or a slice or two of whole-wheat bread with a little butter—but not all these things at once in great quantity.

"But I'll starve on such a restricted diet," you exclaim.

Don't worry. Admit it! What you are really after is *pleasure*, not nourishment, for you know that you are overnourished. But you need not lose any pleasure. If you use your sense of taste, savoring each mouthful, you'll discover endless pleasure in a mere fraction of the breakfast you are eating now. That's the great lesson of this book.

Nor is that all. You can get a lot more fun by also eating vegetables and fruits with your breakfast. Of these you can eat *as much as you like*.

Vegetables at breakfast? Why not? Why not for a change a small sweet potato, or a taste of parsnip, or Jerusalem artichoke, or carrots, or spinach, or chard, or eggplant, or onions, or celery, or coleslaw, or sauerkraut, or tomatoes, or peas, squash, cauliflower, and so on?

Raw vegetables are particularly desirable for your breakfast—celery, tomatoes, yellow turnips, peas, corn, radishes, asparagus tips, cucumbers—all these are better and more valuable raw than cooked; when you eat them raw you know that none of the precious minerals have been wasted in the cooking water.

If you prefer your breakfast vegetables warm, they can be cooked in a hundred appetizing ways, preferably as a soup.

"Soup for breakfast? Are you crazy?"

No, ma'am, I am *not* crazy. I'm from Missouri. Therefore I want to be shown, and no one has ever shown me why I should not eat soup the first thing in the morning. I have never in my life abstained from doing sensible things simply because other people didn't do them.

Breakfast is the very time for *thick* soups. You don't want a thick soup for dinner, because several other nourishing foods follow it; but for breakfast a thick vegetable soup is just the thing. The French eat onion soup for breakfast all the time! Try it; you will be delighted and hugely benefited.

Many years ago, soldiers who were dying on starchy "dead" food were revived with a soup made of wheat bran, cabbage, carrots, parsnips, spinach, onions, turnips, and potato skins (to which were added, gradually, unbuttered whole-wheat bread and egg yolks, orange juice, and milk). Forty-seven of the stricken were dismissed from the hospital in ten days as cured.

If vegetable soup can work such a quick miracle on dying men, think what it can do for you if you are simply tired, sluggish and overweight because you don't eat enough mineral food!

If every man, woman, and child ate such a vegetable soup for breakfast instead of cereals, and sweets, within a year most doctors specializing in obesity would have to find another line of work, and obesity would vanish.

## A WONDERFUL WAY TO START THE DAY!

Try fruits for breakfast! It seems revolutionary, but it's an old American custom! Raw or cooked fruits are always delicious and wholesome, and, with the exception of bananas, grapes, and avocados, can be eaten in unlimited quantities!

Raw fruit is best. If you want it cooked, apple sauce (with little sugar) is preferable to prunes. A prune is a plum which has so much sugar in it that when exposed to the sun it does not decay (like other plums), but dries. Dried apricots, peaches, cherries, tomatoes, have little sugar content and will serve as delectable substitutes for prunes.

There are some persons with whom fruit does not agree. But in most of these cases the trouble is they don't chew it thoroughly. This is particularly true of bananas, apples, pears, and pineapples. Avoid unripe, overripe, and sweet canned fruits. Raw fresh fruits are best. Banish the sugar bowl from your table. You will soon enjoy the natural flavor of fruits, including berries, much more.

After a night's rest the stomach's muscles and glands are refreshed and strengthened. Normal persons can, therefore, eat things at breakfast which it might not be so safe to take later in the day. The breakfast table is for this reason a good place for gastronomic experiments—all sorts of mixtures.

This makes mealtime more interesting—gives us a chance to use our brains, judgment, taste. More than once I have been laughed at for my novel breakfast mixtures by persons who did not realize how funny *they* were.

## SANDWICHES FOR LUNCH!

For city dwellers who are overweight, the lunch question is a serious one. In nine out of ten restaurants, it's difficult to get anything really edible except meats and sweets. Vegetables and fruits are treated as mere trimmings; if you try to make a meal of them the waiter thinks you're crazy. But there are signs of improvement, places where you can get a "vegetable dinner," vegetable soup, and plain or mixed salads. Stick to vegetables and you'll have no trouble eating out.

Your best bet is to pack a lunch, thereby saving money, as well as time for a midday walk. Sandwiches are naturally preferred for office lunches, and there is no reason why you shouldn't have them. Use high fiber toast, diet margarine or diet mayonnaise (high fiber bread has half the calories of regular bread, but needs toasting for flavor). Or you may use a *little* butter. You may eat one or two sandwiches. The filling may be almost anything, although non-fattening ingredients (vegetables and fruits) will, of course, accelerate your weight loss.

Hundreds of sandwich combinations are possible. Sample: lettuce and tomato; egg salad; hard-boiled eggs; preserved fruits, marmalades, and jellies, thinly spread because they are sweet; American or Swiss Cheese (with mustard); ham or ham and cheese; chicken (with ketchup); cold cuts; thin sliced roast beef; even peanut butter and jelly.

There are hundreds of kinds of crackers and fancy biscuits for your office lunch. You don't want to eat sugar wafers or sugar cookies, but among the others there are plenty you can eat—in moderation, of course, as they are all made of flour, which turns to sugar in the system.

If your breakfast has not been fattening and you intend to eat no sweet dessert with your dinner, there is no reason why you should not have a few dates or figs for lunch; or a few nuts—a dozen delicious kinds to choose from and to vary your office menu.

There is more lasting flavor in nuts than in anything else; you can chew and chew forever on an almond or pecan or walnut, or a hazel or Brazil nut, getting no end of pleasure out of its flavor. By adding to nuts or fruits some lettuce or other greens you get a balanced ration to sustain life.

But of all midday meals, fruit lunches are the best because fruit is almost all water and mineral salts, which are absorbed at once, putting no burden on the stomach and keeping your brain clear for the afternoon's work.

## SIX-COURSE DINNERS ARE OKAY!

It's the easiest thing in the world—after you have read the foregoing chapters—to arrange the bill of fare for dinners that are at once enjoyable and not fattening.

You may safely allow yourself five or six courses—soup, hors d'oeuvres, fish or meat, vegetables, dessert. I put soups first because they can be filling, low in calories, and appetizing. Soup is not often included in weight-reducing menus, evidently because of the mistaken notion that they are fattening. But soups are not fattening, unless specially made so. Use clear soups if you plan a heavy dinner.

To make their soups flavorful, the French, as we have seen, use bones (pulverized with a mallet) as well as meats and savory herbs galore. Add the gravy and remains of yesterday's dinner—anything to insure plenty of gastronomic pleasure. There are 700 French soups to choose from!

Hors d'oeuvres are particularly important to overweights; not the Scandinavian and Russian kinds made up of meat and fish sandwiches, sausage and other cold cuts, pickles and diverse things that make a meal in themselves, but the more civilized kind which includes celery, radishes, an olive or two, and—well, yes, a thin slice of brown bread with a teaspoonful of caviar will do no harm—it's very appetizing (if you like it).

Why not vary this by adding raw vegetables? Baby turnips or carrots, asparagus tips, and so on, might be used, with all their mineral salts intact.

If you eat meat or fish, choose the leaner sorts; eat slowly and don't forget to savor it. Meat is distinctly a pleasure food. To eat too much of it is undoubtedly bad for your health; why, therefore, eat a big portion or a second helping, since you know how to get more pleasure from one small portion?

How about vegetables? Of these you may eat aplenty unless they are cooked with cream sauce or too much grease. Eat them with your meat, or as a separate course, as the French do. Same with salads. Every dinner should include a salad, and a cooked vegetable or two, besides the raw ones included among the hors d'oeuvres. That is the way to slimness and health.

Sweets for dessert are permitted in moderation, but fruits, including berries—raw or cooked—are the best.

## FOLLOW THE STARS TO EASY WEIGHT LOSS!

Here are two sets of sample menus, each of them covering three meals a day for a week, one for warm weather—whenever it may come—the other for cold weather. They are intended for the use of busy persons who want to begin to reduce in an easy, effortless, gradual way.

If any of the dishes on the following menus do not appeal to your taste, substitute others of the same value. If you choose wrong ones, the scales will tell at once. I hesitated a moment to prescribe vegetable soup for breakfast because for anyone outside of France that means a startling innovation—and most people are discouragingly stubborn in their food habits. I am, however, convinced that if you will oblige me by trying my plan for a few weeks, you will feel so exhilarated, so delighted with your increased vitality and efficiency, that you will eat vegetable soup for breakfast—or make it lunch if you prefer—from now on. Naturally homemade soup is best. Use fresh or frozen vegetables whenever possible. Use canned tomatoes, corn, pod beans, okra, asparagus, or peas if you cannot get the fresh or frozen kind.

To eliminate the nuisance of having scales and mathematics in the dining room, I have devised the simple plan of marking with one star (*) those dishes of which you should partake sparingly; ** means the things which you may eat somewhat more freely; while *** means eat all you please—and more; you cannot have too much in the way of mineral salts, and you need a lot of roughage to escape autointoxication. If you have two or three complete bowel movements a day there is perhaps no reason why you should not have meat twice a day.

So far as individuals are concerned, these sample menus are of course more or less experimental; some persons have to cut down their food intake more heroically than others. If you find you are losing less than a pound a week you must eat less of the ** dishes and still less of the *

Reduction of weight can be accelerated considerably by omitting one breakfast, one lunch, and one dinner each week; or by taking only two meals a day regularly. Hunger pangs ought to please you; they mean that your fat is being gnawed at. They can be appeased (without stopping that process) by sipping a glass of water or nibbling a raw vegetable.

No sugar or cream or salt, please, with fruit, berries, and cereals. Soon you will not miss them. Learn to like natural flavors. The fruits, vegetables, and salads in these menus are interchangeable—according to what the market provides. If you are constipated, don't forget the roughage foods with each meal.

### Warm Weather Menus

#### Monday

| *Breakfast* | *Lunch* | *Dinner* |
|---|---|---|
| *** Vegetable soup or | *** Lettuce salad (no oil) | ** Chicken soup |
| *** 1 apple, or orange | ** Cheese sandwich (Swiss or American) | ** Roast beef |
| ** 2 slices high fiber toast with margarine | ** 1 pear or 2 peaches | *** Asparagus or stewed carrots (or both) |
| *** Coffee, tea or milk | *** Coffee, tea or milk | ** 2 slices high fiber toast with coffee, tea or milk |
| | | * Ice cream |

Tuesday

| *Breakfast* | *Lunch* | *Dinner* |
|---|---|---|
| *** Vegetable soup or | ** Broiled fish, lean (or cold ham, lean) | *** Tomato soup (clear) |
| *** 1 orange and/or | ** 1 sliced cucumber (fresh) or | ** 2 small lamb chops |
| *** ½ cantaloupe | *** 1 tomato | *** Spinach (or peas, or pod beans) |
| ** A bran muffin with | * 1 slice whole wheat bread | *** Berries (no sugar or cream) |
| *** Coffee, tea or milk | *** Coffee, tea or milk | *** Coffee or tea |

Wednesday

| *Breakfast* | *Lunch* | *Dinner* |
|---|---|---|
| *** 1 orange or ½ cantaloupe | *** Vegetable salad | *** Bouillon (or boiled onions) |
| ** Poached egg on toast | * Tongue sandwich on whole wheat bread (any condiment) | ** Broiled chicken (no skin) |
| *** Coffee, tea or milk | * 2 figs or 3 dates | *** Lettuce and tomato salad |
| | *** Coffee, tea or milk | *** Coffee, tea or milk |
| | | ** Orange or lemon sherbet |

Thursday

| *Breakfast* | *Lunch* | *Dinner* |
|---|---|---|
| *** ½ grapefruit or 1 orange | *** Spinach or carrots | *** Tomato soup |
| ** Oatmeal, with 2 spoonfuls of bran with skim milk | *** Cottage cheese | ** Beefsteak |
| *** Coffee, tea or milk | * Rhubarb or peach or apple pie | ** Steamed potatoes with parsley |
| | *** Coffee, tea or milk | *** Strawberries (no cream) |
| | | *** Coffee, tea or milk |

## Friday

| *Breakfast* | *Lunch* | *Dinner* |
|---|---|---|
| *** ½ cantaloupe | *** Vegetable soup or | ** Consommé with egg poached in it |
| ** Shredded wheat with skim milk | *** Raw, grated carrots with a dash of diet Mayonnaise and a few raisins | *** Sliced tomatoes |
| *** Coffee or tea | * Tongue or egg sandwich | ** Fish, in season, plain or with lemon |
| | *** Coffee, tea or milk | *** Peas or pod beans |
| | ** 1 pear or 2 peaches | *** Coffee, tea or milk |
| | | * Ice cream |

## Saturday

| *Breakfast* | *Lunch* | *Dinner* |
|---|---|---|
| *** ½ grapefruit | *** Lettuce and tomato salad | ** Potato or pea soup |
| * 1 egg, poached, boiled or coddled | * Tongue sandwich | * Olives |
| ** 2 slices high fiber toast with diet margarine | ** ½ cantaloupe or pear | ** Roast lamb |
| *** Coffee, tea or milk | *** Beverage | *** Spinach or carrots |
| | | *** ½ cantaloupe or 2 peaches |

## Sunday

| *Breakfast* | *Lunch* | *Dinner* |
|---|---|---|
| *** ½ grapefruit | *** Stewed tomatoes | ** Clear broth |
| * 1 poached or boiled egg | ** Cheese sandwich (Swiss or American) | ** Chicken, any style |
| ** 2 slices high fiber toast with margarine | *** Coffee, tea or milk | *** Boiled onions (or carrots, peas, or pod beans) |
| *** Beverage | *** Peaches or plums | ** 1 steamed potato |
| | | *** Beverage |
| | | * Ice cream |

## Cold Weather Menus

Monday

| *Breakfast* | *Lunch* | *Dinner* |
|---|---|---|
| *** Vegetable soup | *** Spinach with 1 | *** Tomato soup |
| ** 2 slices high | poached egg | (fresh or |
| fiber toast with | ** Cheese and | canned) |
| diet margarine | crackers | *** Raw celery |
| *** Coffee, tea or | *** Coffee, tea or | ** Roast lamb |
| milk | milk | ** 1 steamed |
| *** 1 orange | | potato |
| | | *** Romaine or |
| | | lettuce salad |
| | | *** Sliced oranges |
| | | or ½ grapefruit |

Tuesday

| *Breakfast* | *Lunch* | *Dinner* |
|---|---|---|
| ** 1 apple or pear | *** ½ grapefruit or | *** Mutton broth |
| or preserved | 1 orange | ** Roast chicken |
| blueberries | * 1 tongue or beef | (no skin or |
| * 1 poached egg | sandwich | stuffing) |
| ** 2 slices high | *** Celery salad or | *** Boiled onions |
| fiber toast with | plain celery | *** Cranberry |
| diet margarine | *** Beverage | sauce |
| *** Beverage | | *** Endive or |
| | | lettuce salad |
| | | *** 1 apple |

Wednesday

| *Breakfast* | *Lunch* | *Dinner* |
|---|---|---|
| *** Vegetable soup, | * Spaghetti with | ** Chicken soup |
| or | tomato sauce | *** Raw celery |
| * 2 thin slices of | *** Vegetable salad | ** Fish or roast |
| broiled bacon | *** Apple or pear | beef, lean |
| with 1 egg (not | *** Beverage | *** Vegetable salad |
| fried) | | *** Coffee, tea or |
| *** Coffee or tea | | milk |
| ** 1 slice high | | ** Orange or |
| fiber toast | | lemon sherbet |

## Thursday

| Breakfast | Lunch | Dinner |
|---|---|---|
| *** ½ grapefruit or 1 orange | ** Stewed fruit | *** Tomato soup |
| * 1 corn muffin or 2 slices high fiber toast | *** Squash | *** Grated carrots |
| *** Coffee, tea or milk | * Deep dish apple pie | ** Roast turkey |
| | *** Coffee, tea or milk | *** Cranberry sauce |
| | | *** Endive, romaine or lettuce salad |
| | | ** Cheese and crackers |
| | | *** Coffee, tea or milk |

## Friday

| Breakfast | Lunch | Dinner |
|---|---|---|
| *** Vegetable soup | ** Potato salad | ** Cream of celery soup |
| ** 2 slices high fiber toast with diet margarine | *** Cottage cheese and crackers | *** Broiled mushrooms or stewed carrots |
| *** Coffee, tea or milk | *** Coffee, tea or milk | ** Broiled fish (in season) |
| *** 1 orange | | *** Lettuce and tomato salad |
| | | *** 1 sliced orange, or an apple or pear |

## Saturday

| Breakfast | Lunch | Dinner |
|---|---|---|
| ** Finnan haddie, or fish soufflé | *** ½ grapefruit | *** Vegetable soup |
| * Toast and coffee | ** Plain omelette | *** Raw celery or stewed knob celery |
| *** 1 apple or pear | * Toast and coffee | ** Broiled steak |
| | *** Blueberries or strawberries | * Canned corn |
| | | *** Lettuce or escarole salad |
| | | *** 1 sliced orange |
| | | *** Coffee or tea |

Sunday

| *Breakfast* | *Lunch* | *Dinner* |
|---|---|---|
| *** Vegetable soup, or 4 raw soaked prunes | *** Spinach with 1 poached egg | *** Mutton, beef, or clam broth |
| * 2 slices broiled bacon | *** Fruit cocktail | *** Raw celery or radishes |
| ** 2 slices high fiber toast (diet margarine) | *** Coffee or tea | ** Roast or boiled chicken (no skin or dressing) |
| *** Coffee or tea | * 3 dates or 2 figs | *** Vegetable salad |
| | | ** 2 slices high fiber toast (diet margarine) |
| | | * Ice cream |

## HITCH YOUR WAGON TO THREE STARS!

Make up your mind to eat more slowly, which makes one helping equal to two, so far as pleasure is concerned, and *more pleasure* is what you want, not more food. Don't fool yourself by enriching the allowed dishes with sugar or oil, or eating anabolic (fattening) foods between meals. If you want to snack, munch on *catabolic* (speed reducing) foods, instead.

Watch the scales! They will tell whether these menus are right for you. If not, I have just told you how you can make them so. Hitch your wagon to three stars and you will soon startle your friends by your improved appearance, health, and efficiency. All aboard for a long life and a happy one!

# 21

## Your Instant Guide
## to Speed Reducing Foods!

On the following pages, you will find the calorie values of four-ounce portions of some 600 common foods and dishes.

All the definitely catabolic (speed reducing) foods have been underlined and marked with an asterisk. Remember please that these are actually *reducing* foods. For example, fresh orange is catabolic (it breaks down fat) because energy is required to digest the pulp. While fresh orange juice is not fattening, it is definitely not catabolic because no great energy expense is needed to digest it.

Soups, while low-caloried, cannot be considered catabolic because there is no great digestion expense.

Study the charts and try to remember the catabolic foods. The more you eat of these, the easier it will be to hold down your weight.

In general, you can reckon that any food which has a calorie value of 150 and under, for a four-ounce portion, will not be particularly fattening. The higher the calorie value, the more likely the food is to be fattening.

Please note especially how methods of preparation affect the calorie values of foods. Thus fried eggs are very much higher in calorie value than boiled eggs; creamed eggs even more so.

You will find a few fish, especially the shell fish, in the catabolic class. They are almost the only protein foods in this division. They are doubly useful, for they supply essential proteins and they do not add to the weight.

We have marked milk, acidophilus milk, buttermilk, and skim milk, in spite of the fact that they are, strictly speaking, not catabolic, because they are so useful in a reducing diet. They provide excellent food values.

Purchase a small notebook and record in it all the low-caloried meats and fish that you like. Note also the low-caloried foods in other divisions such as fruits, desserts, soups. This will be your personal chart, which will meet your tastes and desires and be a constant guide and reminder.

Please remember particularly that it is the gravies, the tidbits, and the dressings that turn a non-fattening dish into a fattening one.

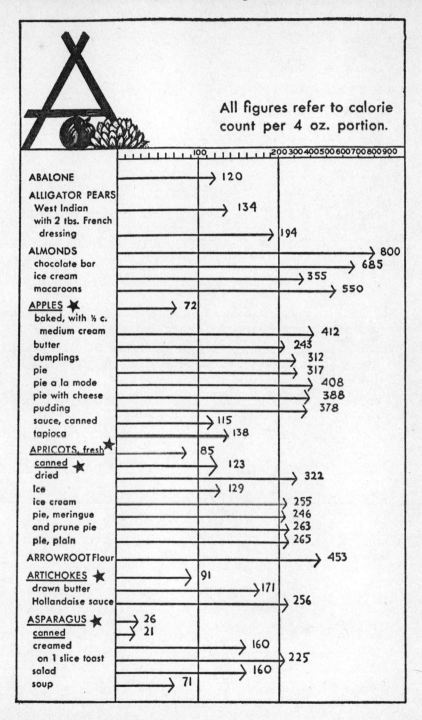

All figures refer to calorie count per 4 oz. portion.

|  |  |
|------|----------|
| ABALONE | 120 |
| ALLIGATOR PEARS West Indian | 134 |
| with 2 tbs. French dressing | 194 |
| ALMONDS | 800 |
| chocolate bar | 685 |
| ice cream | 355 |
| macaroons | 550 |
| APPLES ★ | 72 |
| baked, with ½ c. medium cream | 412 |
| butter | 243 |
| dumplings | 312 |
| pie | 317 |
| pie a la mode | 408 |
| pie with cheese | 388 |
| pudding | 378 |
| sauce, canned | 115 |
| tapioca | 138 |
| APRICOTS, fresh ★ | 85 |
| canned ★ | 123 |
| dried | 322 |
| Ice | 129 |
| ice cream | 255 |
| pie, meringue | 246 |
| and prune pie | 263 |
| pie, plain | 265 |
| ARROWROOT Flour | 453 |
| ARTICHOKES ★ | 91 |
| drawn butter | 171 |
| Hollandaise sauce | 256 |
| ASPARAGUS ★ | 26 |
| canned | 21 |
| creamed | 160 |
| on 1 slice toast | 225 |
| salad | 160 |
| soup | 71 |

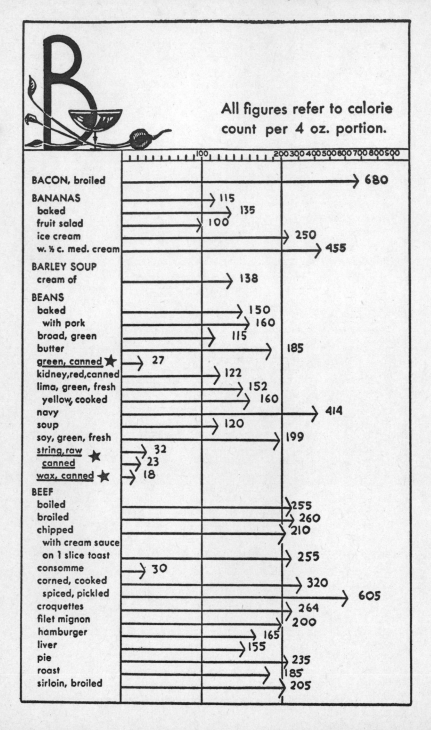

All figures refer to calorie count per 4 oz. portion.

|  |  |
|---|---|
| BACON, broiled | 680 |
| **BANANAS** | 115 |
| baked | 135 |
| fruit salad | 100 |
| ice cream | 250 |
| w. ½ c. med. cream | 455 |
| **BARLEY SOUP** | |
| cream of | 138 |
| **BEANS** | |
| baked | 150 |
| with pork | 160 |
| broad, green | 115 |
| butter | 185 |
| green, canned ★ | 27 |
| kidney, red, canned | 122 |
| lima, green, fresh | 152 |
| yellow, cooked | 160 |
| navy | 414 |
| soup | 120 |
| soy, green, fresh | 199 |
| string, raw ★ | 32 |
| canned | 23 |
| wax, canned ★ | 18 |
| **BEEF** | |
| boiled | 255 |
| broiled | 260 |
| chipped | 210 |
| with cream sauce on 1 slice toast | 255 |
| consomme | 30 |
| corned, cooked | 320 |
| spiced, pickled | 605 |
| croquettes | 264 |
| filet mignon | 200 |
| hamburger | 165 |
| liver | 155 |
| pie | 235 |
| roast | 185 |
| sirloin, broiled | 205 |

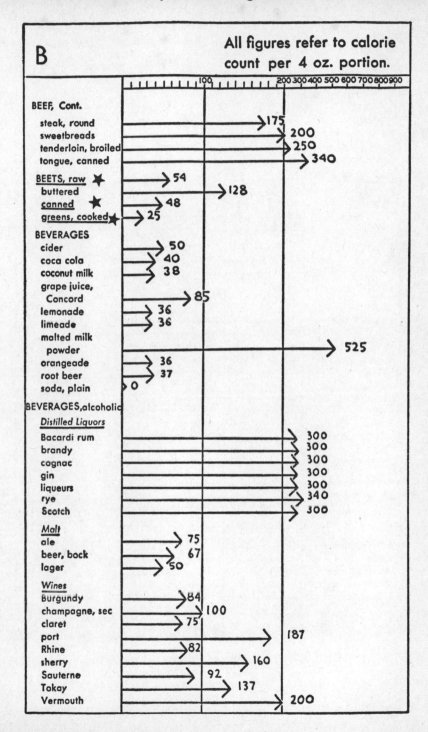

**B**

All figures refer to calorie count per 4 oz. portion.

| | |
|---|---|
| **BEEF, Cont.** | |
| steak, round | 175 |
| sweetbreads | 200 |
| tenderloin, broiled | 250 |
| tongue, canned | 340 |
| **BEETS, raw** ✸ | 54 |
| buttered | 128 |
| canned ✸ | 48 |
| greens, cooked ✸ | 25 |
| **BEVERAGES** | |
| cider | 50 |
| coca cola | 40 |
| coconut milk | 38 |
| grape juice, Concord | 85 |
| lemonade | 36 |
| limeade | 36 |
| malted milk powder | 525 |
| orangeade | 36 |
| root beer | 37 |
| soda, plain | 0 |
| **BEVERAGES, alcoholic** | |
| *Distilled Liquors* | |
| Bacardi rum | 300 |
| brandy | 300 |
| cognac | 300 |
| gin | 300 |
| liqueurs | 300 |
| rye | 340 |
| Scotch | 300 |
| *Malt* | |
| ale | 75 |
| beer, bock | 67 |
| lager | 50 |
| *Wines* | |
| Burgundy | 84 |
| champagne, sec | 100 |
| claret | 75 |
| port | 187 |
| Rhine | 82 |
| sherry | 160 |
| Sauterne | 92 |
| Tokay | 137 |
| Vermouth | 200 |

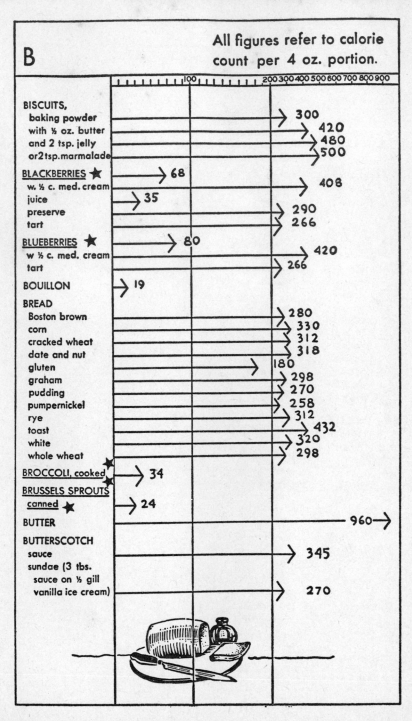

**B**

All figures refer to calorie count per 4 oz. portion.

| | 100 | | 200 300 400 500 600 700 800 900 |

BISCUITS,
  baking powder → 300
  with ½ oz. butter → 420
  and 2 tsp. jelly → 480
  or 2 tsp. marmalade → 500
BLACKBERRIES ★ → 68
  w. ½ c. med. cream → 408
  juice → 35
  preserve → 290
  tart → 266
BLUEBERRIES ★ → 80
  w ½ c. med. cream → 420
  tart → 266
BOUILLON → 19
BREAD
  Boston brown → 280
  corn → 330
  cracked wheat → 312
  date and nut → 318
  gluten → 180
  graham → 298
  pudding → 270
  pumpernickel → 258
  rye → 312
  toast → 432
  white → 320
  whole wheat → 298
BROCCOLI, cooked ★ → 34
BRUSSELS SPROUTS
  canned ★ → 24
BUTTER → 960 →
BUTTERSCOTCH
  sauce → 345
  sundae (3 tbs.
    sauce on ½ gill
    vanilla ice cream) → 270

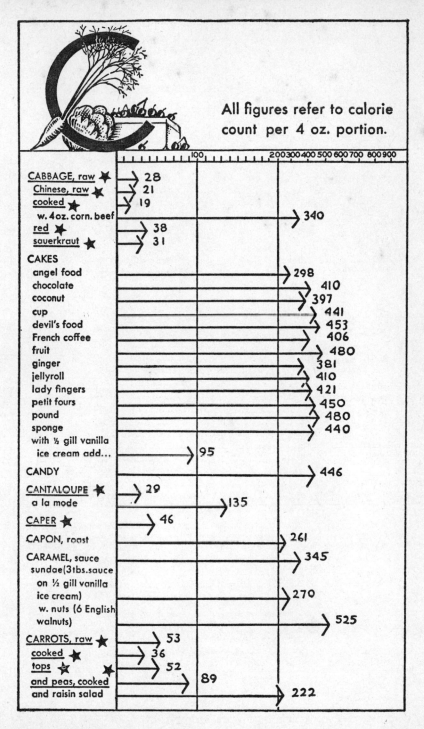

All figures refer to calorie count per 4 oz. portion.

|  | 100 | 200 300 400 500 600 700 800 900 |
|---|---|---|
| CABBAGE, raw ★ | 28 | |
| Chinese, raw ★ | 21 | |
| cooked ★ | 19 | |
| w. 4 oz. corn. beef | | 340 |
| red ★ | 38 | |
| sauerkraut ★ | 31 | |
| CAKES | | |
| angel food | | 298 |
| chocolate | | 410 |
| coconut | | 397 |
| cup | | 441 |
| devil's food | | 453 |
| French coffee | | 406 |
| fruit | | 480 |
| ginger | | 381 |
| jellyroll | | 410 |
| lady fingers | | 421 |
| petit fours | | 450 |
| pound | | 480 |
| sponge | | 440 |
| with ½ gill vanilla ice cream add... | 95 | |
| CANDY | | 446 |
| CANTALOUPE ★ | 29 | |
| a la mode | 135 | |
| CAPER ★ | 46 | |
| CAPON, roast | | 261 |
| CARAMEL, sauce | | 345 |
| sundae (3 tbs. sauce on ½ gill vanilla ice cream) | | 270 |
| w. nuts (6 English walnuts) | | 525 |
| CARROTS, raw ★ | 53 | |
| cooked ★ | 36 | |
| tops ☆  ★ | 52 | |
| and peas, cooked | 89 | |
| and raisin salad | | 222 |

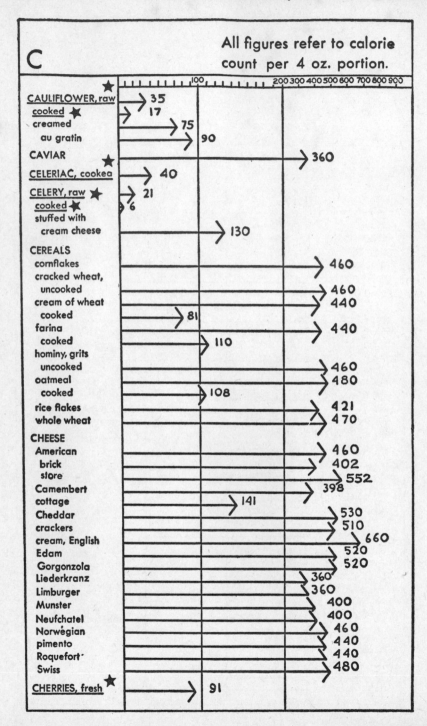

C

All figures refer to calorie count per 4 oz. portion.

|  |  |
|---|---|
| CAULIFLOWER, raw ★ | 35 |
| cooked ★ | 17 |
| creamed | 75 |
| au gratin | 90 |
| CAVIAR ★ | 360 |
| CELERIAC, cooked | 40 |
| CELERY, raw ★ | 21 |
| cooked ★ | 36 |
| stuffed with cream cheese | 130 |
| CEREALS cornflakes | 460 |
| cracked wheat, uncooked | 460 |
| cream of wheat | 440 |
| cooked | 81 |
| farina | 440 |
| cooked | 110 |
| hominy, grits uncooked | 460 |
| oatmeal | 480 |
| cooked | 108 |
| rice flakes | 421 |
| whole wheat | 470 |
| CHEESE American | 460 |
| brick | 402 |
| store | 552 |
| Camembert | 398 |
| cottage | 141 |
| Cheddar | 530 |
| crackers | 510 |
| cream, English | 660 |
| Edam | 520 |
| Gorgonzola | 520 |
| Liederkranz | 360 |
| Limburger | 360 |
| Munster | 400 |
| Neufchatel | 400 |
| Norwegian | 460 |
| pimento | 440 |
| Roquefort | 440 |
| Swiss | 480 |
| CHERRIES, fresh ★ | 91 |

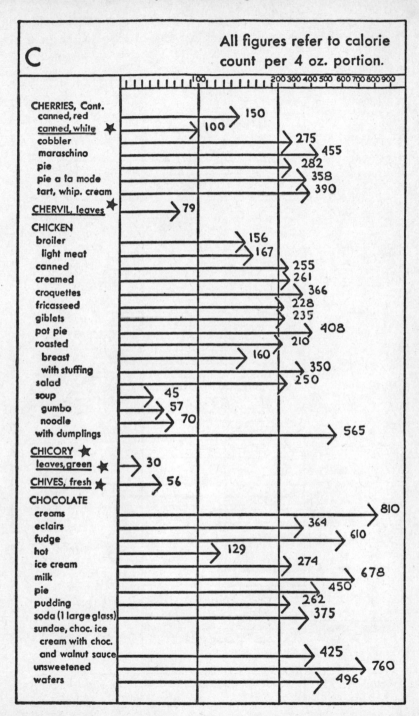

C

All figures refer to calorie count per 4 oz. portion.

|  |  |
|------|----------|
| **CHERRIES, Cont.** | |
| canned, red | 150 |
| canned, white ★ | 100 |
| cobbler | 275 |
| maraschino | 455 |
| pie | 282 |
| pie a la mode | 358 |
| tart, whip. cream | 390 |
| **CHERVIL, leaves ★** | 79 |
| **CHICKEN** | |
| broiler | 156 |
| light meat | 167 |
| canned | 255 |
| creamed | 261 |
| croquettes | 366 |
| fricasseed | 228 |
| giblets | 235 |
| pot pie | 408 |
| roasted | 210 |
| breast | 160 |
| with stuffing | 350 |
| salad | 250 |
| soup | 45 |
| gumbo | 57 |
| noodle | 70 |
| with dumplings | 565 |
| **CHICORY ★** | |
| leaves, green ★ | 30 |
| **CHIVES, fresh ★** | 56 |
| **CHOCOLATE** | |
| creams | 810 |
| eclairs | 364 |
| fudge | 610 |
| hot | 129 |
| ice cream | 274 |
| milk | 678 |
| pie | 450 |
| pudding | 262 |
| soda (1 large glass) | 375 |
| sundae, choc. ice cream with choc. and walnut sauce | 425 |
| unsweetened | 760 |
| wafers | 496 |

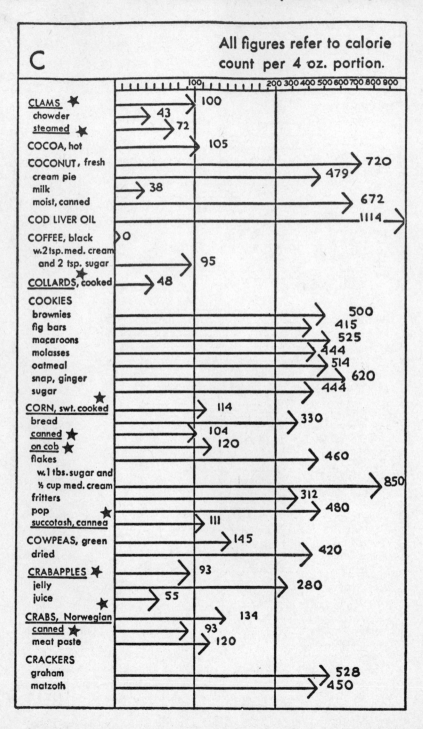

**C**

All figures refer to calorie count per 4 oz. portion.

|  |  |
|---|---|
| CLAMS ★ | 100 |
| chowder | 43 |
| steamed ★ | 72 |
| COCOA, hot | 105 |
| COCONUT, fresh | 720 |
| cream pie | 479 |
| milk | 38 |
| moist, canned | 672 |
| COD LIVER OIL | 1114 |
| COFFEE, black | 0 |
| w. 2 tsp. med. cream and 2 tsp. sugar | 95 |
| COLLARDS, cooked ★ | 48 |
| COOKIES | |
| brownies | 500 |
| fig bars | 415 |
| macaroons | 525 |
| molasses | 444 |
| oatmeal | 514 |
| snap, ginger | 620 |
| sugar | 444 |
| CORN, swt. cooked ★ | 114 |
| bread | 330 |
| canned ★ | 104 |
| on cob ★ | 120 |
| flakes | 460 |
| w. 1 tbs. sugar and ½ cup med. cream | 850 |
| fritters | 312 |
| pop | 480 |
| succotash, canned ★ | 111 |
| COWPEAS, green | 145 |
| dried | 420 |
| CRABAPPLES ★ | 93 |
| jelly | 280 |
| juice | 55 |
| CRABS, Norwegian ★ | 134 |
| canned ★ | 93 |
| meat paste | 120 |
| CRACKERS | |
| graham | 528 |
| matzoth | 450 |

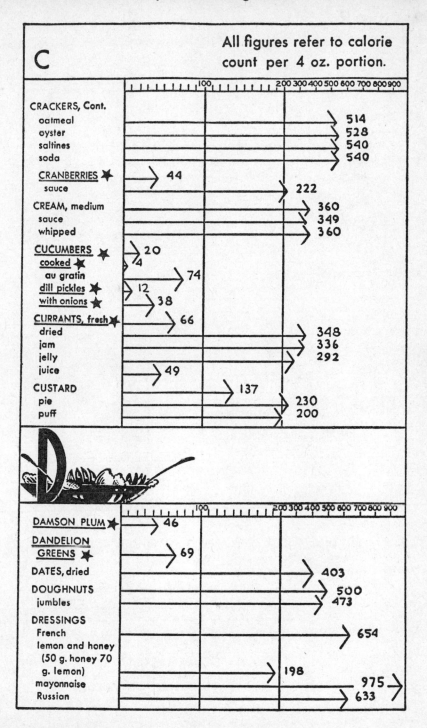

# C

All figures refer to calorie count per 4 oz. portion.

| | |
|---|---|
| **CRACKERS, Cont.** | |
| oatmeal | 514 |
| oyster | 528 |
| saltines | 540 |
| soda | 540 |
| **CRANBERRIES** ✸ | 44 |
| sauce | 222 |
| **CREAM, medium** | 360 |
| sauce | 349 |
| whipped | 360 |
| **CUCUMBERS** ✸ | 20 |
| cooked ✸ | 4 |
| au gratin | 74 |
| dill pickles ✸ | 12 |
| with onions ✸ | 38 |
| **CURRANTS, fresh** ✸ | 66 |
| dried | 348 |
| jam | 336 |
| jelly | 292 |
| juice | 49 |
| **CUSTARD** | 137 |
| pie | 230 |
| puff | 200 |

| | |
|---|---|
| **DAMSON PLUM** ✸ | 46 |
| **DANDELION GREENS** ✸ | 69 |
| **DATES, dried** | 403 |
| **DOUGHNUTS** | 500 |
| jumbles | 473 |
| **DRESSINGS** | |
| French | 654 |
| lemon and honey (50 g. honey 70 g. lemon) | 198 |
| mayonnaise | 975 |
| Russian | 633 |

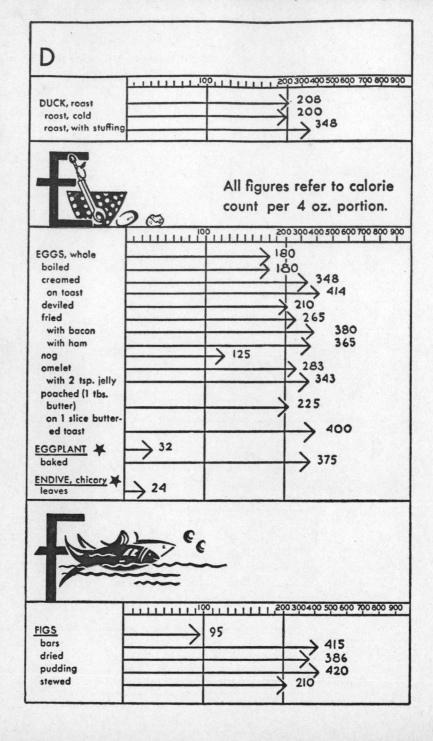

**D**

| | 100 | | 200 300 400 500 600 700 800 900 |
|---|---|---|---|
| DUCK, roast | | | 208 |
| roast, cold | | | 200 |
| roast, with stuffing | | | 348 |

**E**

All figures refer to calorie count per 4 oz. portion.

| | 100 | | 200 300 400 500 600 700 800 900 |
|---|---|---|---|
| EGGS, whole | | | 180 |
| boiled | | | 180 |
| creamed | | | 348 |
| on toast | | | 414 |
| deviled | | | 210 |
| fried | | | 265 |
| with bacon | | | 380 |
| with ham | | | 365 |
| nog | | 125 | |
| omelet | | | 283 |
| with 2 tsp. jelly | | | 343 |
| poached (1 tbs. butter) | | | 225 |
| on 1 slice buttered toast | | | 400 |
| EGGPLANT ✶ | 32 | | |
| baked | | | 375 |
| ENDIVE, chicory ✶ | 24 | | |
| leaves | | | |

**F**

| | 100 | | 200 300 400 500 600 700 800 900 |
|---|---|---|---|
| FIGS | 95 | | |
| bars | | | 415 |
| dried | | | 386 |
| pudding | | | 420 |
| stewed | | | 210 |

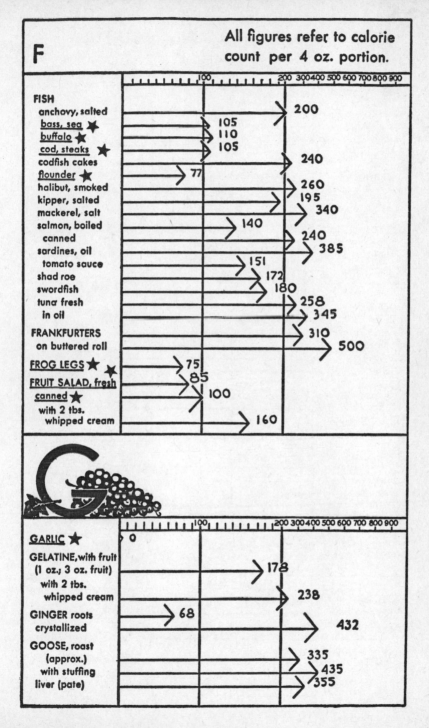

All figures refer to calorie count per 4 oz. portion.

**FISH**
anchovy, salted — 200
bass, sea ★ — 105
buffalo ★ — 110
cod, steaks ★ — 105
codfish cakes — 240
flounder ★ — 77
halibut, smoked — 260
kipper, salted — 195
mackerel, salt — 340
salmon, boiled — 140
canned — 240
sardines, oil — 385
tomato sauce — 151
shad roe — 172
swordfish — 180
tuna fresh — 258
in oil — 345

**FRANKFURTERS** — 310
on buttered roll — 500

**FROG LEGS** ★ — 75

**FRUIT SALAD, fresh** — 85
canned ★ — 100
with 2 tbs. whipped cream — 160

**GARLIC** ★ — 0

**GELATINE, with fruit**
(1 oz.; 3 oz. fruit) — 178
with 2 tbs. whipped cream — 238

**GINGER roots** — 68
crystallized — 432

**GOOSE, roast** (approx.) — 335
with stuffing — 435
liver (pate) — 355

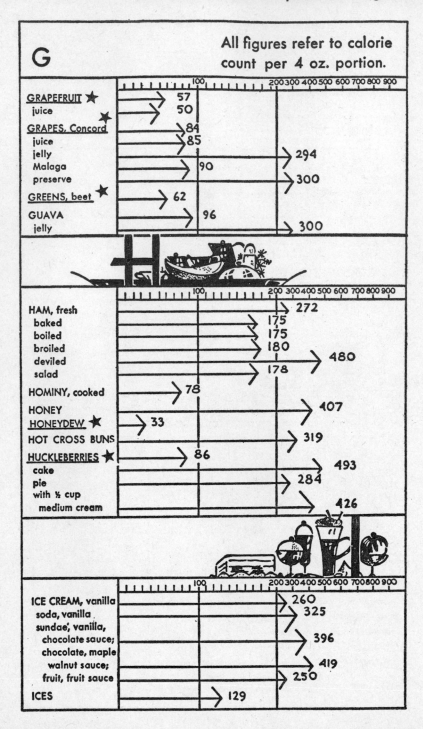

**G**

All figures refer to calorie count per 4 oz. portion.

GRAPEFRUIT ★ → 57
juice → 50
GRAPES, Concord ★ → 84
juice → 85
jelly → 294
Malaga → 90
preserve → 300
GREENS, beet ★ → 62
GUAVA → 96
jelly → 300

HAM, fresh → 272
baked → 175
boiled → 175
broiled → 180
deviled → 480
salad → 178
HOMINY, cooked → 78
HONEY → 407
HONEYDEW ★ → 33
HOT CROSS BUNS → 319
HUCKLEBERRIES ★ → 86
cake → 493
pie → 284
with ½ cup
  medium cream → 426

ICE CREAM, vanilla → 260
soda, vanilla → 325
sundae; vanilla,
  chocolate sauce; → 396
chocolate, maple
  walnut sauce; → 419
fruit, fruit sauce → 250
ICES → 129

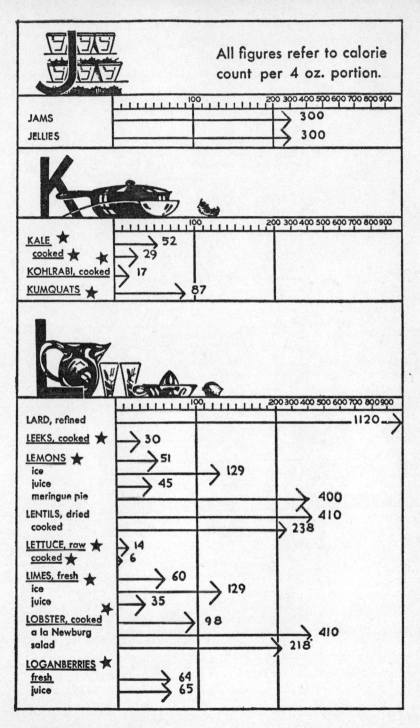

All figures refer to calorie
count per 4 oz. portion.

| | 100 | 200 300 400 500 600 700 800 900 |
|---|---|---|
| JAMS | | 300 |
| JELLIES | | 300 |

| | 100 | 200 300 400 500 600 700 800 900 |
|---|---|---|
| KALE ★ | 52 | |
| cooked ★ ★ | 29 | |
| KOHLRABI, cooked | 17 | |
| KUMQUATS ★ | 87 | |

| | 100 | 200 300 400 500 600 700 800 900 |
|---|---|---|
| LARD, refined | | 1120 → |
| LEEKS, cooked ★ | 30 | |
| LEMONS ★ | 51 | |
| ice | | 129 |
| juice | 45 | |
| meringue pie | | 400 |
| LENTILS, dried | | 410 |
| cooked | | 238 |
| LETTUCE, raw ★ | 14 | |
| cooked ★ | 6 | |
| LIMES, fresh ★ | 60 | |
| ice | | 129 |
| juice | 35 | |
| LOBSTER, cooked | 98 | |
| a la Newburg | | 410 |
| salad | | 218 |
| LOGANBERRIES ★ | | |
| fresh | 64 | |
| juice | 65 | |

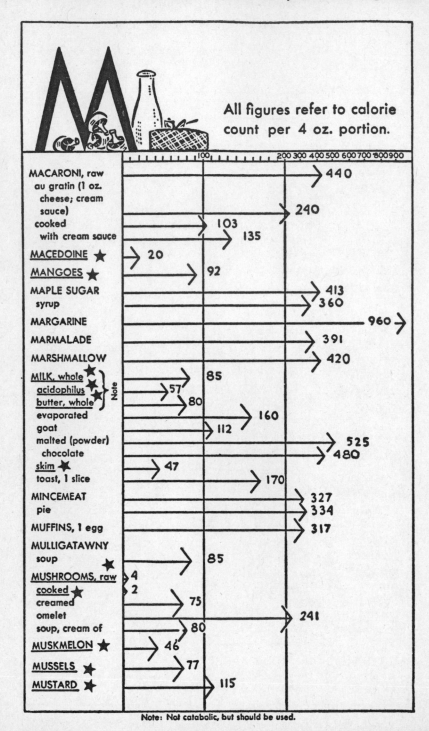

All figures refer to calorie count per 4 oz. portion.

|  |  |
|---|---|
| MACARONI, raw | 440 |
| au gratin (1 oz. cheese; cream sauce) | 240 |
| cooked | 103 |
| with cream sauce | 135 |
| MACEDOINE ★ | 20 |
| MANGOES ★ | 92 |
| MAPLE SUGAR | 413 |
| syrup | 360 |
| MARGARINE | 960 |
| MARMALADE | 391 |
| MARSHMALLOW | 420 |
| MILK, whole ★ | 85 |
| acidophilus ★ | 57 |
| butter, whole ★ | 80 |
| evaporated | 160 |
| goat | 112 |
| malted (powder) | 525 |
| chocolate | 480 |
| skim ★ | 47 |
| toast, 1 slice | 170 |
| MINCEMEAT | 327 |
| pie | 334 |
| MUFFINS, 1 egg | 317 |
| MULLIGATAWNY soup ★ | 85 |
| MUSHROOMS, raw | 4 |
| cooked ★ | 2 |
| creamed | 75 |
| omelet | 241 |
| soup, cream of | 80 |
| MUSKMELON ★ | 46 |
| MUSSELS ★ | 77 |
| MUSTARD ★ | 115 |

Note: Not catabolic, but should be used.

# M

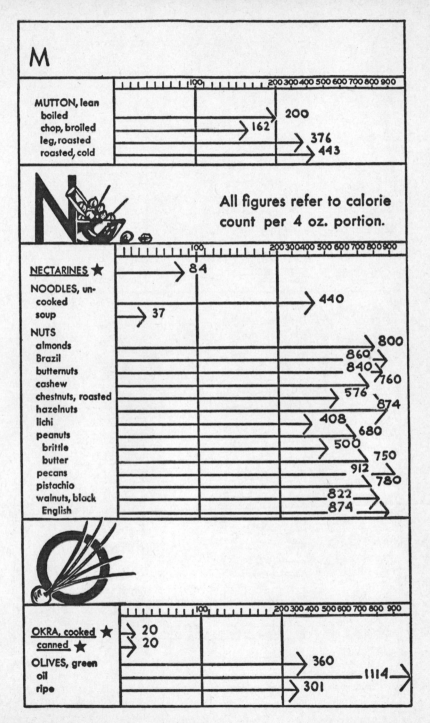

MUTTON, lean
  boiled — 200
  chop, broiled — 162
  leg, roasted — 376
  roasted, cold — 443

**All figures refer to calorie count per 4 oz. portion.**

NECTARINES ★ — 84

NOODLES, un-
  cooked — 440
  soup — 37

NUTS
  almonds — 800
  Brazil — 860
  butternuts — 840
  cashew — 760
  chestnuts, roasted — 576
  hazelnuts — 874
  lichi — 408
  peanuts — 680
    brittle — 500
    butter — 750
  pecans — 912
  pistachio — 780
  walnuts, black — 822
  English — 874

OKRA, cooked ★ — 20
canned ★ — 20

OLIVES, green — 360
  oil — 1114
  ripe — 301

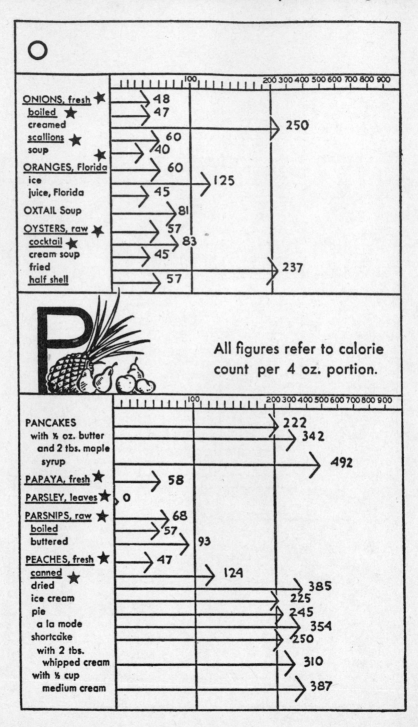

O

| | |
|---|---|
| ONIONS, fresh ★ | 48 |
| boiled ★ | 47 |
| creamed | 250 |
| scallions ★ | 60 |
| soup ★ | 40 |
| ORANGES, Florida ★ | 60 |
| ice | 125 |
| juice, Florida | 45 |
| OXTAIL Soup | 81 |
| OYSTERS, raw ★ | 57 |
| cocktail ★ | 83 |
| cream soup | 45 |
| fried | 237 |
| half shell | 57 |

**All figures refer to calorie count per 4 oz. portion.**

| | |
|---|---|
| PANCAKES | 222 |
| with ½ oz. butter and 2 tbs. maple syrup | 342 |
| | 492 |
| PAPAYA, fresh ★ | 58 |
| PARSLEY, leaves ★ | 0 |
| PARSNIPS, raw ★ | 68 |
| boiled | 57 |
| buttered | 93 |
| PEACHES, fresh ★ | 47 |
| canned ★ | 124 |
| dried | 385 |
| ice cream | 225 |
| pie | 245 |
| a la mode | 354 |
| shortcake | 250 |
| with 2 tbs. whipped cream | 310 |
| with ½ cup medium cream | 387 |

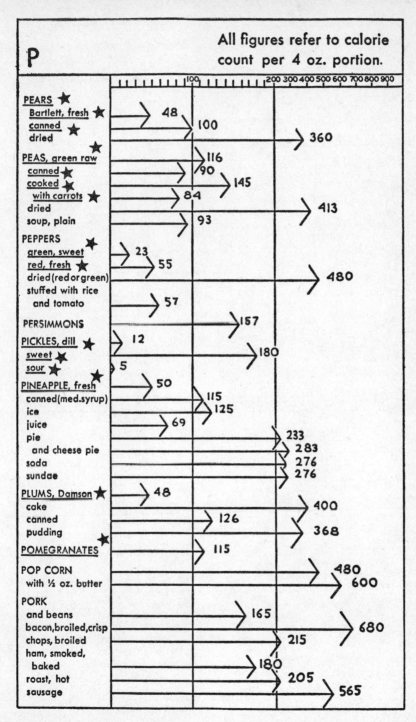

**P**

All figures refer to calorie count per 4 oz. portion.

100    200 300 400 500 600 700 800 900

PEARS ★
  Bartlett, fresh ★ → 48
  canned ★ → 100
  dried → 360
PEAS, green raw → 116
  canned ★ → 90
  cooked ★ → 145
    with carrots ★ → 84
  dried → 413
  soup, plain → 93
PEPPERS ★
  green, sweet → 23
  red, fresh ★ → 55
  dried (red or green) → 480
  stuffed with rice
    and tomato → 57
PERSIMMONS → 157
PICKLES, dill ★ → 12
  sweet ★ → 180
  sour ★ → 5
PINEAPPLE, fresh ★ → 50
  canned (med. syrup) → 115
  ice → 125
  juice → 69
  pie → 233
    and cheese pie → 283
  soda → 276
  sundae → 276
PLUMS, Damson ★ → 48
  cake → 400
  canned → 126
  pudding → 368
POMEGRANATES ★ → 115
POP CORN → 480
  with ½ oz. butter → 600
PORK
  and beans → 165
  bacon, broiled, crisp → 680
  chops, broiled → 215
  ham, smoked,
    baked → 180
  roast, hot → 205
  sausage → 565

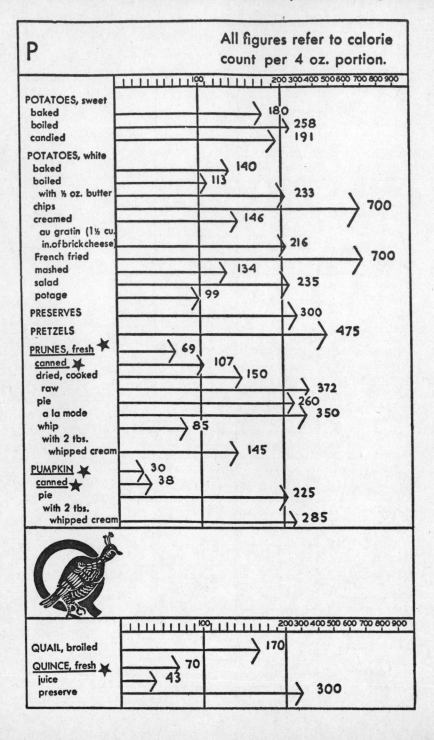

**P**

All figures refer to calorie count per 4 oz. portion.

| | |
|---|---|
| POTATOES, sweet | |
| baked | 180 |
| boiled | 258 |
| candied | 191 |
| POTATOES, white | |
| baked | 140 |
| boiled | 113 |
| with ½ oz. butter | 233 |
| chips | 700 |
| creamed | 146 |
| au gratin (1½ cu. in. of brick cheese) | 216 |
| French fried | 700 |
| mashed | 134 |
| salad | 235 |
| potage | 99 |
| PRESERVES | 300 |
| PRETZELS | 475 |
| PRUNES, fresh ★ | 69 |
| canned ★ | 107 |
| dried, cooked | 150 |
| raw | 372 |
| pie | 260 |
| a la mode | 350 |
| whip | 85 |
| with 2 tbs. whipped cream | 145 |
| PUMPKIN ★ | 30 |
| canned ★ | 38 |
| pie | 225 |
| with 2 tbs. whipped cream | 285 |

| | |
|---|---|
| QUAIL, broiled | 170 |
| QUINCE, fresh ★ | 70 |
| juice | 43 |
| preserve | 300 |

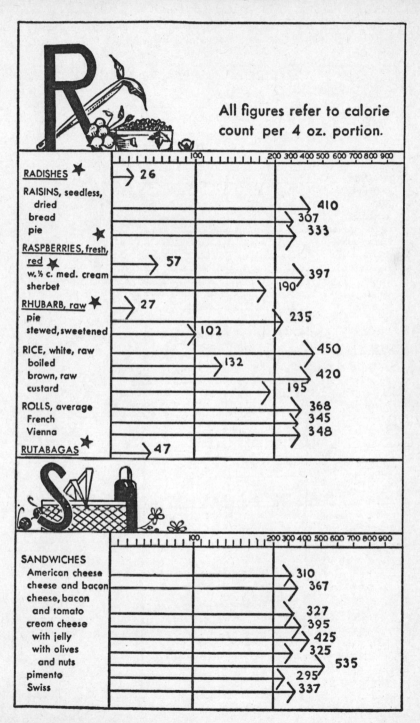

All figures refer to calorie count per 4 oz. portion.

|  |  |
|------|----------|
| RADISHES ★ | 26 |
| RAISINS, seedless, dried | 410 |
| bread | 307 |
| pie ★ | 333 |
| RASPBERRIES, fresh, red ★ | 57 |
| w. ½ c. med. cream | 397 |
| sherbet | 190 |
| RHUBARB, raw ★ | 27 |
| pie | 235 |
| stewed, sweetened | 102 |
| RICE, white, raw | 450 |
| boiled | 132 |
| brown, raw | 420 |
| custard | 195 |
| ROLLS, average | 368 |
| French | 345 |
| Vienna | 348 |
| RUTABAGAS ★ | 47 |

|  |  |
|------|----------|
| SANDWICHES |  |
| American cheese | 310 |
| cheese and bacon | 367 |
| cheese, bacon and tomato | 327 |
| cream cheese | 395 |
| with jelly | 425 |
| with olives and nuts | 325 |
| pimento | 535 |
| | 295 |
| Swiss | 337 |

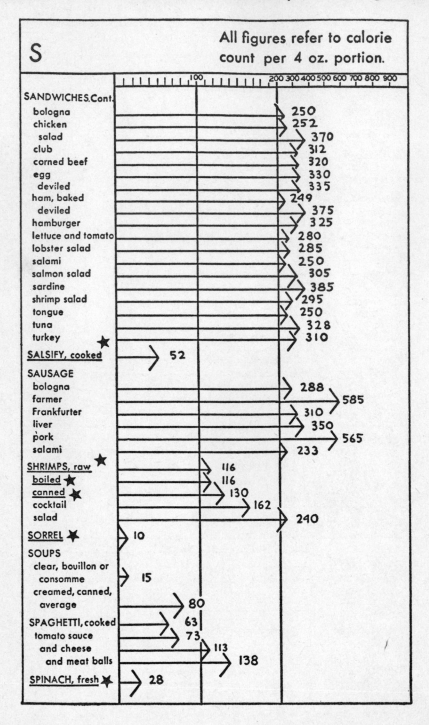

| S | All figures refer to calorie count per 4 oz. portion. |
|---|---|

**SANDWICHES, Cont.**
bologna — 250
chicken — 252
salad — 370
club — 312
corned beef — 320
egg — 330
deviled — 335
ham, baked — 249
deviled — 375
hamburger — 325
lettuce and tomato — 280
lobster salad — 285
salami — 250
salmon salad — 305
sardine — 385
shrimp salad — 295
tongue — 250
tuna — 328
turkey — 310

**SALSIFY, cooked** ★ — 52

**SAUSAGE**
bologna — 288
farmer — 585
Frankfurter — 310
liver — 350
pork — 565
salami — 233

**SHRIMPS, raw** ★ — 116
boiled ★ — 116
canned ★ — 130
cocktail — 162
salad — 240

**SORREL** ★ — 10

**SOUPS**
clear, bouillon or consomme — 15
creamed, canned, average — 80

**SPAGHETTI, cooked** — 63
tomato sauce — 73
and cheese — 113
and meat balls — 138

**SPINACH, fresh** ★ — 28

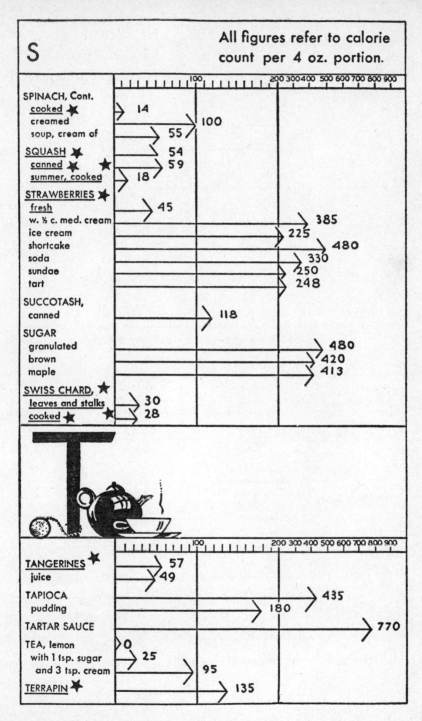

| **S** | All figures refer to calorie count per 4 oz. portion. |
|---|---|

| | |
|---|---|
| SPINACH, Cont. | |
| cooked ★ | 14 |
| creamed | 100 |
| soup, cream of | 55 |
| SQUASH ★ | 54 |
| canned ★ ★ | 59 |
| summer, cooked | 18 |
| STRAWBERRIES ★ | |
| fresh | 45 |
| w. ½ c. med. cream | 385 |
| ice cream | 225 |
| shortcake | 480 |
| soda | 330 |
| sundae | 250 |
| tart | 248 |
| SUCCOTASH, | |
| canned | 118 |
| SUGAR | |
| granulated | 480 |
| brown | 420 |
| maple | 413 |
| SWISS CHARD, ★ | |
| leaves and stalks | 30 |
| cooked ★ ★ | 28 |

**T**

| | |
|---|---|
| TANGERINES ★ | 57 |
| juice | 49 |
| TAPIOCA | 435 |
| pudding | 180 |
| TARTAR SAUCE | 770 |
| TEA, lemon | 0 |
| with 1 tsp. sugar | 25 |
| and 3 tsp. cream | 95 |
| TERRAPIN ★ | 135 |

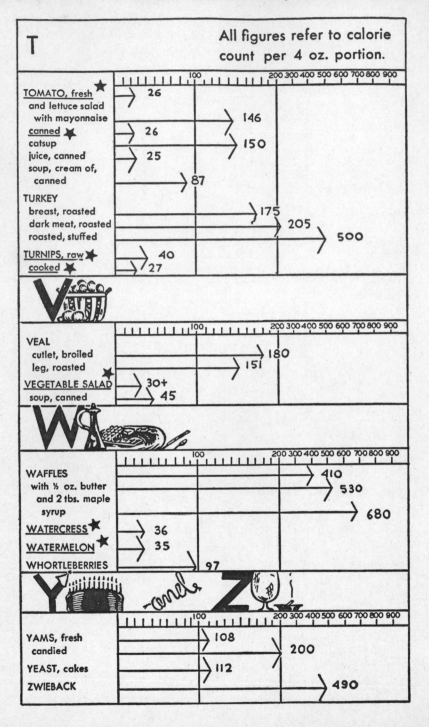

**T**

All figures refer to calorie count per 4 oz. portion.

| | 100 | 200 300 400 500 600 700 800 900 |
|---|---|---|
| TOMATO, fresh ★ | 26 | |
| and lettuce salad with mayonnaise | | 146 |
| canned ★ | 26 | |
| catsup | | 150 |
| juice, canned | 25 | |
| soup, cream of, canned | 87 | |
| TURKEY | | |
| breast, roasted | | 175 |
| dark meat, roasted | | 205 |
| roasted, stuffed | | 500 |
| TURNIPS, raw ★ | 40 | |
| cooked ★ | 27 | |

| | 100 | 200 300 400 500 600 700 800 900 |
|---|---|---|
| VEAL | | |
| cutlet, broiled | | 180 |
| leg, roasted | | 151 |
| VEGETABLE SALAD ★ | 30+ | |
| soup, canned | 45 | |

| | 100 | 200 300 400 500 600 700 800 900 |
|---|---|---|
| WAFFLES | | 410 |
| with ½ oz. butter | | 530 |
| and 2 tbs. maple syrup | | 680 |
| WATERCRESS ★ | 36 | |
| WATERMELON ★ | 35 | |
| WHORTLEBERRIES | 97 | |

| | 100 | 200 300 400 500 600 700 800 900 |
|---|---|---|
| YAMS, fresh | 108 | |
| candied | | 200 |
| YEAST, cakes | 112 | |
| ZWIEBACK | | 490 |

# 22

How to Find
Your Ideal Weight!

Technically, there is no such thing as ideal weight, since no two people are exactly alike in what they require for health. The closest anyone can come to "ideal" weight is determined by the bony framework of the body. Even a competent investigator, using advanced medical methods, can only say that such-and-such is "about right" for an individual.

So-called "normal" weight charts are based on averages, and may have no bearing whatever on individual cases. They do not take such factors into account as widths of shoulders and hips, for example. Therefore, they may not mean much, as far as you are concerned. The best way to find out how much you should weigh is to consult a physician. With the tables and measurements at his command, he can give you a fairly accurate ideal weight range for *you*.

The tables reproduced here—devised by Dr. Lindlahr—will give you a much better idea of what you should weigh than the ordinary average weight tables. These charts of ideal or optimum weights were compiled from different sources, taking into account all kinds of variations in build and body needs. (See pages 287 and 288.)

## FIT YOURSELF INTO THE PICTURE!

A considerable deviation exists between weights which might be ideal for anyone of a given age and height. Thus, a man of 30 who is five feet, six inches tall might weigh from 132 to 161 pounds and still be just about right, depending upon his skeleton. Because of this swing, the first thing you must do before you consult the tables is to determine your particular type of frame and classify yourself as Type 1, Type 2, or Type 3 (wrist size, below, refers to distance around wrist).

> **Type 1:** This is the person of so-called normal or average build. It is the standard frame (skeleton). If you never have trouble buying clothes right off the rack, with little or no alterations, this is your type. Wrist size: about 7 inches for men, 6 inches for women.
>
> **Type 2:** This is the large-boned, heavy-set, stocky or large-framed person. Wrist size: 7½ inches for men, 6½ inches for women.
>
> **Type 3:** Here is the slender, small-boned, small-framed person. Wrist size: 6½ inches for men, 5½ inches for women.

Unless you are *definitely* either Type 2 or 3, consider yourself Type 1. When you know your frame type, read down that column in the charts for your height in inches and your age in years. From the rough figure given, you can judge whether or not your present weight is approximately correct.

## AT AGE 30 YOUR IDEAL WEIGHT IS A LIFETIME GOAL!

At first, those of you over 30 may be amazed to find no allowance made for picking up pounds in the middle years. Dr. Lindlahr stated flatly that this is erroneous. How many overweight men and women sigh sadly at 40 when they remember their trim bodies of ten or twelve years ago! Yet their body frames have not changed, said Dr. Lindlahr! Their skeletons are the same size and should not have to carry any extra pounds. The fact that many people gain with years does not make it right.

Authorities are agreed that the weight which is correct for age 30 is also correct for age 40, said Dr. Lindlahr. At advancing ages, the weight should actually decrease slightly—not increase—for best health, he emphasized! As a person reaches 45, 50, and older ages, his circulatory and digestive systems benefit by a slight decrease in body weight.

The reverse of this is true for people under 30. Here a few extra pounds may be beneficial. For this reason, Dr. Lindlahr does not give weight estimates for youngsters between 14 and 21. A youngster may grow three inches or more in a year, and "fill out" in sporadic spurts. Body framework is still not established. Only an examining physician can decide upon the optimum weight for a given adolescent.

## AN EASY WAY TO ESTIMATE WEIGHT!

Adelle Davis also did not place much value in average height-weight tables. "The adult who uses these tables is doing nothing more than to compare himself to the average weight of thousands of people, the majority of whom were more or less obese," she said. Such tables are compiled as follows. Say 1,000 men, 30 years old and five feet, six inches tall, are weighed. The total weight figure may be 130,000 pounds, which is then divided by 1,000 to give an average weight of 130 pounds for this height and age.

Because these tables proved unsatisfactory in her work, she used this simple method: 100 pounds for an adult of 5 feet, either men or women; for women, 5 additional pounds for each inch over 5 feet; for men, 7 additional pounds for each inch over 5 feet. This proved most satisfactory, she said.

For example, a woman who is 5 feet, 5 inches tall should weigh, according to this standard, 125 pounds. A man who is 5 feet, 10 inches should weigh about 170.

From this standard is allowed a 20-pound range for personal preference and individual bone build. If a woman who is 5 feet, 4 inches tall has small bones or wishes to be particularly slender, she may choose 110 pounds for her ideal weight rather than 120 pounds. If a man who is 5 feet, 11 inches tall has large bones and feels better when he is heavier, he may choose 187 for his ideal weight. This standard, of course, is not ironclad, but it is an easy, "personalized" way to find your ideal weight.

starring Renata Scotto and Luciano Pavarotti. If you missed it, you missed a magnificent performance. If you saw it, then you know you're in store for a magnificent encore. You can see it in four consecutive one hour evenings, April 14 through 17 and again in its entirety on April 19. And on April 13 you can enjoy a preview with a one hour documentary of how it was all put together.

We'll take you from day one to opening night. You'll hear the great voices of Scotto and Pavarotti. You'll see the first meeting with Kurt Adler. The first drawings of the sets. The agonies of rehearsal. The battles. The egos. The loves. The fears. And finally, opening night and triumph.

It'll all be there for you and your family to enjoy. The choice is yours. "La Gioconda" vs. whatever. Give it some serious thought.

"La Gioconda" with English subtitles is produced for PBS by KCET/Los Angeles. And made possible as a public service by BankAmerica Corporation.

BankAmerica NT&SA SPEC-1080 3/80

# La Gioconda

## vs.

# Lou Grant

Or Happy Days or Laverne and Shirley or Charlie's Angels or whatever you might find opposite it on network television.

Because BankAmerica Corporation is again proud to sponsor the San Francisco Opera.

This time in the form of a mini-series "Opera from San Francisco: La Gioconda Act by Act."

## IDEAL WEIGHTS FOR WOMEN *
### In Pounds, According to Age, Height, and Frame

N=Normal frame (type 1).    H=Heavy frame (type 2).    L=Light frame (type 3).

*Age Groups*

| Height in Feet and Inches | 14 | | | 15-20 | 21-24 | | | 25-29 | | | 30-34 | | | 35-39 | | | 40-44 | | | 45-49 | | | 50-54 | | | 55-59 | | | 60-64 | | | 65-69 | | |
|---|---|---|---|---|---|---|---|---|---|---|---|---|---|---|---|---|---|---|---|---|---|---|---|---|---|---|---|---|---|---|---|---|---|---|---|---|
| | N | H | L | | N | H | L | N | H | L | N | H | L | N | H | L | N | H | L | N | H | L | N | H | L | N | H | L | N | H | L | N | H | L |
| 4' 9" | 88 | 101 | 74 | | 108 | 121 | 99 | 110 | 123 | 101 | 112 | 125 | 103 | 112 | 125 | 103 | 111 | 124 | 103 | 110 | 123 | 103 | 109 | 122 | 102 | 108 | 121 | 101 | 105 | 117 | 98 | 104 | 116 | 97 |
| 4' 10" | 93 | 104 | 79 | | 110 | 123 | 101 | 112 | 125 | 103 | 114 | 127 | 105 | 114 | 127 | 105 | 113 | 126 | 105 | 112 | 125 | 105 | 111 | 124 | 104 | 110 | 123 | 103 | 107 | 119 | 100 | 106 | 118 | 99 |
| 4' 11" | 96 | 110 | 81 | | 112 | 125 | 103 | 114 | 127 | 105 | 116 | 129 | 107 | 116 | 129 | 107 | 115 | 128 | 107 | 114 | 127 | 107 | 113 | 126 | 106 | 112 | 125 | 105 | 109 | 121 | 102 | 108 | 120 | 101 |
| 5' 0" | 101 | 114 | 85 | | 114 | 127 | 105 | 116 | 129 | 107 | 118 | 131 | 109 | 118 | 131 | 109 | 117 | 130 | 109 | 116 | 129 | 109 | 115 | 128 | 108 | 114 | 127 | 107 | 111 | 123 | 104 | 110 | 122 | 103 |
| 5' 1" | 105 | 120 | 89 | | 116 | 129 | 107 | 118 | 130 | 109 | 120 | 132 | 111 | 120 | 132 | 111 | 119 | 131 | 111 | 118 | 130 | 111 | 117 | 129 | 110 | 116 | 128 | 109 | 113 | 124 | 106 | 112 | 123 | 105 |
| 5' 2" | 109 | 123 | 93 | | 119 | 133 | 110 | 121 | 135 | 112 | 123 | 137 | 114 | 123 | 137 | 114 | 122 | 136 | 114 | 121 | 135 | 114 | 120 | 134 | 113 | 119 | 133 | 112 | 116 | 129 | 109 | 115 | 128 | 108 |
| 5' 3" | 112 | 128 | 95 | | 123 | 134 | 112 | 125 | 136 | 114 | 127 | 138 | 116 | 127 | 138 | 116 | 126 | 138 | 116 | 125 | 135 | 116 | 124 | 135 | 115 | 123 | 134 | 114 | 120 | 130 | 111 | 119 | 129 | 110 |
| 5' 4" | 117 | 132 | 100 | | 126 | 141 | 116 | 128 | 143 | 118 | 130 | 145 | 120 | 130 | 145 | 120 | 129 | 144 | 120 | 128 | 143 | 120 | 127 | 142 | 119 | 126 | 141 | 118 | 123 | 137 | 115 | 122 | 136 | 114 |
| 5' 5" | 121 | 139 | 103 | | 130 | 142 | 119 | 132 | 144 | 121 | 134 | 146 | 123 | 134 | 146 | 123 | 133 | 145 | 123 | 132 | 144 | 123 | 131 | 143 | 122 | 130 | 142 | 121 | 127 | 138 | 118 | 126 | 137 | 117 |
| 5' 6" | 124 | 140 | 106 | | 134 | 150 | 123 | 136 | 152 | 125 | 138 | 154 | 127 | 138 | 154 | 127 | 137 | 153 | 127 | 136 | 152 | 127 | 135 | 151 | 126 | 134 | 150 | 125 | 131 | 146 | 122 | 130 | 145 | 121 |
| 5' 7" | 130 | 149 | 111 | | 138 | 152 | 127 | 140 | 154 | 129 | 142 | 156 | 131 | 142 | 156 | 131 | 141 | 155 | 131 | 140 | 154 | 131 | 139 | 153 | 130 | 138 | 152 | 129 | 135 | 148 | 126 | 134 | 147 | 125 |
| 5' 8" | 133 | 150 | 114 | | 142 | 158 | 131 | 144 | 160 | 133 | 146 | 162 | 135 | 146 | 162 | 135 | 145 | 161 | 135 | 144 | 160 | 135 | 143 | 159 | 134 | 142 | 158 | 133 | 139 | 154 | 130 | 138 | 153 | 129 |
| 5' 9" | 135 | 155 | 115 | | 146 | 161 | 134 | 148 | 163 | 136 | 150 | 165 | 138 | 150 | 165 | 138 | 149 | 164 | 138 | 148 | 163 | 138 | 147 | 162 | 137 | 146 | 161 | 136 | 143 | 157 | 133 | 142 | 156 | 132 |
| 5' 10" | 136 | 156 | 116 | | 149 | 167 | 138 | 151 | 169 | 140 | 153 | 171 | 142 | 153 | 171 | 142 | 152 | 170 | 142 | 151 | 169 | 142 | 150 | 168 | 141 | 149 | 167 | 140 | 146 | 163 | 137 | 145 | 162 | 136 |
| 5' 11" | 138 | 158 | 118 | | 153 | 170 | 141 | 155 | 172 | 143 | 158 | 175 | 146 | 158 | 175 | 146 | 157 | 174 | 146 | 156 | 173 | 146 | 155 | 172 | 145 | 154 | 171 | 144 | 151 | 167 | 141 | 150 | 166 | 140 |

(15-20 age group: Indeterminate)

* Undressed. For clothing and shoes, allow 4 pounds.

## IDEAL WEIGHTS FOR MEN *

### In Pounds, According to Age, Height, and Frame

N=Normal frame (type 1).　　　H=Heavy frame (type 2).　　　L=Light frame (type 3).

Age Groups

| Height in Feet and Inches | 14 N | 14 H | 14 L | 15-20 | 21-24 N | 21-24 H | 21-24 L | 25-29 N | 25-29 H | 25-29 L | 30-34 N | 30-34 H | 30-34 L | 35-39 N | 35-39 H | 35-39 L | 40-44 N | 40-44 H | 40-44 L | 45-49 N | 45-49 H | 45-49 L | 50-54 N | 50-54 H | 50-54 L | 55-59 N | 55-59 H | 55-59 L | 60-64 N | 60-64 H | 60-64 L | 65-69 N | 65-69 H | 65-69 L |
|---|---|---|---|---|---|---|---|---|---|---|---|---|---|---|---|---|---|---|---|---|---|---|---|---|---|---|---|---|---|---|---|---|---|---|
| 4' 9" | 83 | 95 | 70 | Indeterminate | | | | | | | | | | | | | | | | | | | | | | | | | | | | | | |
| 4' 10" | 86 | 96 | 73 | Indeterminate | | | | | | | | | | | | | | | | | | | | | | | | | | | | | | |
| 4' 11" | 90 | 103 | 76 | Indeterminate | 112 | 134 | 106 | 116 | 138 | 110 | 118 | 140 | 112 | 118 | 140 | 112 | 117 | 139 | 112 | 116 | 138 | 112 | 115 | 137 | 111 | 114 | 136 | 110 | 111 | 132 | 107 | 110 | 131 | 106 |
| 5' 0" | 94 | 106 | 79 | Indeterminate | 114 | 136 | 108 | 118 | 140 | 112 | 120 | 142 | 114 | 120 | 142 | 114 | 119 | 141 | 114 | 118 | 140 | 114 | 117 | 139 | 113 | 116 | 138 | 112 | 113 | 134 | 109 | 112 | 133 | 108 |
| 5' 1" | 99 | 113 | 84 | Indeterminate | 116 | 138 | 110 | 120 | 142 | 114 | 122 | 144 | 116 | 122 | 144 | 116 | 121 | 143 | 116 | 120 | 142 | 116 | 119 | 141 | 115 | 118 | 140 | 114 | 115 | 136 | 111 | 114 | 135 | 110 |
| 5' 2" | 103 | 116 | 87 | Indeterminate | 120 | 140 | 112 | 123 | 143 | 115 | 125 | 145 | 117 | 125 | 145 | 117 | 124 | 144 | 117 | 123 | 143 | 117 | 122 | 142 | 116 | 121 | 141 | 115 | 118 | 137 | 112 | 117 | 136 | 111 |
| 5' 3" | 108 | 124 | 92 | Indeterminate | 124 | 144 | 116 | 125 | 145 | 117 | 128 | 148 | 120 | 128 | 148 | 120 | 127 | 147 | 120 | 126 | 146 | 120 | 125 | 145 | 119 | 124 | 144 | 118 | 121 | 140 | 115 | 120 | 139 | 114 |
| 5' 4" | 113 | 127 | 96 | Indeterminate | 128 | 148 | 120 | 128 | 148 | 120 | 132 | 152 | 124 | 132 | 152 | 124 | 131 | 151 | 124 | 130 | 150 | 124 | 129 | 149 | 123 | 128 | 148 | 122 | 125 | 144 | 119 | 124 | 143 | 118 |
| 5' 5" | 118 | 135 | 101 | Indeterminate | 132 | 152 | 123 | 130 | 150 | 123 | 136 | 156 | 127 | 136 | 156 | 127 | 135 | 155 | 127 | 134 | 154 | 127 | 133 | 153 | 126 | 132 | 152 | 125 | 129 | 148 | 122 | 128 | 147 | 121 |
| 5' 6" | 122 | 138 | 104 | Indeterminate | 135 | 156 | 127 | 134 | 154 | 125 | 140 | 161 | 132 | 140 | 161 | 132 | 139 | 160 | 132 | 138 | 159 | 132 | 137 | 158 | 131 | 136 | 157 | 130 | 133 | 153 | 127 | 132 | 152 | 126 |
| 5' 7" | 128 | 147 | 109 | Indeterminate | 139 | 160 | 130 | 138 | 159 | 127 | 144 | 165 | 135 | 144 | 165 | 135 | 143 | 164 | 135 | 142 | 163 | 135 | 141 | 162 | 134 | 140 | 161 | 133 | 137 | 157 | 130 | 136 | 156 | 129 |
| 5' 8" | 134 | 152 | 114 | Indeterminate | 143 | 164 | 133 | 142 | 163 | 130 | 148 | 169 | 138 | 148 | 169 | 138 | 147 | 168 | 138 | 146 | 167 | 138 | 145 | 166 | 137 | 144 | 165 | 136 | 141 | 161 | 133 | 140 | 160 | 132 |
| 5' 9" | 137 | 157 | 117 | Indeterminate | 147 | 170 | 137 | 146 | 167 | 136 | 153 | 176 | 143 | 153 | 176 | 143 | 152 | 175 | 143 | 151 | 174 | 143 | 150 | 173 | 142 | 149 | 172 | 141 | 146 | 168 | 138 | 145 | 167 | 137 |
| 5' 10" | 143 | 162 | 122 | Indeterminate | 152 | 175 | 140 | 150 | 173 | 140 | 158 | 181 | 146 | 158 | 181 | 146 | 157 | 180 | 146 | 156 | 179 | 146 | 155 | 178 | 146 | 154 | 177 | 144 | 151 | 173 | 141 | 150 | 172 | 140 |
| 5' 11" | 148 | 170 | 127 | Indeterminate | 156 | 180 | 144 | 155 | 178 | 143 | 164 | 188 | 152 | 164 | 188 | 152 | 163 | 187 | 152 | 162 | 186 | 152 | 161 | 185 | 151 | 160 | 184 | 150 | 157 | 180 | 147 | 156 | 179 | 146 |
| 6' 0" | | | | Indeterminate | 161 | 184 | 148 | 161 | 185 | 149 | 170 | 193 | 157 | 170 | 193 | 157 | 169 | 192 | 157 | 168 | 191 | 157 | 167 | 190 | 156 | 166 | 189 | 155 | 163 | 185 | 151 | 162 | 184 | 151 |
| 6' 1" | | | | Indeterminate | 167 | 187 | 153 | 167 | 190 | 154 | 176 | 196 | 162 | 176 | 196 | 162 | 175 | 195 | 162 | 174 | 194 | 162 | 173 | 193 | 161 | 172 | 192 | 160 | 169 | 188 | 157 | 168 | 187 | 156 |
| 6' 2" | | | | Indeterminate | 171 | 192 | 157 | 173 | 196 | 159 | 182 | 203 | 168 | 182 | 203 | 168 | 181 | 202 | 168 | 180 | 201 | 168 | 179 | 200 | 167 | 178 | 199 | 166 | 175 | 195 | 163 | 174 | 194 | 162 |

* Undressed. For clothing and shoes, allow 8 pounds.